CHARTED
KNITTING
DESIGNS

CHARTED KNITTING DESIGNS

A Third Treasury of Knitting Patterns

By Barbara G. Walker

CHARLES SCRIBNER'S SONS · NEW YORK

Charles Scribner's Sons
Macmillan Publishing Company
866 Third Avenue, New York, NY 10022
Collier Macmillan Canada, Inc.

Library of Congress Catalog Card Number 72-169114

ISBN 0-684-17462-6

Macmillan books are available at special discounts for bulk purchases
for sales promotions, premiums, fund-raising, or educational use.
For details, contact:

> Special Sales Director
> Macmillan Publishing Company
> 866 Third Avenue
> New York, NY 10022

10 9 8 7

Printed in the United States of America

To all dispersed sorts of ARTS and TRADES,
I writ the needles prayse (that never fades)
So long as children shall be got or borne,
So long as garments shall be made or worne,
So long as Hemp or Flax or Sheep shall bear
Their linnen woollen fleeces yeare by yeare:
So long as Silk-wormes, with exhausted spoile,
Of their own Entrailes for mans gaine shall toyle:
Yea till the world be quite dissolv'd and past;
So long at least, the Needles use shall last.

—JOHN TAYLOR, *The Praise of the Needle*
London, 1640

Acknowledgements

I am grateful to my husband, Gordon N. Walker, and my editor, Elinor Parker, for their help and encouragement; to my photographer, William J. Williams, whose consistently superlative work enriches this volume as well as *A Treasury of Knitting Patterns* and *A Second Treasury of Knitting Patterns;* to Coats & Clark, Inc., and the Spinnerin Yarn Company for materials used in swatches and samples; and to Dorothy Reade for the inspiration leading to new circular designs in lace.

Those patterns that are not the author's originals have been contributed to this collection by the following people: Winnifred H. Angus, Toronto, Canada; Pauline Balbes, Hollywood, California; Eugen K. Beugler, Dexter, Oregon; Janida R. Bultman, Milwaukee, Wisconsin; Virginia C. Dewey, Amherst, Massachusetts; Hildegard M. Elsner, Aldan, Pennsylvania; Peggy Ferber, Seattle, Washington; Bernice Haedike, Oak Park, Illinois; Leona Hughes, Sarasota, Florida; Ruth Kanaris, Laramie, Wyoming; Patricia M. Shannon, Decatur, Alabama; and Dorothy M. Singer, Concord, Vermont.

Contents

Introduction

The twelve-hundred-odd patterns presented in my two previous books, *A Treasury of Knitting Patterns* and *A Second Treasury of Knitting Patterns*, were mostly other people's. Although they included some of my own invention, the majority were traditional patterns, passed down through generations of knitters in many parts of the world.

The patterns in this book are different. Most are newborn, and have never appeared in any other book. They are almost all my own original designs, with only a dozen or so examples of other people's. Not only are the patterns themselves original, but often the techniques used in making them are original too. That is to say, certain knitting operations are combined in unusual ways, to make shapes that have never before translated themselves into a knitted fabric. Taken individually, however, these knitting operations are standard ones that almost every knitter has used at one time or another. There is nothing in this book so radically new that it would require special instruction or demonstration. Some of the patterns are simple little things, well within the grasp of any beginner; others are quite fancy, to provide some degree of excitement and enjoyment for the expert. But anyone who knows how to knit can master and use any of these original designs. It is my belief that most knitters like to learn new pattern stitches, and it is my hope that some of the newborns offered in this book will bring pleasure to fellow knitters, who will therefore graciously grant them long and useful lives.

To satisfy the curiosity of those who would like to invent original patterns of their own, and wonder how it is done, a few words on this matter might not be amiss. There are two possible approaches to the problem of designing a new pattern. One approach is internal, the other external. The internal approach begins with an existing pattern and changes it around somehow. Many of the designs in this book represent variations on variations on variations of older patterns, rearranged to make new shapes. Frequently, this kind of invention is done by accident. A knitter who is a little careless in working an old pattern may make a few interesting mistakes that make the pattern look different and, perhaps, better. It is remarkable how much you can do with an old pattern, just by knitting it wrong in various ways. Naturally, you must master the right way too, so as to know where the variations occur and how to reproduce them.

The external approach begins with a design, not necessarily having anything to do with knitting: some geometric figure or form either originating in the designer's head or copied from nature, art, or history. Some of the patterns in this book have been inspired by such apparently improbable things as Scandinavian woodcarving, Etruscan pottery, Gothic choir stalls, Indian rugs, Moorish screens, rococo mirror frames, roof shingles, maps, building facades, steel girders, pavements, blueprints, chess moves, and microscopic cell structures. To give just two examples, the pattern entitled "Temple of Zeus" really is a copy of a tiled floor in the ancient temple at Olympia; and the one entitled "Optical Illusion" comes from the design on a pillar in the cathedral at Chartres.

Having chosen or invented a design, the creator must then decide which knitting techniques would best express it. Do the lines lend themselves to reproduction in lace, or cables, or mosaic knitting, or twist stitches, or something else? Certain forms suggest certain types and weights of yarn, certain colors, or certain qualities of fabric, from delicate openwork to heavy embossed knitting. After this decision is made, the next ones concern the construction of the pattern itself. How many stitches and rows should be allotted to each portion of the design? What techniques should be used to make the lines go left, right, up, down? Where should the holes, or the crossings, or the increases, or the decreases be placed? What adjustments are necessary to maintain the desired number of stitches?

All these decisions are greatly facilitated by some method of working the pattern on paper before beginning the actual knitting. Along with its collection of original patterns, this book also presents such a method. It is unusual because it is my own system of pattern charting, painfully developed through innumerable hours and reams of graph paper. Like all other systems for doing anything, my system of charting is based on things that have been done before. But it includes many novel refinements and renovations that combine to make it different from any other method of paper knitting.

This book will teach you, in addition to new patterns, this system of charting. It is a system that I have found useful in many ways. It has helped me to understand pattern stitches while learning them, to create new pattern stitches, to design garments, to keep handy records of knitting directions, and to visualize patterns at a glance without having to work through a series of written formulae. I offer it here, in the hope that it may help other knitters in the same ways. It is not difficult to learn, and it can be applied to all kinds of knitting patterns, both old and new.

Most American knitters already know how to follow charts for the Fair Isle type of color knitting, which is all done in stockinette stitch. Knitters of European backgrounds may know also how to follow charts for other sorts of pattern stitches, because pattern directions are often given in chart form in European countries. This has been so for many years. Written-out directions, rather than charts, have been the rule in the United States, however; and it is possible that we Americans have missed out on a good thing. A chart is an efficient, economical way to convey knitting directions, especially for long and complicated patterns whose written-out rows would take up an excessive amount of space. A chart also does what written-out directions cannot do: it shows the knitter something resembling a picture of the finished work. This can be very useful for learning an unfamiliar pattern. With this in mind, I have tried to develop charts that are as graphic as possible, imitating the actual knitted fabric with a reasonable degree of fidelity. Patterns presented in this way do not have to be decoded with the aid of yarn and needles; they can almost be seen before they are knitted. After learning how to chart patterns, you will probably find yourself not *knitting* your way through a set of written-out directions, but *drawing* your way through them the first time around. Drawing goes a lot faster than knitting, and when your chart is finished, you have captured the pattern on paper once and for all. The chart will show you how every row relates to every other row, and how the entire pattern repeat should look when it is worked.

A system of charting makes it much easier for anyone to be a designer of knitting patterns when working from the external approach. The design can be drawn on graph paper and translated almost directly into stitches and rows. Most of us notice patterns in everything, every day, indoors or outdoors. Some of us, who happen to be obsessed with knitting, think in terms of reproducing those patterns on a knitted fabric. It's as simple as that.

Charting is an extremely valuable aid to the knitter who wishes to do her own garment designing—and that means almost every knitter, sooner or later. If you doubt that you will ever do your own garment designing, consider whether you have ever (1) altered the number of stitches given anywhere in a commercial garment design, because the number given would not suit your own measurements, (2) substituted a different pattern stitch for the one shown in the garment, (3) inserted cables, or some other vertical pattern panels, where they were not, (4) changed a border, a collar, a cuff, a pocket, or any other detail, (5) converted a cardigan design into a pullover, or vice versa, (6) re-figured a garment to suit a different stitch gauge from the recommended one, or (7) constructed a basic garment shape several times, using a different pattern stitch each time to make different garments. If you have done any of these things, you have already had experience in designing. Not many knitters find it possible to follow a commercial garment design exactly, because individual figures differ, and a correct fit usually must involve some alterations.

From these bits and pieces of alteration it is a very short step to designing a whole garment from scratch, starting with the desired measurements (taken from a garment that does fit well) and multiplying them by the stitch gauge (number of stitches and rows to the inch). To design a sweater, all you really need to know is the multiplication table. 5 stitches to the inch times 20 inches = 100 stitches, and you're off. What could be simpler? Anyone who has made three or four knitted garments knows how the shaping around the shoulder area ought to be done, just as anyone who has made three or four dresses with a sewing machine knows where to expect the darts, the seams, and the facings. There are no special, arcane secrets to knitwear design. It's just measure and multiply. The directions for the original garment designs in the last chapter of this book will give you a basic idea of how it is done.

Charting helps both the measuring and the multiplying. On a large piece of graph paper, you can chart an entire garment piece, with every stitch in its proper place, before the first stitch is cast on the needle. It's easy to count inch measurements, because if your gauge is 5 stitches to the inch, then 5 squares on the chart represent an inch; 6 stitches to the inch, 6 squares; and so on. You can measure any part of your garment long before it has begun to exist, just by counting squares. Shaping is shown by widening or narrowing the chart at the right heights, which are ascertained by counting squares vertically according to your row gauge. So you can see exactly which rows are increase or decrease rows, and how many stitches are to be added or removed on each. The pattern stitch itself is charted right along with the rest, so there is never any doubt about how to keep the pattern correct while shaping. As the narrowing part of the chart eats into the pattern repeat, or the widening part of the chart adds more of a new pattern repeat, your drawing of the pattern shows you how to work each stitch.

Even when there is no shaping involved, charting is a great help in straight pattern knitting. Sometimes you cannot fit the number of stitches you need into an exact multiple, so you have to work a partial repeat of the pattern at the beginning or end of each row. This is very tedious to figure out from written pattern directions, especially when you are not entirely familiar with the pattern. But when the directions are given in chart form, it is simplicity itself. An extra, temporary "repeat line" (see How To Read Charts) can be drawn right on the chart, at the place where you want to cut into or out of the pattern when working a partial repeat. One glance at this line on each row, and you know just where to start off. It even works for most patterns in which the stitch count varies on different rows. Furthermore, a chart makes it easy to match up increases and decreases on any given row, even when they are separated from each other by several intervening stitches, because you can see them and count them. One "k2 tog" here equals one "yo" there, etc. So a chart is a comforting assurance that you can keep the pattern correct while adding, subtracting, or just maintaining the desired total number of stitches.

Learning to read pattern charts is fun, and a lot easier than it may seem at first glance. The few basic principles of these charts are thoroughly described under How To Read Charts, and the symbol-alphabet is also thoroughly described in the Complete List of Symbols. Give your undivided attention for a while to these two preliminary lessons, then you can go on to learn and use these original patterns. Since the majority of these patterns are quite new and different, it follows that you can use them to knit articles that are unlike any others. In short, you can create something that has never been seen before. Time spent on doing *that* is time well spent, in anyone's book.

BARBARA G. WALKER

MOUNT KEMBLE LAKE
MORRISTOWN, NEW JERSEY

How To Read Charts

This is the most important section in this book. In order to work these original designs, you must read and understand the following information—all of it. Since the method of charting given here differs from other methods in some respects, it is necessary for you to know the ground rules for this method even if you are accustomed to working patterns from other kinds of charts.

If you are not used to knitting from a chart, all those queer little dots and squiggles look perplexing at first. But once you have learned what each symbol stands for, and used it by following the chart as you knit, you will find that charting is the easiest and simplest way to convey the directions for pattern knitting.

Each chart is an accurate picture of one repeat, or sometimes two repeats, of the operations required to make the pattern. It is read exactly as the knitting is worked: from the bottom to the top, going from right to left on right-side rows, and from left to right on wrong-side rows. The numbers at the edges of the chart are row numbers. After the last row at the top of the chart has been worked, you begin again at the bottom with Row 1. This number 1 may be either at the right-hand edge of the chart or at the left-hand edge, depending on whether the pattern begins with a right-side row or a wrong-side row. If the number 1 is at the right-hand edge, the first row is a right-side row and so are all the other odd-numbered rows. If the number 1 is at the left-hand edge, the first row is a wrong-side row and so are all the other odd-numbered rows.

It is important to know whether you are working on a right-side or a wrong-side row, because *all* rows are shown on the chart *as they appear from the right side* of the fabric. Therefore, most of the symbols stand for two opposite things, or, more precisely, the same thing worked from one of two directions, front or back. So a dot, for instance, always means a purl bump on the *right* side; therefore dotted squares mean purl stitches if they are on a right-side row, and knit stitches if they are on a wrong-side row. Conversely, a blank square stands for a knit stitch on the *right* side; so it is knitted on a right-side row, purled on a wrong-side row. The advantages of this system are threefold: first, it allows the chart to show the pattern as it really looks, instead of showing a mishmash of opposite symbols that reverse themselves every other row; second, it makes circular knitting much easier, because in circular knitting all rows—or rounds—are worked from the right side; third, it trains the knitter to understand which knitting operations are the reverse versions of which others, so that a really thorough knowledge of the craft can be acquired. The Complete List of Symbols, immediately following, gives directions for working each symbol on both sides of the fabric. The chances are that if you study this list carefully, you will know more about alternative methods of doing things in knitting than you ever knew before.

When a chart shows a pattern that makes an allover design (rather than a single panel on a fixed number of stitches), there are two vertical lines near the side edges of the chart. These lines mean the same thing as asterisks in printed pattern directions, i.e., "repeat from °." Therefore these vertical lines are called repeat lines. Outside the repeat lines are the edge stitches, which are *not* repeated as you continue to work the pattern across the row. Inside the repeat lines is the material to be repeated. So for example, when beginning a right-side row, you work the right-hand edge stitch or stitches as shown, and arrive at the first (right-hand) repeat line. This is your first "°." Pass it, and work across the pattern to the second (left-hand) repeat line, and stop. Now go back to the first repeat line, and repeat the pattern from there. Continue in this way, working between the two lines over and over, until you have used up all the stitches in your row except the final left-hand edge stitches. Then—and only then—pass the second repeat line and finish the row according to whatever the left-hand edge stitches tell you to do. The same principle applies on a wrong-side row, except that you begin with the left-hand edge stitches and work between the repeat lines from left to right until you arrive at the right-hand edge again.

If there are no repeat lines on a chart, this means that the pattern is a one-repeat panel, like a cable, or else that the pattern has no edge stitches. In either case you simply begin at one side edge and work straight across to the other; and if you want to work the pattern more than once, begin again at the first side edge. In some patterns, a repeat line will be broken occasionally to show the passage of a twist or cable across it; but it is still considered to be in the same place.

If you are working in rounds on a circular needle, instead of in rows on straight needles, of course you do not use the edge stitches. For circular knitting you cast on the multiple only, omitting the "plus" number (edge stitches) altogether. In this way the rounds are made continuous, without being interrupted by extra stitches. So to work any pattern in circular knitting, you cast on the correct multiple *without* edge stitches, and begin each round with the first stitch *inside* the first repeat line. In circular knitting all rounds are on the right side, so all rows of the chart are read from right to left, no matter where their row numbers may be. Therefore the first repeat line, where you begin, is always the one on the right-hand side; and you never pass the second, or left-hand, repeat line at all. Circular-knitting fans should be delighted by this method of charting, which clearly depicts all patterns from the circular knitter's point of view, that is from the right side. (Dear reader, do you still laboriously sew the side seams of your sweaters? Why bother, when it's so easy to work the back and front of a sweater at the same time on a circular needle, thus eliminating both sewing and seams?)

The multiple of stitches required for each pattern, along with the "plus" or edge stitches, is given with the pattern title at the top of each chart. In addition, the multiple number is given also at the bottom of the chart between the repeat lines. These numbers tell you how many stitches to cast on (or mark, in the case of a panel) for the pattern. On many charts, the number of stitches to cast on for each repeat is *not* the same as the number of squares across the width of the chart; it is less. This occurs when the pattern is one that changes its stitch count on different rows. Charts must be drawn to accommodate the maximum number of stitches in the pattern at its widest point; therefore the narrower rows will have empty or stitchless spaces. Each of these spaces is marked with an X.

The X in a square anywhere on any chart means nothing—absolutely nothing. There is no stitch there. You will find in your knitting that the stitches corresponding to the X squares simply don't exist. So when counting stitches on the chart for any purpose (casting on, following the pattern, or re-checking your work), you must skip, ignore, and refuse to recognize the X squares. If the pattern says to cast on a multiple of 12, for example, and yet it looks like 16 squares between the repeat lines on the first row, you may be sure that that first row contains four X's somewhere. Go ahead and cast on the correct multiple, 12, and let the nonexistent stitches take care of themselves. They will turn up, sooner or later.

Symbols have been designed with considerable attention to the actual appearance of the knitting, so that the shape of each symbol can serve to some extent as a memory cue, and save the reader from making too many trips back to the Complete List to see what a chart is saying. In addition, an unusual method of charting cable and twist patterns has been devised in order to make these charts as representational as possible. This method involves outlining the stitches that are crossed over, so they stand out from the chart just as they stand out from the knitted fabric. This method is fully explained in the introductory remarks to the Cable and Twist sections, so these remarks must be looked upon as further lessons in How To Read Charts. Still another charting technique is presented by the mosaic patterns, which are special slip-stitch designs worked in two colors. This technique too is explained at length in another section.

All of the charts in this book try—some with more, some with less success—to be pictures of the actual knitting. But they are not only pictures; they are precise directions for making the stitches. Each horizontal row of squares on each chart is a line of knitting directions, stitch by stitch. So when you are working from a chart, you have to forget the total picture for the moment and get down to the knitty-gritty process of looking at one square at a time, row after row. A straight edge—a ruler, pencil, or card—laid along the row you are working on is a great help. It's surprisingly easy for the eye to jump a row now and then, and it's very awkward to discover that your eye is doing Row 27 while your hands are still toiling along Row 26; so do use a straight edge as you work. Most knitters prefer to lay the straight edge along the top of the row rather than beneath it, because it is more helpful to see what has gone before than to see what comes next.

Do take time, also, to study the Complete List of Symbols thoroughly, and *try out* all the alternative ways of working each stitch operation from both right and wrong sides. When there are several possible ways to do one thing, know them all so you will be able to choose the right one. The right one, in such cases, is the one that pleases you and looks best in the pattern you are working. Don't hang on to the old left-slanting decrease, "sl 1, k1, psso," for example, if you haven't tried "ssk"—you may find that "ssk" looks nicer.

The Complete List should be your bible for a little while, until you get used to following the charts.

Each different type of pattern is represented by one or two examples that are given in written-out directions as well as in chart form. The examples are not necessarily the simplest patterns in the group. On the contrary, they contain as many different stitch operations as possible, to provide better practice. But it is earnestly recommended that you begin your career as a chartist by working each one of these example patterns in a test swatch, following both the chart and the printed directions at the same time. Comparison will teach you just how the charts express, in their picture language, the same things expressed by the abbreviations of "knitter's English."

When you work through the first repeat of a charted pattern, especially a complicated one, you do a lot of counting. Do it with care, and do it always. Count each square along each horizontal row as you work the corresponding stitches. If there are X's in the pattern, you can't always depend on the vertical alignment of squares to show you what to do next. Sometimes the X's have to be jogged right or left to provide room for other symbols, so the squares cannot be lined up from top to bottom exactly as the stitches are. Great efforts have been made to preserve the correct vertical alignment of patterns wherever possible, but occasionally you will come across a pattern that doggedly refuses to be charted this way. Don't worry about it. Trust the chart, and knit on!

Complete List of Symbols

I. GENERAL

On a right-side row (row number at right of chart) this symbol means:

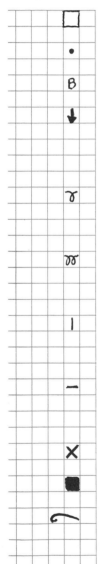

K1—knit one stitch (blank).

P1—purl one stitch.

K1-b—knit one stitch in back loop.

K1 in the row below, inserting needle from front through the st in the row below left-hand needle instead of the st on left-hand needle.

K1 elongated—knit one stitch wrapping yarn twice; drop extra wrap from needle on next row.

K1 elongated twice—knit one stitch wrapping yarn three times; drop extra wraps from needle on next row.

Sl 1 wyib—slip one stitch as if to purl, holding yarn in back (i.e., on wrong side).

Sl 1 wyif—slip one stitch as if to purl, holding yarn in front (i.e., on right side).

No stitch.

Color symbol; see Mosaic Patterns.

Bind 2—yo, k2, pass the yo over the 2 knit sts (may apply to 1, 2, 3 or more sts).

On a wrong-side row (row number at left of chart) this symbol means:

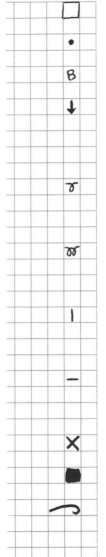

P1—purl one stitch (blank).

K1—knit one stitch.

P1-b—purl one stitch in back loop.

P1 in the row below, inserting needle from behind through the st in the row below left-hand needle instead of the st on left-hand needle.

P1 elongated—purl one stitch wrapping yarn twice; drop extra wrap from needle on next row.

P1 elongated twice—purl one stitch wrapping yarn three times; drop extra wraps from needle on next row.

Sl 1 wyif—slip one stitch as if to purl, holding yarn in front (i.e., on wrong side).

Sl 1 wyib—slip one stitch as if to purl, holding yarn in back (i.e., on right side).

No stitch.

Color symbol: see Mosaic Patterns.

Bind 2—yo, p2, pass the yo over the 2 purl sts (may apply to 1, 2, 3 or more sts).

On a right-side row (row number at right of chart) this symbol means:

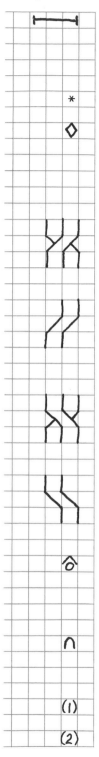

Cluster 3—sl 3 wyib, pass yarn to front, sl the same 3 sts back to left-hand needle, pass yarn to back, k3. (May apply to 2, 3 or more sts).

Special instructions, given with chart.

MB—make bobble: (k1, yo, k1, yo, k1) in one st, turn and p5, turn and k5, turn and p2 tog, p1, p2 tog, turn and sl 1—k2 tog—psso, completing bobble. (Alternate methods of making bobbles are given with charts.)

RT—Right Twist: k2 tog, leave on needle; then insert right-hand needle between the sts just knitted tog, and knit the first st again; then sl both sts from left-hand needle.
OR
Skip 1 st and knit the 2nd st in front loop, then knit the skipped st in front loop, then sl both sts from needle together.

LT—Left Twist: skip 1 st and knit the 2nd st in back loop, then k2 tog-b (the skipped st and the knit st); sl both sts from needle together.
OR
Skip 1 st and knit the 2nd st in back loop, then knit the skipped st in front loop; sl both sts from needle together.

Daisy Cluster—same as for wrong-side rows.

K1 under the loose strand or strands of a preceding row, or rows, on front of fabric.

Numbers in parentheses indicate special directions for that space (temporarily increased stitches).

On a wrong-side row (row number at left of chart) this symbol means:

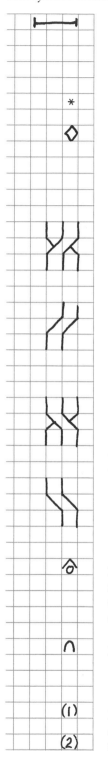

Cluster 3—sl 3 wyif, pass yarn to back, sl the same 3 sts back to left-hand needle, pass yarn to front, p3. (May apply to 2, 3 or more sts).

Special instructions, given with chart.

MB—not used on wrong-side rows.

PRT—Purl Right Twist: skip 1 st and purl the 2nd st, then p2 tog (the skipped st and the 2nd st); sl both sts from needle together.
OR
Skip 1 st and purl the 2nd st, then purl the skipped st, then sl both sts from needle together.

PLT—Purl Left Twist: skip 1 st and purl the 2nd st in back loop (i.e., from behind), then purl the skipped st; sl both sts from needle together.

Also see special charts for CABLES.

Daisy Cluster—p3 tog, leave on needle; yo, then purl the same 3 sts tog again; sl all 3 sts from needle together.

Not used on wrong-side rows.

Numbers in parentheses indicate special directions for that space (temporarily increased stitches).

II. INCREASES

On a right-side row (row number at right of chart) this symbol means:

O Yo—yarn over.

O O (Yo) twice—yarn over twice; on the next row work (k1, p1) into the double loop unless otherwise specified.

M M1—Make One; lift running thread between the st just worked and the next st, and knit into the back of this thread.

V Inc 1—increase 1 stitch; knit into the back of the st in the row below first st on left-hand needle (inserting needle point from the top down into the purled head of st); then knit into the front (or back, if preferred) of the first st on left-hand needle.

OR

Insert left-hand needle from front into the st in the row below the first st on right-hand needle; pick up right-hand loop of this st onto left-hand needle and knit into the front of this loop.

OR

(K1-b, k1) in one stitch.

OR

(K1, k1-b) in one stitch.

OR

(K1, p1) in one stitch.

OR

K1 in the row below, then knit the st on needle.

V̇ (K1, p1, k1) in 1 st—knit, purl, and knit again, all in the same st, to make 3 sts from 1.

On a wrong-side row (row number at left of chart) this symbol means:

O Yo—yarn over.

O O (Yo) twice—yarn over twice; on the next row work (k1, p1) into the double loop unless otherwise specified.

M M1—Make One; lift running thread between the st just worked and the next st, and purl into the back of this thread.

V Inc 1—increase 1 stitch; purl into the top loop of the st in the row below first st on left-hand needle (inserting needle point downward from front, *not* through the st from behind, which would be "p1 in the row below"); then purl into the first st on left-hand needle. (This increase is used when the st in the row below is a purl st.)

OR

(P1-b, p1) in one stitch.

OR

(P1, p1-b) in one stitch.

OR

(P1, k1) in one stitch.

OR

P1 in the row below, then purl the st on needle.

V̇ (P1, k1, p1) in 1 st—purl, knit, and purl again, all in the same st, to make 3 sts from 1.

On a right-side row (row number at right of chart) this symbol means:

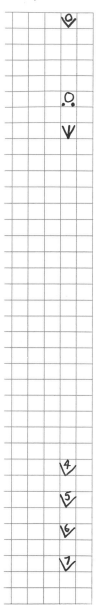

(K1, yo, k1) in 1 st—k1, leave on needle; yo right-hand needle, then knit again into the same st, to make 3 sts from 1.

(P1, yo, p1) in 1 st.

Central double increase—(k1-b, k1) in one stitch, then insert left-hand needle point behind the vertical strand that runs downward from between the 2 sts just made, and k1-b into this strand to make the 3rd st of the group.

OR

Knit into the back of the st in the row below (as in 1st version of **V**); then knit into the back of first st on left-hand needle; then with left-hand needle point pick up *left* side strand of the same st in the row below, and k1-b into this strand to make the 3rd st of the group. (This second version is an excellent, invisible double increase for any stockinette fabric, especially for raglan seams worked from the top down.)

Multiple increases—from one stitch, make the total number shown above the increase V symbol. For example, if the number is 4, (k1, p1, k1, p1) in 1 st; if the number is 5, (k1, yo, k1, yo, k1) in 1 st; etc. For even numbers, knit and purls are usually preferable; for odd numbers, knits and yo's.

On a wrong-side row (row number at left of chart) this symbol means:

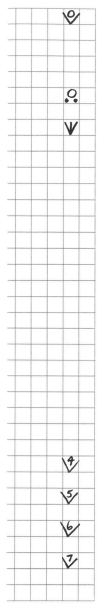

(P1, yo, p1) in 1 st—p1, leave on needle; yo right-hand needle, then purl again into the same st, to make 3 sts from 1.

(K1, yo, k1) in 1 st.

Central double increase—not used on wrong-side rows in this collection of patterns, but it may be worked as follows: (p1-b, p1) in 1 st, then insert left-hand needle into strand between the 2 sts just made, and p1 into this strand to make the 3rd st of the group.

Multiple increases—from one stitch, make the total number shown above the increase V symbol. For example, if the number is 4, (p1, k1, p1, k1) in 1 st; if the number is 5, (p1, yo, p1, yo, p1) in 1 st; etc. For even numbers, purls and knits are usually preferable; for odd numbers, purls and yo's.

III. DECREASES

On a right-side row (row number at right of chart) this symbol means:

On a wrong-side row (row number at left of chart) this symbol means:

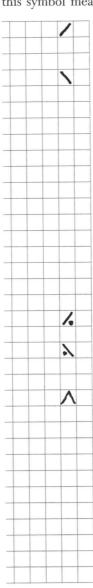

K2 tog—knit two stitches together in front loops as one stitch.

Ssk (slip, slip, knit)—slip the first and second stitches one at a time as if to knit, then insert point of left-hand needle into the fronts of these 2 sts, and knit them together from this position.

OR

K2 tog-b—knit two stitches together in back loops as one stitch.

OR

Sl 1, k1, psso—slip one stitch with yarn in back, knit next stitch, then pass the slipped stitch over the knit stitch and off needle.

P2 tog—purl 2 sts together.

P2 tog-b—same as the wrong-side versions of \.

Sl 1—k2 tog—psso—slip 1 st with yarn in back, knit next two stitches together, then pass the slipped stitch over the knit stitch (this makes a double decrease slanting to the left).

OR

Ssk, return resulting st to left-hand needle, then pass the *next* st over it and off needle; then slip the st back to right-hand needle (this makes a double decrease slanting to the right).

P2 tog—purl two stitches together as one stitch.

P2 tog-b—purl two stitches together in back loops, inserting needle from the left, behind, into the backs of the 2nd and 1st stitches, in that order, then wrapping yarn in front to complete the purl stitch in the usual way.

OR

Purl 1 st, return it to left-hand needle, then with point of right-hand needle pass the *next* st over it and off needle; then slip the st back to right-hand needle.

K2 tog—knit 2 sts together.

Ssk—same as the right-side versions of \.

P2 tog, return resulting st to left-hand needle (keeping yarn in front), then pass the *next* st over it and off needle; then slip the st back to right-hand needle (this makes a double decrease slanting to the left).

OR

Sl 1 wyif, p2 tog-b, then pass the slip-stitch over the p2 tog-b stitch and off needle (this makes a double decrease slanting to the right).

On a right-side row (row number at right of chart) this symbol means:

K3 tog—knit three stitches together as one stitch (double decrease slanting strongly to the right).

OR

Knit 2 sts together, return resulting st to left-hand needle, pass the next st over it and off needle, then slip the st back to right-hand needle (double decrease slanting strongly to the right).

K3 tog-b—knit three stitches together through back loops (double decrease slanting strongly to the left).

OR

Sl 1, ssk, psso.

OR

Sssk (slip, slip, slip, knit)—slip 3 sts knitwise, one at a time, then insert left-hand needle into the fronts of the 3 sts and knit them together from this position.

P3 tog—same as the wrong-side versions of ◿ .

P3 tog-b—same as the wrong-side versions of ◺ .

Sl 2—k1—p2sso—vertical double decrease: insert needle into the 2nd and 1st stitches as if to k2 tog, and slip both stitches at once from this position; knit next stitch, then pass the 2 slipped stitches together over the knit stitch.

On a wrong-side row (row number at left of chart) this symbol means:

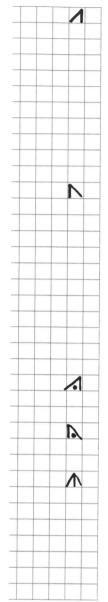

P3 tog—purl three stitches together as one stitch (double decrease slanting strongly to the right).

OR

Sl 1—p2 tog—psso—slip one stitch with yarn in front, purl 2 stitches together, pass the slipped stitch over the purl stitch (double decrease slanting strongly to the right).

P3 tog-b—purl three stitches together through back loops, inserting needle from the left, behind, into the 3rd, 2nd, and 1st stitches (double decrease slanting strongly to the left).

OR

Work the same as the *first* wrong-side version of ◺ .

K3 tog—same as the right-side versions of ◿ .

K3 tog-b—same as the right-side versions of ◺ .

Sl 2—p1—p2sso—vertical double decrease: insert needle into the 2nd and 1st stitches as if to p2 tog-b, and slip both stitches at once from this position; purl next stitch, then pass the 2 slipped stitches together over the purl stitch.

On a right-side row (row number at right of chart) this symbol means:

Work 4 sts tog—ssk, k2 tog, then pass the ssk stitch over the k2-tog stitch.

OR

K4 tog in front or back loops.

OR

See multiple slipped decrease, below.

Work 5 sts tog by multiple slipped decrease: sl 3 with yarn in back, drop yarn; then ° pass the 2nd st on right-hand needle over the 1st (center) st; slip the center st back to left-hand needle and pass the 2nd st on left-hand needle over it; ° slip the center st back to right-hand needle again and repeat from ° to ° once more. Pick up yarn and knit (if the background is knit) or purl (if the background is purl) the center st.

OR

Ssk, k3 tog, pass the ssk st over the k3-tog st.

Other numbers within the "decrease tent" mean that that many stitches are to be decreased to one. The multiple slipped decrease is to be preferred. For example, on seven stitches: sl 4 wyib, ° pass the 2nd st on right-hand needle over the 1st (center) st; sl the center st back to left-hand needle and pass the 2nd st on left-hand needle over it; ° slip the center st back to right-hand needle again and repeat from ° to ° twice more. Pick up yarn and work the center st.

On a wrong-side row (row number at left of chart) this symbol means:

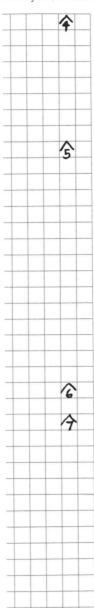

Work 4 sts tog—p2 tog, p2 tog-b, then pass the p2-tog stitch over the p2-tog-b stitch.

OR

P4 tog.

OR

See multiple slipped decrease, below.

Work 5 sts tog by multiple slipped decrease: sl 3 with yarn in front, drop yarn; then ° pass the 2nd st on right-hand needle over the 1st (center st; slip the center st back to left-hand needle and pass the 2nd st on left-hand needle over it; ° slip the center st back to right-hand needle again and repeat from ° to ° once more. Pick up yarn and knit (if the background is knit) or purl (if the background is purl) the center st.

OR

P2 tog, p3 tog-b, pass the p2-tog st over the p3-tog-b st.

Other numbers within the "decrease tent" mean that that many stitches are to be decreased to one. The multiple slipped decrease is to be preferred. For example, on seven stitches: sl 4 wyif, ° pass the 2nd st on right-hand needle over the 1st (center) st; sl the center st back to left-hand needle and pass the 2nd st on left-hand needle over it; ° slip the center st back to right-hand needle again and repeat from ° to ° twice more. Pick up yarn and work the center st.

Quick-Reference List of Symbols

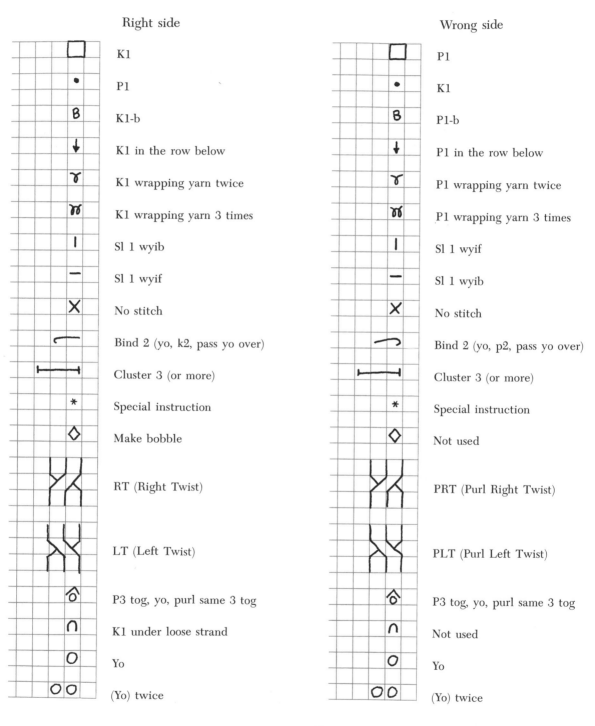

	Right side		Wrong side
☐	K1	☐	P1
•	P1	•	K1
β	K1-b	β	P1-b
↓	K1 in the row below	↓	P1 in the row below
ϓ	K1 wrapping yarn twice	ϓ	P1 wrapping yarn twice
ϻ	K1 wrapping yarn 3 times	ϻ	P1 wrapping yarn 3 times
I	Sl 1 wyib	I	Sl 1 wyif
—	Sl 1 wyif	—	Sl 1 wyib
✕	No stitch	✕	No stitch
⌒	Bind 2 (yo, k2, pass yo over)	⌒	Bind 2 (yo, p2, pass yo over)
⊢—⊣	Cluster 3 (or more)	⊢—⊣	Cluster 3 (or more)
✳	Special instruction	✳	Special instruction
◇	Make bobble	◇	Not used
	RT (Right Twist)		PRT (Purl Right Twist)
	LT (Left Twist)		PLT (Purl Left Twist)
⌂	P3 tog, yo, purl same 3 tog	⌂	P3 tog, yo, purl same 3 tog
∩	K1 under loose strand	∩	Not used
O	Yo	O	Yo
OO	(Yo) twice	OO	(Yo) twice

Right side		Wrong side	
M	M1 (Make One)	M	M1 (Make One)
V	Inc 1	V	Inc 1
ѷ	(K1, p1, k1) in 1 st	ѷ	(P1, k1, p1) in 1 st
ⱷ	(K1, yo, k1) in 1 st	ⱷ	(P1, yo, p1) in 1 st
ⱷ	(P1, yo, p1) in 1 st	ⱷ	(k1, yo, k1) in 1 st
Ѵ	Central double increase	Ѵ	Not used
4 5 6 7	Make 4 (or more) sts from 1	4 5 6 7	Make 4 (or more) sts from 1
/	K2 tog	/	P2 tog
\	Ssk—or etc.	\	P2 tog-b—or etc.
/.	P2 tog	/.	K2 tog
\.	P2 tog-b—or etc.	\.	Ssk—or etc.
∧	Sl 1—k2 tog—psso; or etc.	∧	Sl 1—p2 tog-b—psso; or etc.
⋀	K3 tog—or etc.	⋀	P3 tog—or etc.
⋀	K3 tog-b—or etc.	⋀	P3 tog-b—or etc.
⋀.	P3 tog	⋀.	K3 tog
⋀.	P3 tog-b	⋀.	K3 tog-b
⋀	Sl 2—k1—p2sso	⋀	Sl 2—p1—p2sso
4 5 6 7	Work 4 (or more) sts tog into 1 st: see Complete List	4 5 6 7	Work 4 (or more) sts tog into 1 st: see Complete List
(1) (2)	Special directions for a particular space	(1) (2)	Special directions for a particular space
■	Color symbol: see Mosaic Patterns	■	Color symbol: see Mosaic Patterns
	Cable charts: see Cables		Cable charts: see Cables

CHAPTER 1

Textured Fabrics

A group of various fabric textures will give practice in using various kinds of symbols. Some of these patterns are worked with simple knit and purl stitches; some use increases and decreases to form their designs; some use slip-stitches, or elongated stitches, or yarn-over stitches. There are also bobbles, "made" stitches, and stitches worked in the row below—an assortment of knitting operations to help you become accustomed to translating the Complete List of Symbols into real things to do with your hands.

The only quality that these patterns have in common is the quality of texture. They all make designs on the knitted surface, to render it more interesting to look at than plain stockinette stitch or garter stitch. Some of the patterns are lacy, some of average density, some very thick and close; this depends, of course, on the various knitting techniques used in each. Your test swatches will tell you, as you try out each design, which patterns might be used for general garment construction (sweaters, dresses, mittens) or for soft, loosely-knit articles (shawls, bedjackets, baby blankets, scarves) or for heavy outdoor wear (coats, jackets, ski pants, bulky sweaters). Much depends on the yarn weight and needle size that you use. A pattern that is loose and lacy when worked with fine yarn on large needles might be tight and firm when worked with heavier yarn on smaller needles. So no hard and fast rules can be made for textured fabrics. In most cases they will be what you want them to be; colors, weights, stitch gauges, tensions all are decided by individual preferences and individual knitting style. Types of yarn make a difference, too. Most of the photographs show these patterns worked in smooth, standard yarns such as knitting worsted or sport yarn; but if you choose to work them in some fancy, fuzzy, slubbed or hairy yarn, of course they will look different.

So have fun with them, and don't be afraid to be inventive. Knitting is not one of the exact sciences. There is always room for individualism; indeed, a little individualism is essential if you want to create anything that stands out from the general run. As long as you count stitches accurately and read the charts with understanding, you can use textured fabrics almost any way you want. Many of these patterns will reward you with some neat effects that neither you nor anyone else has ever seen before.

Increase-and-Decrease Smocking

Example Textured Fabric:

Increase-and-Decrease Smocking

For the first example, here is a simple diamond design formed by increases and decreases alone. The chart will give you a little practice in ignoring X's and reversing knits and purls on the wrong-side rows. Two repeats are shown on this chart, instead of the usual single repeat, because the last repeat of the row sometimes has to end differently from the others. The left-hand half of the chart therefore applies only to the last repeat, and all others work back and forth between the vertical lines as usual. Thus the asterisks in the printed directions will not coincide exactly with the vertical lines, but they hardly ever do so anyway, in any pattern. As you work this example from both directions and chart at the same time, you'll see why.

Multiple of 18 sts plus 1—(37 sts minimum)

Notes: M1 (Make One)—insert needle from behind under running thread between the st just worked and the next st, and purl this thread; *except* in Rows 18 and 36: in these rows lift running thread and knit into the back of it in the usual way.

  Double increase—(k1-b, k1) in one st, then insert left-hand needle behind the vertical strand that runs downward from between the 2 sts just made, and knit into the back of this strand to make the third stitch of the group.

Row 1 (Wrong side)—P2, ° k5, p5, k5, yo, p3, pass yo over the 3 purl sts; rep from °, end k5, p5, k5, p2.

Row 2—Inc in first st, ° k1, p5, ssk, k1, k2 tog, p5, k1, double inc; rep from °, end last repeat with plain single inc instead of double inc in last st.

Row 3—P3, ° k5, p3, k5, p5; rep from °, end last repeat p3.

Row 4—Inc in first st, ° k2, p5, sl 2-k1-p2sso, p5, k2, double inc; rep from °, end last repeat with plain single inc instead of double inc in last st.

Row 5—K1, ° p3, k11, p3, k1; rep from °.

Row 6—P1, ° M1, k2, ssk, p9, k2 tog, k2, M1, p1; rep from °.

Row 7—K2, ° p3, k9, p3, k3; rep from °, end last repeat k2.

continued on page 4

INCREASE-AND-DECREASE SMOCKING

Multiple of 18 sts plus 1—37 sts minimum. Two repeats shown

NOTE: *Rows* 6, 8, 10, 12, 14, 24, 26, 28, 30, and 32—M1 by purling under running thread from behind.

Rows 18 and 36—M1 in the usual way by knitting into back of running thread.

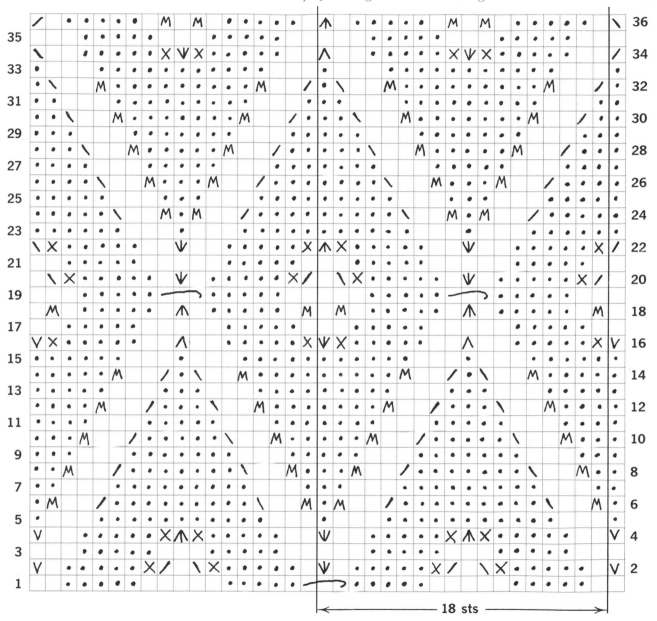

Row 8—P2, ° M1, k2, ssk, p7, k2 tog, k2, M1, p3; rep from °, end last repeat p2.

Row 9—K3, ° p3, k7, p3, k5; rep from °, end last repeat k3.

Row 10—P3, ° M1, k2, ssk, p5, k2 tog, k2, M1, p5; rep from °, end last repeat p3.

Row 11—K4, ° p3, k5, p3, k7; rep from °, end last repeat k4.

Row 12—P4, ° M1, k2, ssk, p3, k2 tog, k2, M1, p7; rep from °, end last repeat p4.

Row 13—K5, ° p3, k3, p3, k9; rep from °, end last repeat k5.

Row 14—P5, ° M1, k2, ssk, p1, k2 tog, k2, M1, p9; rep from °, end last repeat p5.

Row 15—K6, ° p3, k1, p3, k11; rep from °, end last repeat k6.

Row 16—Inc in first st, ° p5, k2, sl 1-k2 tog-psso, k2, p5, double inc; rep from °, end last repeat with plain single inc instead of double inc in last st.

Row 17—P2, ° k5, p5, k5, p3; rep from °, end last repeat p2.

Row 18—K1, ° M1, k1, p5, k1, sl 2-k1-p2sso, k1, p5, k1, M1, k1; rep from °.

Row 19—P3, ° k5, yo, p3, pass yo over the 3 purl sts, k5, p5; rep from °, end last repeat p3.

Row 20—K1, ° k2 tog, p5, k1, double inc, k1, p5, ssk, k1; rep from °.

Rows 21, 23, 25, 27, 29, 31, 33, and *35*—Repeat Rows 17, 15, 13, 11, 9, 7, 5, and 3.

Row 22—K2 tog, ° p5, k2, double inc, k2, p5, sl 2-k1-p2sso; rep from °, end last repeat ssk instead of sl 2-k1-p2sso.

Row 24—P5, ° k2 tog, k2, M1, p1, M1, k2, ssk, p9; rep from °, end last repeat p5.

Row 26—P4, ° k2 tog, k2, M1, p3, M1, k2, ssk, p7; rep from °, end last repeat p4.

Row 28—P3, ° k2 tog, k2, M1, p5, M1, k2, ssk, p5; rep from °, end last repeat p3.

Row 30—P2, ° k2 tog, k2, M1, p7, M1, k2, ssk, p3; rep from °, end last repeat p2.

Row 32—P1, ° k2 tog, k2, M1, p9, M1, k2, ssk, p1; rep from °.

Row 34—K2 tog, ° k2, p5, double inc, p5, k2, sl 1-k2 tog-psso; rep from °, end last repeat ssk instead of sl 1-k2 tog-psso.

Row 36—Ssk, ° k1, p5, (k1, M1) twice, k1, p5, k1, sl 2-k1-p2sso; rep from °, end last repeat k2 tog instead of sl 2-k1-p2sso.

Repeat Rows 1–36.

SEMI-WOVEN LATTICE WITH MOSS STITCH

Multiple of 15 sts plus 2.

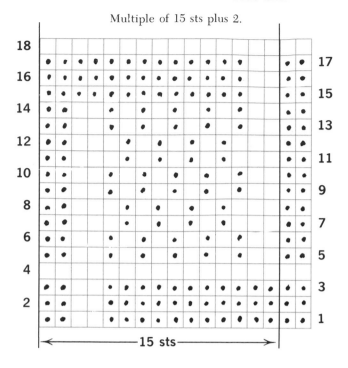

Semi-Woven Lattice with Moss Stitch

Broken Chevron

BROKEN CHEVRON

Multiple of 12 sts.

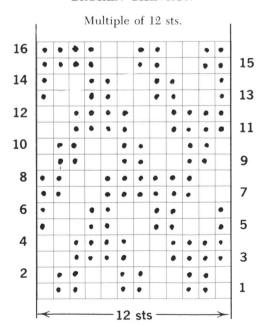

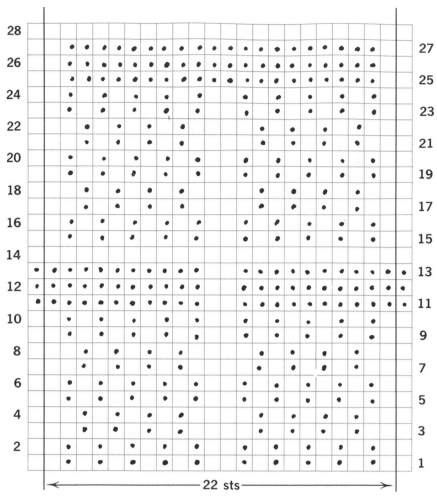

SQUARE LATTICE WITH MOSS STITCH

Multiple of 22 sts plus 2.

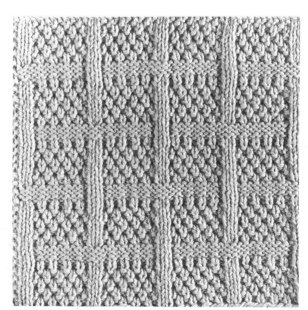

Square Lattice with Moss Stitch

ALAN'S PATTERN

Multiple of 8 sts.

Alan's Pattern

FOUR-AND-TWO BASKETWEAVE

Multiple of 6 sts plus 1.

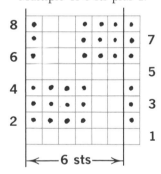

← 6 sts →

GARTER BASKETWEAVE

Multiple of 6 sts plus 1.

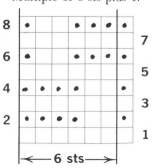

← 6 sts →

ABOVE: **Four-and-Two Basketweave**
BELOW: **Garter Basketweave**

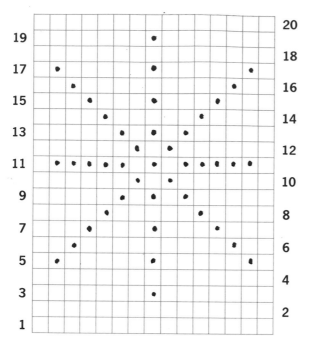

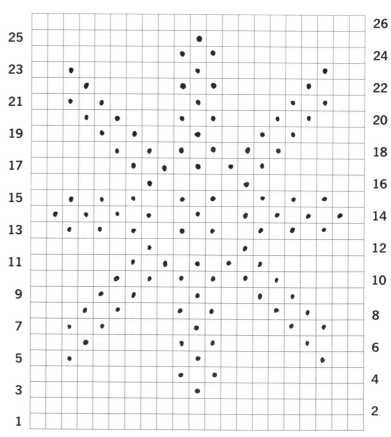

LEFT: Thin Star
CENTER: Latin Star
RIGHT: Flying Wedge

THIN STAR

Panel of 15 sts.

LATIN STAR

Panel of 21 sts.

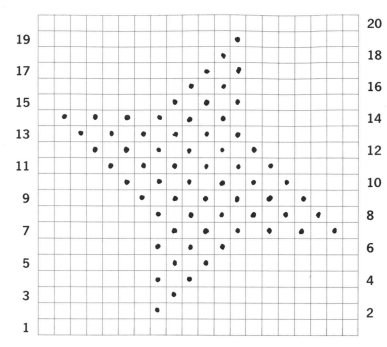

FLYING WEDGE

Panel of 20 sts.

CLOVER CHAIN

Multiple of 9 sts plus 4.

Clover Chain

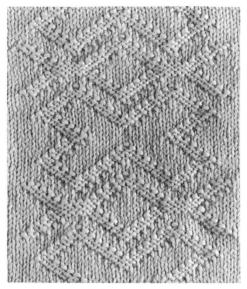

Celtic Pattern

Bubble Pattern

CELTIC PATTERN

Panel of 33 sts.

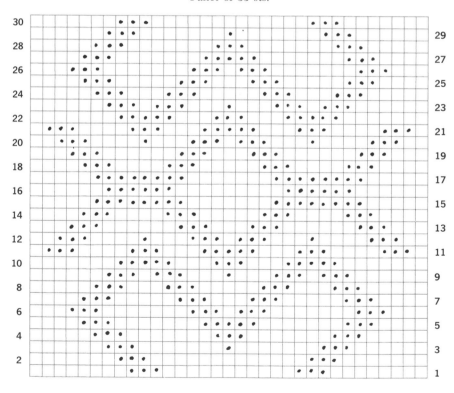

BUBBLE PATTERN

Multiple of 4 sts plus 3.
Two repeats shown

◊—Note: MB (make bobble) as follows: (k1, p1, k1, p1, k1) in one st, (turn and k5) twice, then pass 2nd, 3rd, 4th, and 5th sts on right-hand needle one at a time over the first st, completing bobble.

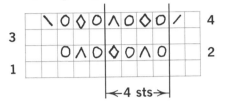

DOUBLE-BAR SMOCKING

Multiple of 6 sts plus 2.
Two repeats shown

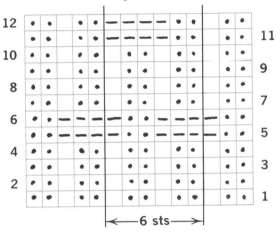

AUSTRIAN SMOCKING

Multiple of 8 sts plus 5.

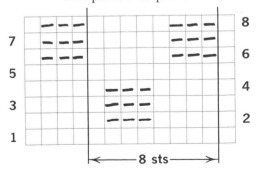

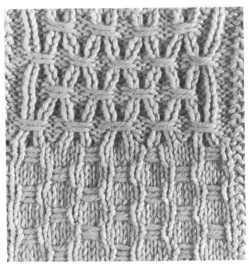

ABOVE: **Double-Bar Smocking**
BELOW: **Austrian Smocking**

Palm Leaf and Bobble Pattern

PALM LEAF AND BOBBLE PATTERN

Multiple of 16 sts plus 3.

◊ ° *Rows 10* and *20*—Make bobble as follows: (k1, yo, k1, yo, k1) in one st, turn and k5, turn and p5, turn and k2 tog, k1, k2 tog, turn and p3 tog.

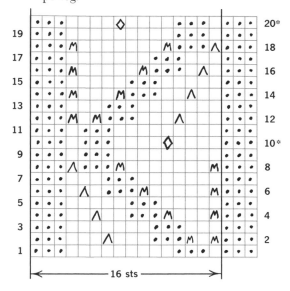

EMBOSSED WAVE

Multiple of 8 sts.

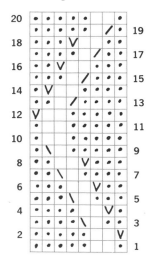

Embossed Wave

KNIT-PURL BOBBLE PATTERN

Multiple of 10 sts plus 1. Two repeats shown

° *Row 12*—make Knit Bobble as in Complete List of Symbols.

° *Row 24*—make Purl Bobble as in Palm Leaf and Bobble Pattern.

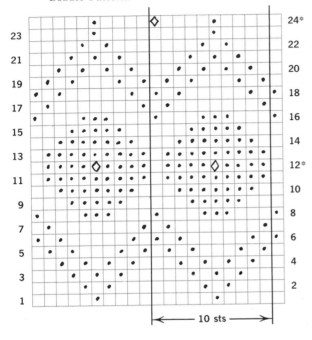

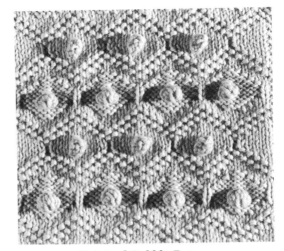

Knit-Purl Bobble Pattern

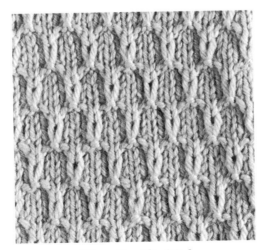

Alternating Slip-Stitch

ALTERNATING SLIP-STITCH

Multiple of 4 sts plus 3.

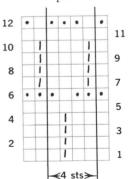

The Pine Tree

THE PINE TREE

Panel of 23 sts.

34	•	•	•	•	•	•	•	•	•	•	•	•	•	•	•	•	•	•	•	•	•	•	•
33	•	•	•	•	•	•	•	•	•	•	•		•	•	•	•	•	•	•	•	•	•	•
32	•	•	•	•	•	•	•	•	•	•	•	∣	•	•	•	•	•	•	•	•	•	•	•
31	•	•	•	•	•	•	•	•	•	•	•			•	•	•	•	•	•	•	•	•	•
30	•	•	•	•	•	•	•	•	•	•		∣		•	•	•	•	•	•	•	•	•	•
29	•	•	•	•	•	•	•	•	•						•	•	•	•	•	•	•	•	•
28	•	•	•	•	•	•	•	•	•	∣		∣		∣	•	•	•	•	•	•	•	•	•
27	•	•	•	•	•	•	•	•					•		▵	▵	▵	•	•	•	•	•	•
26	•	•	•	•	•	•	•	∣			∣			∣	•	•	•	•	•	•	•	•	•
25	•	•	•	•	•	•								•	•	•	•	•	•	•	•	•	•
24	•	•	•	•	•	∣	∣	•		∣		•	∣	∣	•	•	•	•	•	•	•	•	•
23	•	•	•	•	▵			•				•			•	•	•	•	•	•	•	•	•
22	•	•	•	•	•	∣		∣	•	∣		•	∣		∣	•	•	•	•	•	•	•	•
21	•	•	•	•				•				•				•	•	•	•	•	•	•	•
20	•	•	•	•	∣	∣	•	∣	•	∣		•	∣	•	∣	∣	•	•	•	•	•	•	•
19	•	•	•	•			•		•			•		•			•	•	•	•	•	•	•
18	•	•	•	∣		∣	•	∣	•	∣		•	∣	•	∣		∣	•	•	•	•	•	•
17	•	•	•				•		•			•		•			•	•	•	•	•	•	•
16	•	•	∣	∣	∣	•	∣	•	∣	•	∣		•	∣	•	∣	•	∣	∣	•	•	•	•
15	•	•			•		•		•			•		•				•	•	•	•	•	•
14	•	•	∣		∣	•	∣	•	∣	•	∣		•	∣	•	∣	•	∣		∣	•	•	•
13	•	•				•		•		•			•		•				•	•	•	•	•
12	•	•	∣	•	∣	•	∣	•	∣	•	∣		•	∣	•	∣	∣	•	∣	•	∣	•	•
11	•	•		•		•		•		•			•		•			•		•	•	•	•
10	•	•	∣	•	∣	•	∣	•	∣	•	∣		•	∣	•	∣	•	∣	•	∣	•	•	•
9	•	•		•		•		•		•			•		•		•		•		•	•	•
8	•	•	•	•	•	•	•	•	•	•		∣		•	•	•	•	•	◂	•	•	•	•
7	•	•	•	•	•	•	•	•	•	•				•	•	•	•	•	•	•	•	•	•
6	•	•	•	•	•	•	•	•	•	•		∣		•	•	•	•	•	•	•	•	•	•
5	•	•	•	•	•	•	•	•	•	•				•	•	•	•	•	•	•	•	•	•
4	•	•	•	•	•	•	•	•	•	•		∣		•	•	•	•	•	•	•	•	•	•
3	•	•	•	•	•	•	•	•	•	•				•	•	•	•	•	•	•	•	•	•
2	•	•	•	•	•	•	•	•	•	•		∣		•	•	•	•	•	•	•	•	•	•
1	•	•	•	•	•	•	•	•	•	•				•	•	•	•	•	•	•	•	•	•

TRIPLE-SLIP COATING

Multiple of 6 sts plus 3.

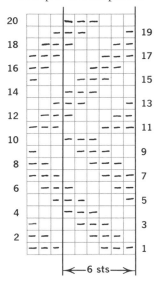

Triple-Slip Coating

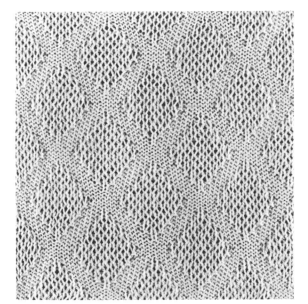

Puff Diamond

PUFF DIAMOND

Multiple of 16 sts plus 1.

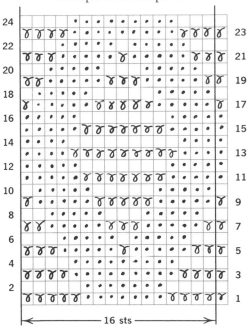

Daisy Cluster Patterns
ABOVE: # 1
BELOW, LEFT: # 2
BELOW, RIGHT: # 3

DAISY CLUSTER PATTERNS

#1—Multiple of 4 sts plus 1.
Two repeats shown

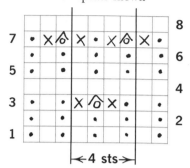

#3—Multiple of 4 sts plus 1.
Two repeats shown

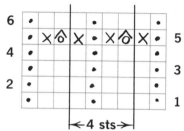

#2—Multiple of 4 sts plus 1.
Two repeats shown

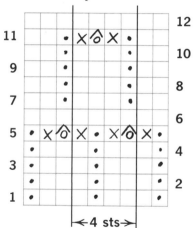

Clustered Sheaves

CLUSTERED SHEAVES

Multiple of 23 sts plus 2.

° Thirteen stitch cluster, Rows 15 and 31—sl 13 sts to dpn, wind yarn 3 times counterclockwise around these 13 sts, then from dpn (k1-b, p1) 6 times, k1-b.

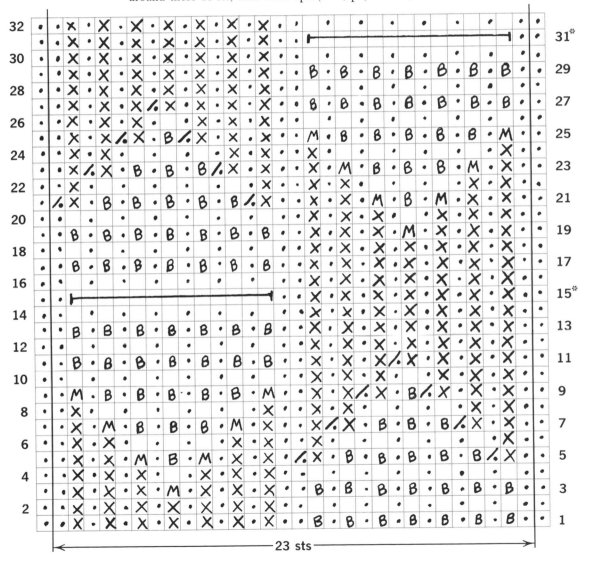

LOLLIPOP STITCH

Multiple of 12 sts plus 1.

(1)—P5

(2)—Inc, k3, inc

(3)—P7

(4)—Inc, k5, inc

(5)—P9

(6)—Ssk, k5, k2 tog

(7)—P2 tog, p3, p2 tog-b

(8)—Ssk, k1, k2 tog

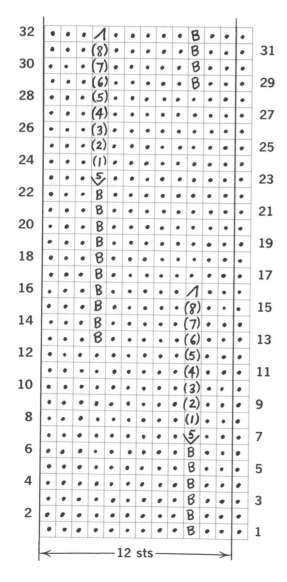

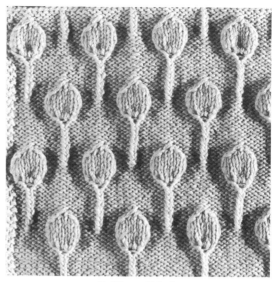

Lollipop Stitch

Lazy Ribbing

LAZY RIBBING

Multiple of 30 sts plus 1.

V—Increase by purling into front and back of same st.

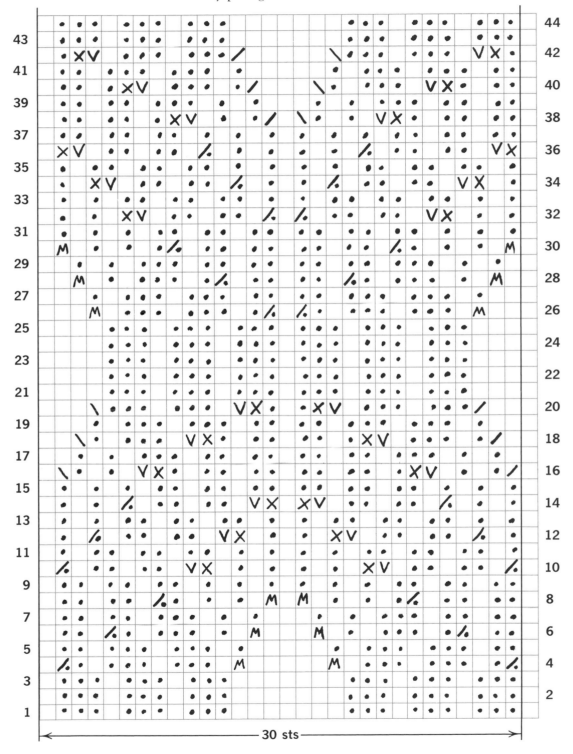

30 sts

ABOVE: Windblown Leaf Border
BELOW: Triple Lily-Bud Border

WINDBLOWN LEAF BORDER

Multiple of 6 sts plus 5. Two repeats shown

(1)—P3

(2)—K1, yo, k1, yo, k1

(3)—P5

(4)—K2, yo, k1, yo, k2

(5)—P7

(6)—K3, yo, k1, yo, k3

(7)—P9

(8)—Ssk, k5, k2 tog

(9)—Ssk, k3, k2 tog

(10)—Ssk, k1, k2 tog

V —Increase by purling into
back and front of same st.

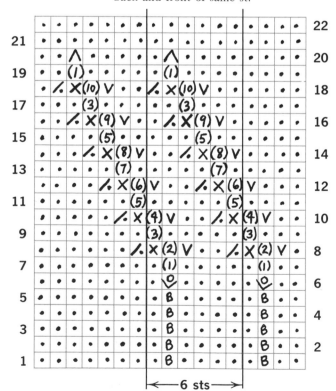

TRIPLE LILY-BUD BORDER

Multiple of 12 sts plus 5.

° *Rows 6 and 8—see chapter on Twist Stitch Patterns.*

(1)—Yo, k1
(2)—P2, yo
(3)—Yo, k3
(4)—P4, yo
(5)—Yo, k5
(6)—P6
(7)—Ssk, k4
(8)—P2 tog, p3
(9)—Ssk, k2
(10)—P2 tog, p1

LOOSE STITCH

Multiple of 12 sts.

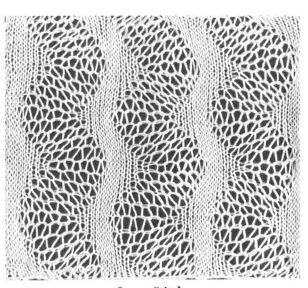

Loose Stitch

Diamond and Rib

DIAMOND AND RIB

Multiple of 16 sts plus 11.

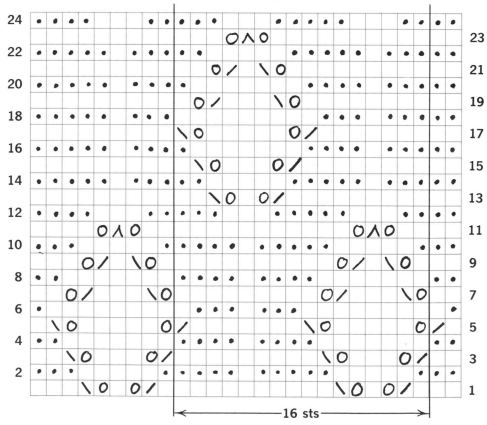

ABOVE: Reverse Fern Stitch
BELOW: Panel Version

REVERSE FERN STITCH

Multiple of 12 sts plus 1. Two repeats shown

NOTE: For Panel Version, repeat Rows 1–10 only.

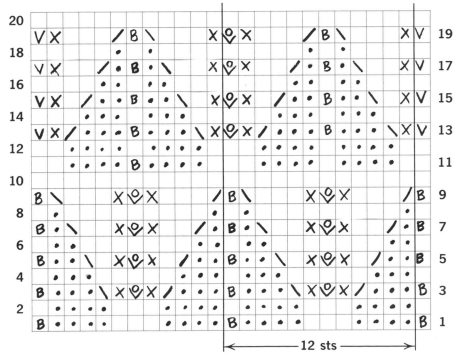

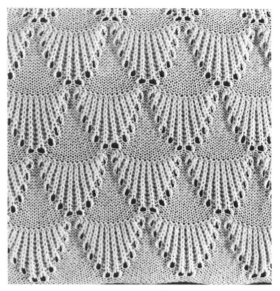

Cockleshells

LITTLE COCKLESHELLS

Multiple of 10 sts plus 3 (increased to 18 plus 3)

NOTE: ↓ to k1 in the row below, over the yo's on Rows 4, 8, 12, etc., insert needle into the yo space 1 row below, and knit.

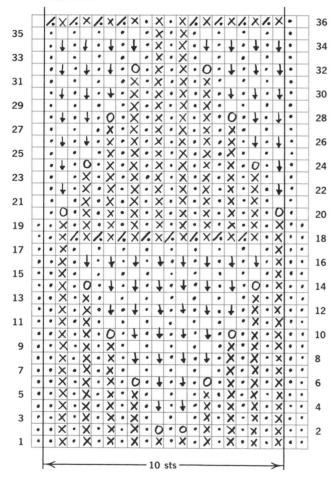

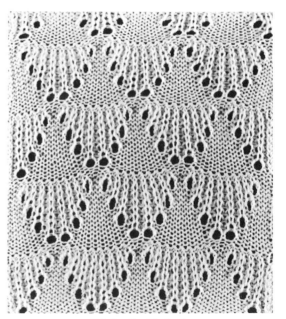

Little Cockleshells

COCKLESHELLS

Multiple of 14 sts plus 3 (increased to 26 plus 3)

NOTE: ↓—see Little Cockleshells. Also, in this pattern, this symbol ↓ means *knit* (not purl) one stitch in the row below, on *all* rows, both right and wrong sides.

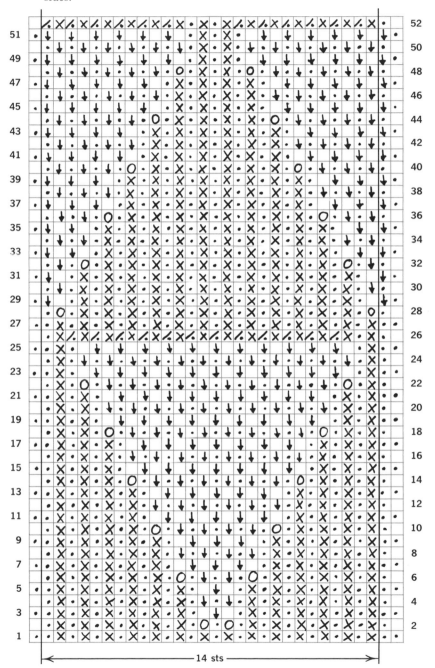

14 sts

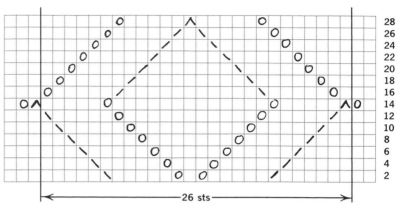

BROAD WAVE PATTERN

Multiple of 26 sts plus 5.

NOTE: *Row 1* (wrong side) and all other wrong-side rows—Purl.
These rows are not shown.

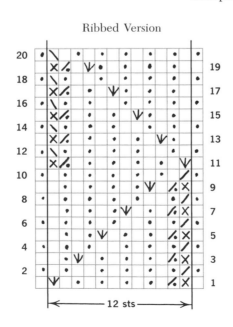

ABOVE: **Ripple Weave, Ribbed Version**
BELOW: **Ripple Weave, Plain Version**

RIPPLE WEAVE

Multiple of 12 sts plus 2.

Ribbed Version

Plain Version

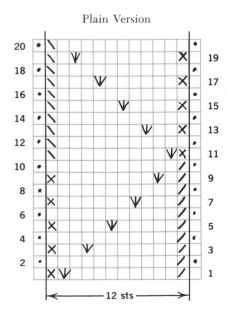

Broad Wave Pattern

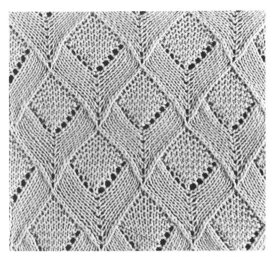

Optical Illusion

OPTICAL ILLUSION

Multiple of 18 sts plus 1 (increased to 20 plus 1)— Two repeats shown

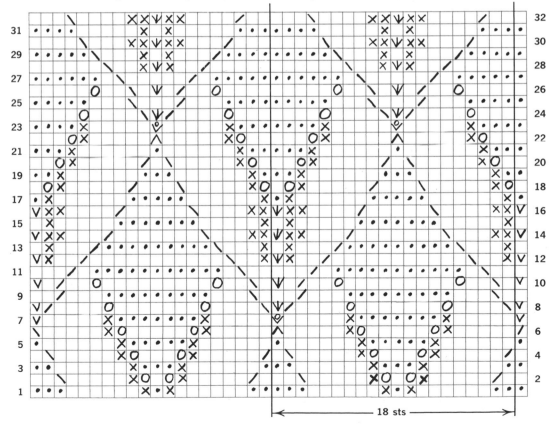

Tassels

Embossed Heart

TASSELS

Multiple of 24 sts plus 5 (increased to 24 sts plus 7)

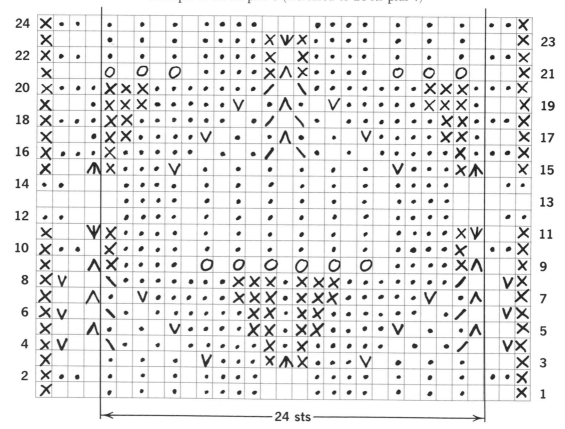

EMBOSSED HEART

Panel of 15 sts (increased to 21)

° *Row 16*— V Increase by purling into front and back of same st.

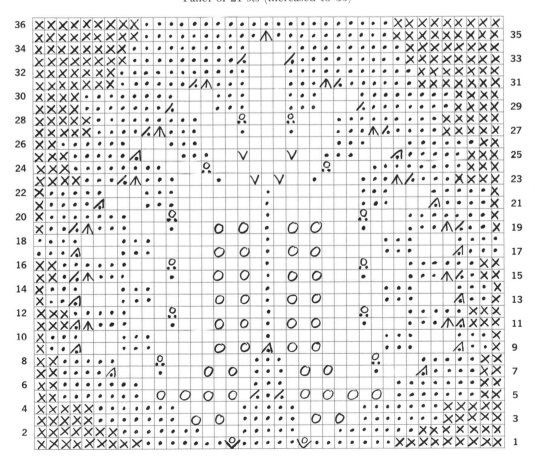

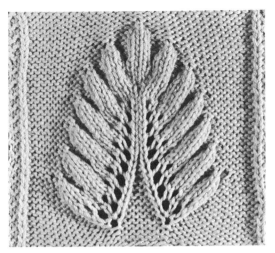

Acanthus Leaf

ACANTHUS LEAF

Panel of 21 sts (increased to 39)

SEVEN-RIB SHELL, SOLID VERSION

Multiple of 29 sts plus 17 (variable stitch count)
Note jog of repeat lines between Rows 14 and 15
V—Increase by purling into front and back of the same st.

Seven-Rib Shell, Solid Version

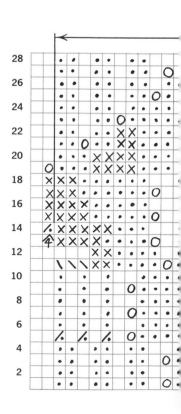

SEVEN-RIB SHELL, OPENWORK VERSION

Multiple of 29 sts plus 17 (variable stitch count)
Note jog of repeat lines between Rows 14 and 15

Seven-Rib Shell, Openwork Version

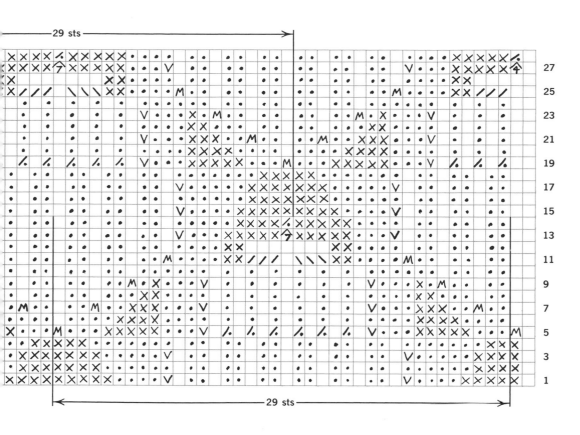

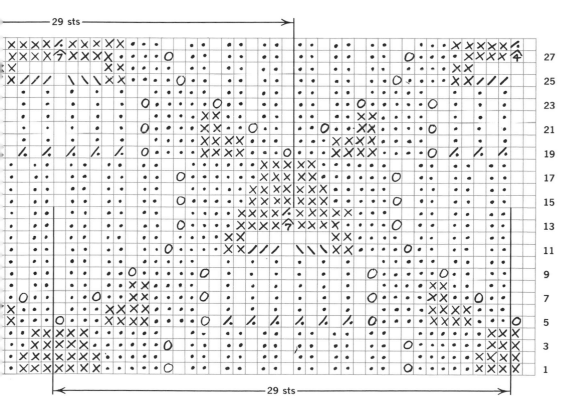

CHAPTER 2

Twist Stitch Patterns

Twist stitches are almost the same as one-over-one cable crossings. The only difference between them is that twists are worked without the aid of a cable needle, so that the rear, or background, stitch usually is not purled. In most twists, two stitches exchange positions, one passing in front and the other behind. Of course it is possible to twist more than two stitches, though the appearance of wider twists is often rather ungainly.

In the two-stitch twist, if the left-hand stitch crosses in front of the right-hand stitch, the result is a Right Twist—that is, a stitch progressing upward from left to right. The reverse is a Left Twist. Two ways of doing each sort of twist are given in the Complete List of Symbols, and the knitter is advised to try them both, to see which one feels better. Purl twists are the same thing worked from the wrong side. They are not much used, except in those patterns which require twists on several consecutive rows to make a broader diagonal line.

In this method of charting twist patterns, the stitches that are to be twisted are outlined at each side, to make them and the direction in which they are going more obvious. On the row where the twist occurs, the outlines of the *front* stitch pass diagonally across the two squares representing the two twisting stitches, from the lower corners of the squares to the opposite upper corners. If these two diagonal outlines go upward from left to right, it is a Right Twist; if they go upward from right to left, it is a Left Twist.

The outlines of the rear, or background, stitch sometimes are included too, but not always. If the background is made up of purl stitches, across which the twists form a clear diagonal rib, the outlines of the rear stitches are usually omitted. On the other hand, if the twist is embedded in knit stitches, or both stitches continue upward and downward as knit ribs, then the additional outlines will be shown on the chart. At times, also, the outlines of the front twist stitches will cut across the vertical repeat lines for greater clarity.

Such charts are very graphic, enabling the knitter to visualize the pattern with precision because they look so much like the knitting itself. Charts for Cables (which see) are constructed on exactly the same principle.

Most of the patterns in this section are especially easy to knit, and suitable for all kinds of knitted articles. Combining different twist patterns in a series of panels, or combining them with assorted cables, will make beautiful Aran-style sweaters. Twist panels make nice afghans, too, and some of the allover patterns are particularly good-looking in coats, jackets, and vests. Twist patterns give a firm fabric that will wear well, because they pull the knitting together laterally. Remember this when you are setting out to make a garment with twist stitches, because you will need to cast on more stitches than you would use for the same width in stockinette. Always make test swatches and check your gauge (number of stitches to the inch), then use the right number of stitches for the right number of inches. Every knitting teacher on earth has said this hundreds of times, but would you believe there are still some knitters who don't do it? However, you, dear reader, surely are not one of these intransigents; so of course your garments always come out the right size and shape.

When you are working a twist pattern from a chart, you will find it possible in many cases to hold the chart upside down if you want to. If you like the pattern better upside down, go ahead and work it that way. Usually it will look the same either way round, but sometimes there is a difference. You can see the difference, if any, on the chart itself.

Of course if you don't like working twist stitches, and prefer to use the cable needle to make one-over-one cable crossings instead, you can do that too. The pattern will still look the same, maybe even a little tidier. But most people like twist stitches because they are faster and more convenient than cabling. You can also work twist stitches by the "drop" method, which is used by a few bold knitters who never get nervous about dropped stitches. It goes like this: for a Right Twist, drop the first stitch off the left-hand needle to the back, and either leave it hanging there, or hold it with the thumb and forefinger of the left hand; work the second stitch, then work the first stitch. For a Left Twist, drop the first stitch off the left-hand needle to the front, work the second stitch, then work the first stitch. In both cases the dropped first stitch is put back on the left-hand needle after the second stitch has been worked; then it can be knitted or purled off with ease (provided it hasn't slid away from you in the meantime). Another way of working the "drop" method is to slide both stitches off the left-hand needle, holding them at the base so they can't unravel, reverse their positions with either the left-hand stitch in front (for a Right Twist) or the right-hand stitch in front (for a Left Twist), and put them back on the left-hand needle; then work them. In either version of the "drop" method the rear stitch can be purled to match a purl background.

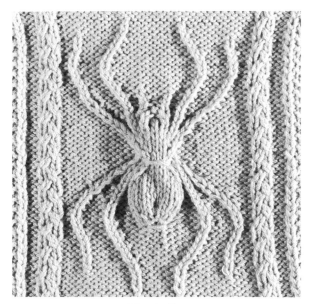

The Spider

Example Twist Pattern:

The Spider

HERE's Arachne herself, the great-grand-mother of all the world's spinners and weavers, and still one of the best of them. Who among us can match her skill?

What's that—you don't think she's very pretty? Well, never mind. The pattern techniques that make her in yarn (as well as all her busy real-life children in your garden) have much to teach you. As twist-stitch patterns go, this one is fairly complex. It has been chosen deliberately as an example to show you almost every kind of knitting operation that you might encounter in a twist-stitch design.

First of all, notice the unbroken diagonal lines of Arachne's outer legs, formed or Rows 19–27 and 29–37. These are made by twisting the stitches on every row instead of every right-side row, as is more usual. There is nothing approximate about these diagonal lines; taken one row at a time, they depict each twist in exactly the right position. To demonstrate this to yourself, look at Row 20 on the chart (the first wrong-side twist row). Cover Rows 19 and 21 with the edges of two pieces of paper, so you see only Row 20. Starting from the left-hand edge, which is where you normally begin on a wrong-side row, you see four dots, or purl bumps, first: four wrong-side knit stitches. Then comes the twist, which moves from the bottom of the left-hand square to the top of the right-hand square; therefore it is a twist to the *right*. Since you are on a wrong-side row, you know you must work the wrong-side version of a Right Twist; that is, a PRT (Purl Right Twist). At the right-hand side of the chart, you see the opposing twist traveling to the left—hence, a PLT—followed by the four dots, or knit stitches, that finish the row. You can check each row in the same way if you are ever in doubt about the position of a wrong-side twist; but if you count carefully the stitches that precede it, you will never have any difficulty in knowing just where it comes. Whenever diagonal lines are continued through the corners of several squares at once on a chart, they indicate that the stitch is to be continuously twisted, once on every row.

The other operations in this pattern are more or less routine—a few "made" stitches, a few assorted decreases, two yarn-overs (for the eyes) and two clusters. The little braided ribs at each side of the illustration are not included in the directions or the chart; they are just arbitrary embellishment. You can probably see how they are worked just by looking at the photograph. But for the record, each braid is made of three stitches, purled on every wrong-side row, with the right-side rows alternately "LT, k1" and "K1, RT."

THE SPIDER

Panel of 29 sts (increased to 35)

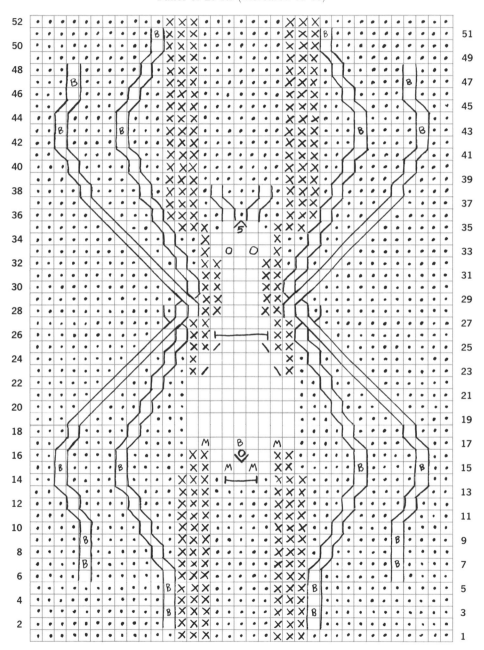

Panel of 29 sts (increased to 35)

Notes: RT (Right Twist)—K2 tog, leave on needle; then insert right-hand needle between the sts just knitted tog, and knit the first st again; sl both sts together from left-hand needle.

LT (Left Twist)—Skip 1 st and knit the 2nd st in back loop, then knit the skipped st in front loop; sl both sts together from left-hand needle.

PRT (Purl Right Twist)—Skip 1 st and purl the 2nd st, then purl the skipped st; sl both sts together from left-hand needle.

PLT (Purl Left Twist)—Skip 1 st and purl the 2nd st in back loop (from behind), then purl the skipped st in front loop; sl both sts together from left-hand needle.

M1 (Make One)—Lift running thread between the st just worked and the next st, and knit into the back of this thread.

Cluster (wrong side)—sl the given number of sts wyif, pass yarn to back, sl the same number of sts back to left-hand needle, pass yarn to front, purl the sts.

Row 1 (Right side)—Purl.
Rows 2 and 4—K11, p1, k5, p1, k11.
Rows 3 and 5—P11, k1-b, p5, k1-b, p11.
Row 6—K4, p1, k6, p1, k5, p1, k6, p1, k4.
Row 7—P4, k1-b, p5, RT, p5, LT, p5, k1-b, p4.
Row 8—K4, p1, k5, p1, k7, p1, k5, p1, k4.
Row 9—P4, k1-b, p4, RT, p7, LT, p4, k1-b, p4.
Row 10—(K4, p1) twice, k9, (p1, k4) twice.
Row 11—(P3, RT) twice, p9, (LT, p3) twice.
Row 12—K3, p1, k4, p1, k11, p1, k4, p1, k3.
Row 13—P2, RT, p3, RT, p11, LT, p3, LT, p2.
Row 14—K2, p1, k4, p1, k5, cluster 3, k5, p1, k4, p1, k2.
Row 15—P2, k1-b, p4, k1-b, p5, (k1, M1) twice, k1, p5, k1-b, p4, k1-b, p2. (31 sts)
Row 16—K2, p1, k4, p1, k5, p2, (p1, yo, p1) in next st, p2, k5, p1, k4, p1, k2. (33 sts)
Row 17—P2, LT, p3, LT, p4, k1, M1, k2, k1-b, k2, M1, k1, p4, RT, p3, RT, p2. (35 sts)
Row 18—K3, (p1, k4) twice, p9, (k4, p1) twice, k3.
Row 19—(P3, LT) twice, p3, k9, p3, (RT, p3) twice.
Row 20—K4, PRT, k3, p1, k3, p9, k3, p1, k3, PLT, k4.
Row 21—P5, (LT, p2) twice, k9, (p2, RT) twice, p5.
Row 22—K6, PRT, k2, p1, k2, p9, k2, p1, k2, PLT, k6.
Row 23—P7, (LT, p1) twice, ssk, k5, k2 tog, (p1, RT) twice, p7. (33 sts)
Row 24—K8, PRT, k1, p1, k1, p7, k1, p1, k1, PLT, k8.
Row 25—P9, (LT) twice, ssk, k3, k2 tog, (RT) twice, p9. (31 sts)
Row 26—K10, PRT, p1, cluster 5, p1, PLT, k10.
Row 27—P11, LT, k5, RT, p11.
Row 28—K12, p7, k12.
Row 29—P12, RT, k3, LT, p12.
Row 30—K11, PLT, p5, PRT, k11.
Row 31—P10, (RT) twice, k3, (LT) twice, p10.

Row 32—K9, PLT, k1, p1, k1, p3, k1, p1, k1, PRT, k9.

Row 33—P8, (RT, p1) twice, (k1, yo) twice, k1, (p1, LT) twice, p8. (33 sts)

Row 34—K7, PLT, k2, p1, k2, p5, k2, p1, k2, PRT, k7.

Row 35—P6, RT, p2, RT, p1, k1, ssk, k3 tog, pass ssk st over the k3-tog st; k1, p1, LT, p2, LT, p6. (29 sts)

Row 36—K5, PLT, k3, p1, k2, p1, k1, p1, k2, p1, k3, PRT, k5.

Row 37—P4, RT, p3, (RT, p1) twice, LT, p1, LT, p3, LT, p4.

Row 38—(K4, p1) twice, k2, p1, k3, p1, k2, (p1, k4) twice.

Rows 39, 40, and *41*—Repeat Rows 11, 12, and 13.

Row 42—K2, p1, k4, p1, k13, p1, k4, p1, k2.

Row 43—P2, k1-b, p4, k1-b, p13, k1-b, p4, k1-b, p2.

Row 44—Repeat Row 42.

Row 45—P2, LT, p3, LT, p11, RT, p3, RT, p2.

Row 46—Repeat Row 12.

Row 47—P3, k1-b, p4, LT, p9, RT, p4, k1-b, p3.

Row 48 K3, p1, k5, p1, k9, p1, k5, p1, k3.

Row 49—P9, LT, p7, RT, p9.

Row 50—K10, p1, k7, p1, k10.

Row 51—P10, k1-b, p7, k1-b, p10.

Row 52—Knit.

Repeat Rows 1–52.

NUBBY STITCH

Multiple of 3 sts plus 1.

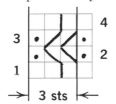

LITTLE TWIST HONEYCOMB

Multiple of 4 sts.

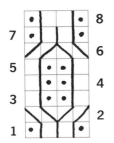

ABOVE: Nubby Stitch
BELOW: Little Twist Honeycomb

LEFT: **Rabbit Ears**
CENTER: **Mirror Cable**
RIGHT: **Ear of Corn Pattern**

RABBIT EARS

Panel of 8 sts.

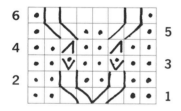

EAR OF CORN PATTERN

Panel of 8 sts.

MIRROR CABLE

Panel of 8 sts.

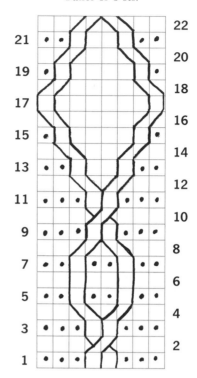

POD PATTERN

Multiple of 14 sts plus 1 (increased to 20 sts plus 1).

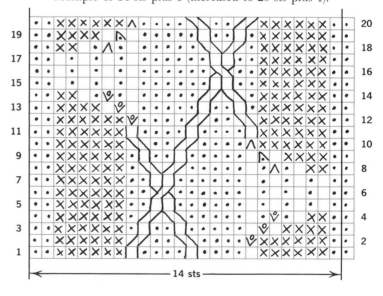

VINE STEM

Panel of 15 sts.

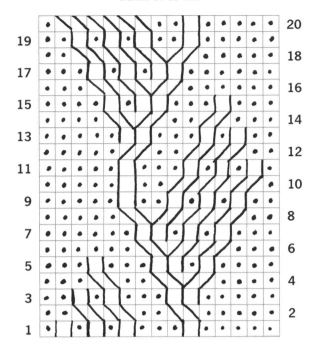

LEFT: Vine Stem
RIGHT: Inside Twist

INSIDE TWIST

Panel of 16 sts.

Pod Pattern

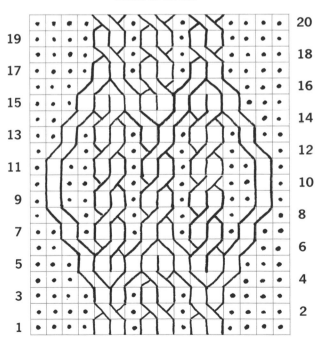

CENTER PANEL: **Three Diamonds**
SIDE PANELS: **Braid X**

BRAID X

Panel of 14 sts.

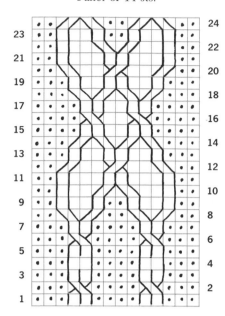

THREE DIAMONDS

Panel of 24 sts.

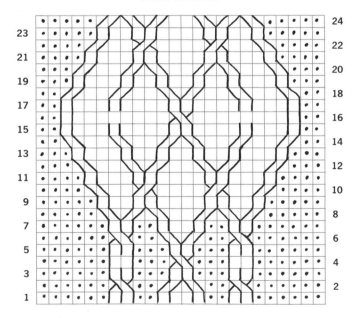

LABYRINTH

Labyrinth

Multiple of 12 sts (24 minimum)
Two repeats shown

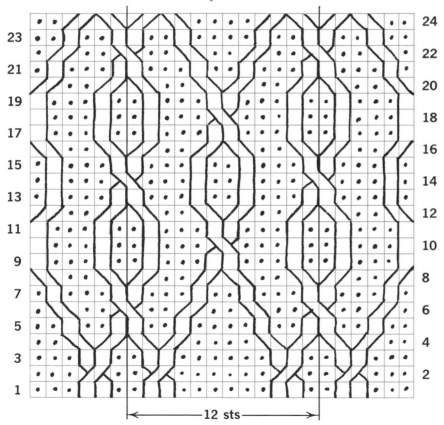

PHARAOH'S CROWN

Panel of 28 sts.

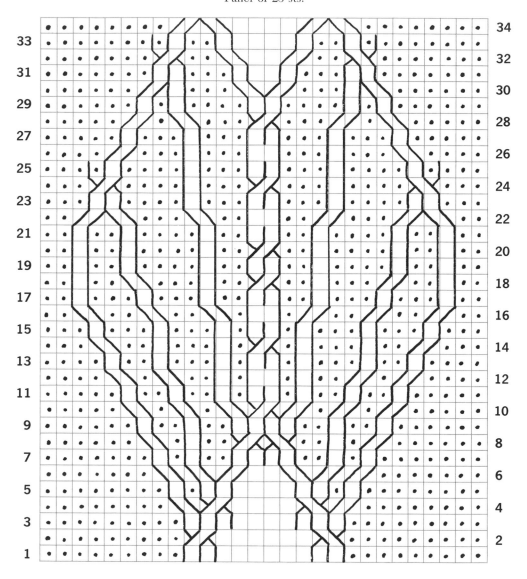

CENTER PANEL: Pharaoh's Crown
LEFT SIDE PANEL: Peanut Chain, Version I
RIGHT SIDE PANEL: Peanut Chain, Version II

PEANUT CHAIN, VERSION I

Panel of 14 sts.

(For Version II, work LT instead of RT in Row 14.)

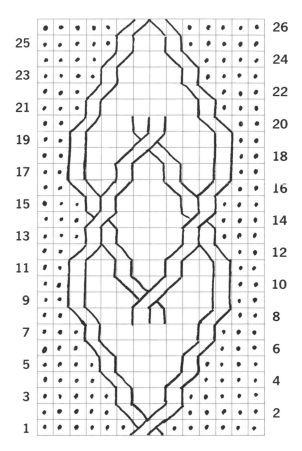

SPOT-PATTERN TWIST

Multiple of 4 sts.

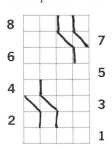

Spot-Pattern Twist

LEFT: Lanterns
RIGHT: Bowmen of Tintagel

LANTERNS

Panel of 24 sts.

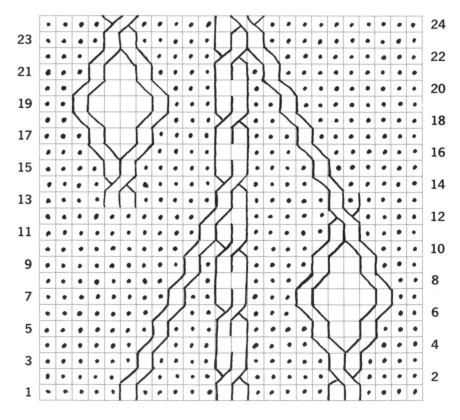

BOWMEN OF TINTAGEL

Panel of 18 sts.

° *Row 16*—Work the 4 center sts as follows: sl 3 sts to dpn
and hold in back, k1, then k3 from dpn.

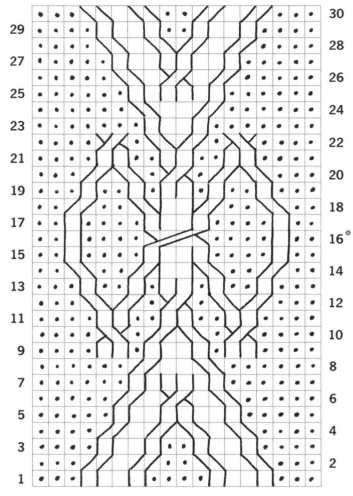

ELEGANT RIBBING

Multiple of 4 sts.

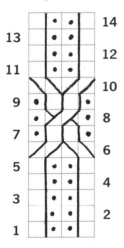

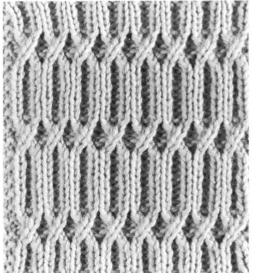

Elegant Ribbing

LEFT: Wrought Iron Panel I
RIGHT: Wrought Iron Panel II

WROUGHT IRON PANEL I

Panel of 32 sts.

WROUGHT IRON PANEL II

Panel of 26 sts.

Northern Lights

NORTHERN LIGHTS

Multiple of 18 sts plus 1.

NOTE: To work this pattern upside down (producing heart-shaped motifs), turn chart around and begin at the top with a wrong-side row.

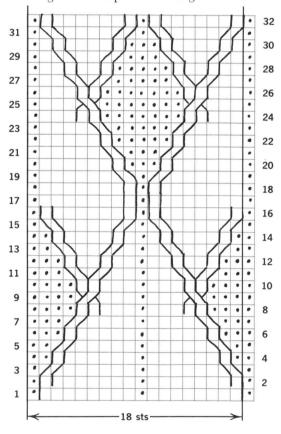

HALF-TWIST LATTICE

Multiple of 6 sts.
Two repeats shown

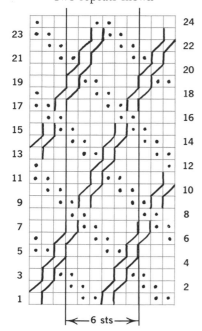

← 6 sts →

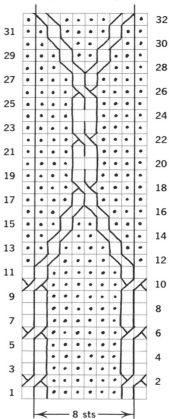

Half-Twist Lattice

GOTHIC LATTICE

Multiple of 8 sts plus 2.

← 8 sts →

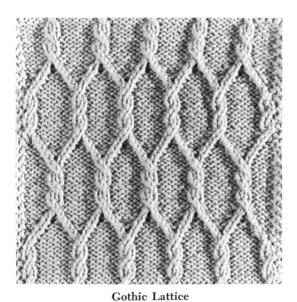

Gothic Lattice

Braided Lattice
ABOVE: **with purl background**
CENTER: **with knit background**
BELOW: **with garter-stitch background**

BRAIDED LATTICE

With choice of 3 backgrounds

Multiple of 14 sts plus 2.

Three repeats shown (one for each background)

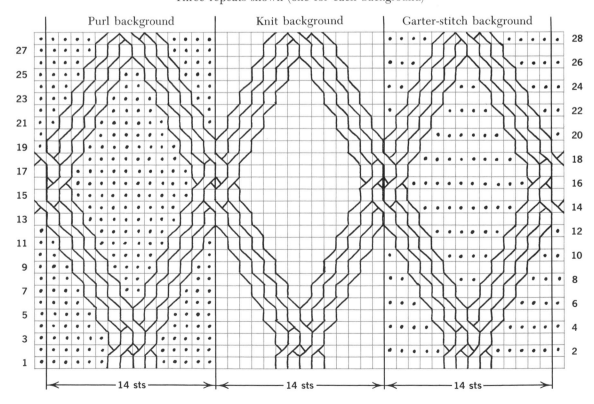

Purl background   Knit background   Garter-stitch background

|—— 14 sts ——| |—— 14 sts ——| |—— 14 sts ——|

Ribbed Lattice

RIBBED LATTICE

Multiple of 12 sts. Two repeats shown

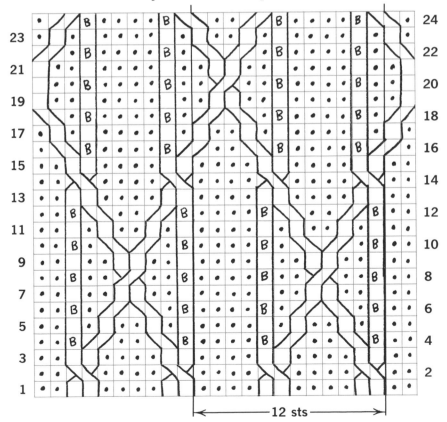

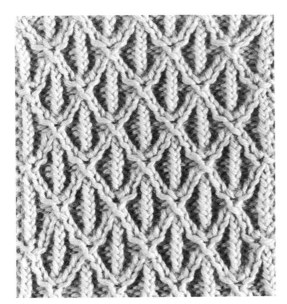

Trinity Rib Lattice

TRINITY RIB LATTICE

Multiple of 8 sts plus 1.
Two repeats shown

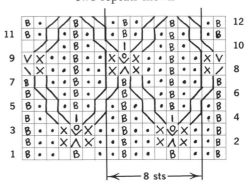

BRAIDED LATTICE WITH MOCK CABLES

Multiple of 16 sts plus 4.

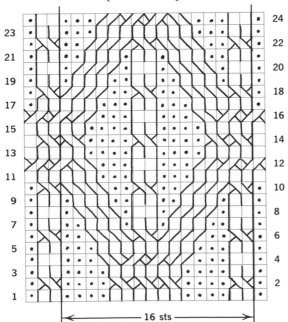

Braided Lattice with Mock Cables

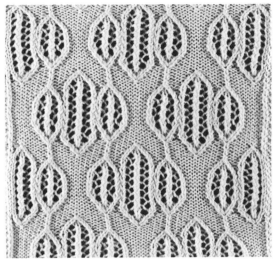

Triptych

TRIPTYCH

Multiple of 26 sts plus 5.

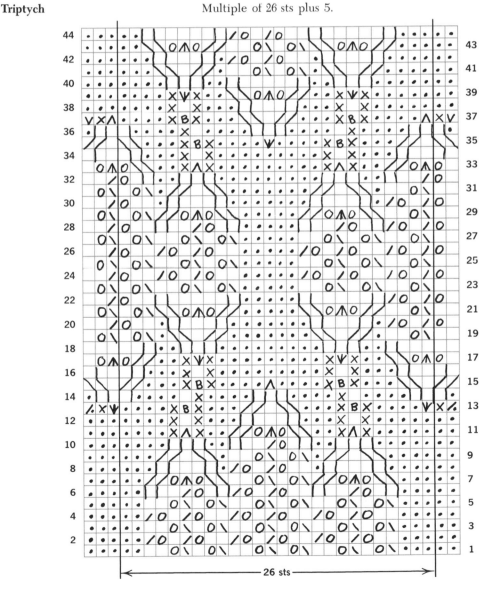

ABOVE: **Balloon Border**
CENTER: **Stump and Branch**
BELOW: **Egg and Dart Frieze**

STUMP AND BRANCH

Multiple of 9 sts plus 2.

(1)—P5

(2)—K5

(3)—P1, p3 tog, p1

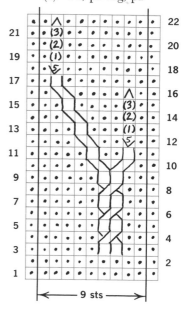

EGG AND DART FRIEZE

Multiple of 17 sts plus 7

(1)—P5

(2)—Inc, k3, inc

(3)—P7

(4)—Inc, k5, inc

(5)—P9

(6)—K9

(7)—Ssk, k5, k2 tog

(8)—Ssk, k3, k2 tog

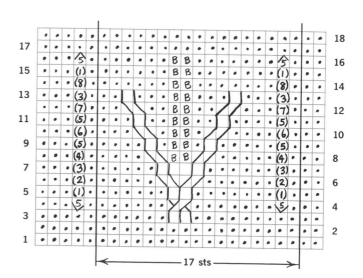

BALLOON BORDER

Multiple of 11 sts plus 4.

(1)—P5

(2)—Inc, k3, inc

(3)—P7

(4)—Inc, k5, inc

(5)—P9

(6)—Ssk, k5, k2 tog

(7)—P2 tog, p3, p2 tog-b

(8)—Ssk, k1, k2 tog

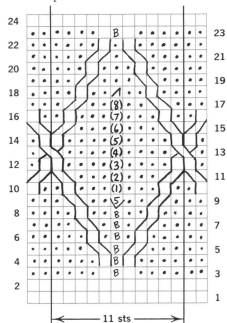

← 11 sts →

TRIPLE-TWIST LACE

Multiple of 10 sts plus 1. Two repeats shown

 Row 5 and *11*—twist 3 sts as follows: knit into 3rd, 2nd, and 1st stitches on left-hand needle, then sl all 3 sts from needle together.

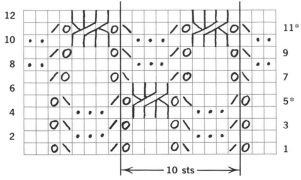

← 10 sts →

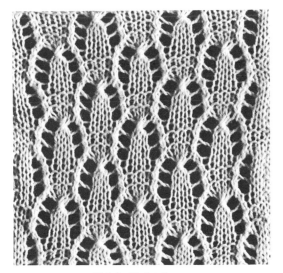

Triple-Twist Lace

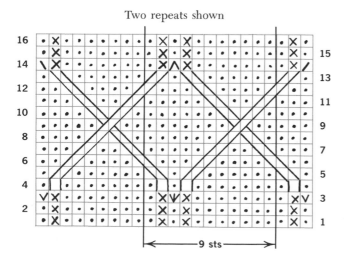

ABOVE: Frogged Border
CENTER: Baghdad Border
BELOW: Plain Lacing Border

PLAIN LACING BORDER

Multiple of 9 sts plus 1 (increased
to 11 sts plus 1)

Two repeats shown

FROGGED BORDER

Multiple of 7 sts plus 2
(increased to 8 sts plus 2)

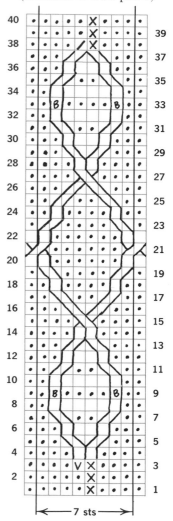

BAGHDAD BORDER

Multiple of 8 sts plus 1 (increased to
10 sts plus 1)

Two repeats shown

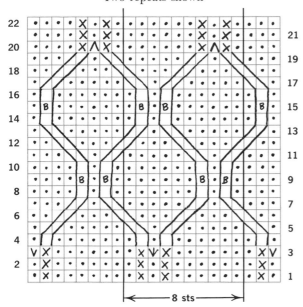

8 sts

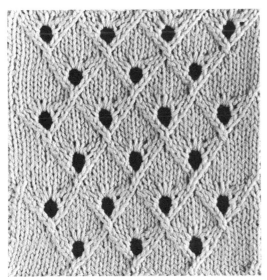

Chinese Checkers

CHINESE CHECKERS

Multiple of 8 sts plus 2 (18 sts minimum).
Two repeats shown

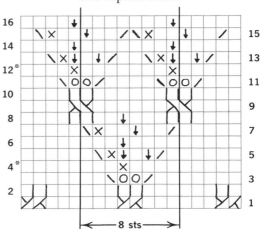

8 sts

° *Rows 4* and *12*—purl *once* into each double yo,
letting the extra loop drop from needle.

↓—Knit (on right side) or purl (on wrong side)
always into the *same* yo space below.

Persian Twist

PERSIAN TWIST

Multiple of 14 sts plus 4
(increased to 16 sts plus 4)

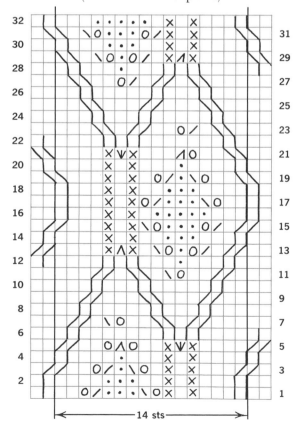

JUGHANDLE RIB

Multiple of 12 sts plus 3 (increased to 14 plus 3)

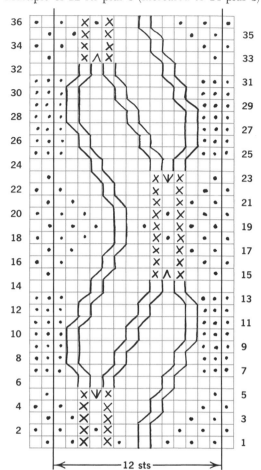

Jughandle Rib

CHAPTER 3

Cables

Most methods of charting cables have been notable for their incomprehensibility. Cable charts, as a rule, steadfastly refuse to look anything like the patterns they represent; also, they perplex the knitter with tangles of interlocking arrows and lines going in all sorts of directions. It's not hard to understand why cable charting can be a problem when you consider that there are well over a hundred possible ways of working a cable crossing. The following diagram shows eighty of them, and these are only basics. So you can see that any charting system is hard put to spread itself over all these possibilities for variation.

This system strives to solve some of the difficulties by making pictures of the cables. The knit ribs are outlined at each side, and when the ribs cross each other, the outlines show where the cabled stitches go—how many stitches over, and in which direction. Even though these outlines have to squeeze a bit when stretching over four or more squares, still they remain readable enough so that this system can cover nearly all types of crossings.

Before studying the diagram of the 80 Basics, you must understand the fundamental nature of cable crossings. Each crossing makes two sorts of stitches: the cable stitches and the background stitches. The cable stitches are the ones that lie in front, on the right side of the fabric, after the crossing is made. The background stitches are behind, and hidden by, the cable stitches. On a front cross, the cable stitches travel from right to left (like a Left Twist). A front cross is worked as follows: sl x number of cable sts to dpn and hold in front, work x number of background sts, then work the cable sts from dpn. On a back cross, the cable stitches travel from left to right (like a Right Twist). A back cross is worked as follows: sl x number of background sts to dpn and hold in back, work x number of cable sts, then work the background sts from dpn.

The cable stitches are almost always knit stitches on the right side, but the background stitches may be either knit or purl. If the background is made of knit stitches, it is an all knit cross. If the background is made of purl stitches, it is a purl background cross. Of course the background stitches in some patterns may change during the crossing from knit stitches (on the row below) to purl stitches (on the row above), or vice versa; but this is not usual.

Now look at the diagram of the 80 Basic Cable Crossings. You will see that each little picture occupies three horizontal rows of squares. Therefore each picture shows three rows of knitting, the crossing row (a right-side row) in the middle, and the two wrong-side rows above and below it. The directions under each picture explain what is happening on the crossing row only. The stitches on the two wrong-side rows are stationary. The outlines are continued on these rows just to show you where the crossed stitches come from and where they are going. You must imagine that the outlines extend even farther, upward and downward, so as to see the crossing as a small portion of a continuous vertical rib.

On the all knit crosses, the background stitches are outlined too. On the purl background crosses, they are not. Instead of outlines you see the dots that indicate a purled fabric. The number of dots above and below each crossing row tells you the number of stitches that are involved in the crossing. This number always begins and ends in a vertical line with the outermost line that sets off the knit rib, as shown.

On the crossing row itself, each purl background cross has *one* dot where the knit rib pulls away. This single dot means that *all* the background stitches are to be purled, no matter how many of them there might be. When there is no dot in the takeoff square, it is an all knit cross and *all* the background stitches are to be knitted. Of course, in other kinds of crossings not included in these 80 Basics, it is possible to work background stitches in a combination of knits and purls; but a crossing of this sort occurs only rarely.

The last sixteen examples in the 80 Basics show double crossings with a single central stitch. This central stitch is purled if it shows dots on the wrong-side rows above and below the crossing, and knitted if it does not. The directions tell you just how these crossings are worked.

If you have not done much cable knitting, it is a good idea to try out some of the 80 Basics before going on to the charted cables. Make a little test swatch by casting on some knit ribs of varying widths, with 3 or 4 purl stitches in between them. Rib plain for a few rows and then take up your cable needle and work some crossings appropriate to the number of stitches in each rib, following the directions in the diagram. You will soon grasp the principles of cabling, and be ready to cope with any sort of crossing that comes along. Then work the example cables from directions and charts together. Then you are ready to pick out even the fanciest cables from this section, and work them into garments or afghans that will dazzle your friends.

You may notice that the sequence of the 80 Basic stops at ribs four stitches in width. Of course it could go on to wider ribs, listing crossings of 5-over-1, -2, -3, -4, and -5 stitches, or 6-over-1, -2, -3, -4, -5, and -6, etc. Thus we could list 80 more Basics with no trouble at all; but these larger numbers of stitches are not often used, and from the examples given you can understand how they would look. Always check the number of stitches in each charted crossing with care, because most of the cables and cable patterns use several different ones on different rows.

You may notice also that a 1-over-1 cross looks just like a twist stitch, both on the chart and in the knitting. So you may substitute twist stitches for 1-over-1 crossings from time to time. In an ordinary twist stitch, you do not purl the rear stitch as in the purl background cable cross; but this can be done if the twist is worked by the "drop" method.

80 BASIC CABLE CROSSINGS

NUMBER OF STS.	FRONT CROSS		BACK CROSS	
	All Knit	*Purl Background*	*All Knit*	*Purl Background*
1-over-1 cross (2 sts)	Sl 1 st to dpn and hold in front, k1, then k1 from dpn.	Sl 1 st to dpn and hold in front, p1, then k1 from dpn.	Sl 1 st to dpn and hold in back, k1, then k1 from dpn.	Sl 1 st to dpn and hold in back, k1, then p1 from dpn.
1-over-2 cross (3 sts)	Sl 1 st to dpn and hold in front, k2, then k1 from dpn.	Sl 1 st to dpn and hold in front, p2, then k1 from dpn.	Sl 2 sts to dpn and hold in back, k1, then k2 from dpn.	Sl 2 sts to dpn and hold in back, k1, then p2 from dpn.
1-over-3 cross (4 sts)	Sl 1 st to dpn and hold in front, k3, then k1 from dpn.	Sl 1 st to dpn and hold in front, p3, then k1 from dpn.	Sl 3 sts to dpn and hold in back, k1, then k3 from dpn.	Sl 3 sts to dpn and hold in back, k1, then p3 from dpn.
1-over-4 cross (5 sts)	Sl 1 st to dpn and hold in front, k4, then k1 from dpn.	Sl 1 st to dpn and hold in front, p4, then k1 from dpn.	Sl 4 sts to dpn and hold in back, k1, then k4 from dpn.	Sl 4 sts to dpn and hold in back, k1, then p4 from dpn.
2-over-1 cross (3 sts)	Sl 2 sts to dpn and hold in front, k1, then k2 from dpn.	Sl 2 sts to dpn and hold in front, p1, then k2 from dpn.	Sl 1 st to dpn and hold in back, k2, then k1 from dpn.	Sl 1 st to dpn and hold in back, k2, then p1 from dpn.
2-over-2 cross (4 sts)	Sl 2 sts to dpn and hold in front, k2, then k2 from dpn.	Sl 2 sts to dpn and hold in front, p2, then k2 from dpn.	Sl 2 sts to dpn and hold in back, k2, then k2 from dpn.	Sl 2 sts to dpn and hold in back, k2, then p2 from dpn.

80 BASIC CABLE CROSSINGS

NUMBER OF STS.	FRONT CROSS		BACK CROSS	
	All Knit	*Purl Background*	*All Knit*	*Purl Background*
2-over-3 cross (5 sts)	Sl 2 sts to dpn and hold in front, k3, then k2 from dpn.	Sl 2 sts to dpn and hold in front, p3, then k2 from dpn.	Sl 3 sts to dpn and hold in back, k2, then k3 from dpn.	Sl 3 sts to dpn and hold in back, k2, then p3 from dpn.
2-over-4 cross (6 sts)	Sl 2 sts to dpn and hold in front, k4, then k2 from dpn.	Sl 2 sts to dpn and hold in front, p4, then k2 from dpn.	Sl 4 sts to dpn and hold in back, k2, then k4 from dpn.	Sl 4 sts to dpn and hold in back, k2, then p4 from dpn.
3-over-1 cross (4 sts)	Sl 3 sts to dpn and hold in front, k1, then k3 from dpn.	Sl 3 sts to dpn and hold in front, p1, then k3 from dpn.	Sl 1 st to dpn and hold in back, k3, then k1 from dpn.	Sl 1 st to dpn and hold in back, k3, then p1 from dpn.
3-over-2 cross (5 sts)	Sl 3 sts to dpn and hold in front, k2, then k3 from dpn.	Sl 3 sts to dpn and hold in front, p2, then k3 from dpn.	Sl 2 sts to dpn and hold in back, k3, then k2 from dpn.	Sl 2 sts to dpn and hold in back, k3, then p2 from dpn.
3-over-3 cross (6 sts)	Sl 3 sts to dpn and hold in front, k3, then k3 from dpn.	Sl 3 sts to dpn and hold in front, p3, then k3 from dpn.	Sl 3 sts to dpn and hold in back, k3, then k3 from dpn.	Sl 3 sts to dpn and hold in back, k3, then p3 from dpn.
3-over-4 cross (7 sts)	Sl 3 sts to dpn and hold in front, k4, then k3 from dpn.	Sl 3 sts to dpn and hold in front, p4, then k3 from dpn.	Sl 4 sts to dpn and hold in back, k3, then k4 from dpn.	Sl 4 sts to dpn and hold in back, k3, then p4 from dpn.

80 BASIC CABLE CROSSINGS

NUMBER OF STS.	FRONT CROSS		BACK CROSS	
	All Knit	*Purl Background*	*All Knit*	*Purl Background*
4-over-1 cross (5 sts)	Sl 4 sts to dpn and hold in front, k1, then k4 from dpn.	Sl 4 sts to dpn and hold in front, p1, then k4 from dpn.	Sl 1 st to dpn and hold in back, k4, then k1 from dpn.	Sl 1 st to dpn and hold in back, k4, then p1 from dpn.
4-over-2 cross (6 sts)	Sl 4 sts to dpn and hold in front, k2, then k4 from dpn.	Sl 4 sts to dpn and hold in front, p2, then k4 from dpn.	Sl 2 sts to dpn and hold in back, k4, then k2 from dpn.	Sl 2 sts to dpn and hold in back, k4, then p2 from dpn.
4-over-3 cross (7 sts)	Sl 4 sts to dpn and hold in front, k3, then k4 from dpn.	Sl 4 sts to dpn and hold in front, p3, then k4 from dpn.	Sl 3 sts to dpn and hold in back, k4, then k3 from dpn.	Sl 3 sts to dpn and hold in back, k4, then p3 from dpn.
4-over-4 cross (8 sts)	Sl 4 sts to dpn and hold in front, k4, then k4 from dpn.	Sl 4 sts to dpn and hold in front, p4, then k4 from dpn.	Sl 4 sts to dpn and hold in back, k4, then k4 from dpn.	Sl 4 sts to dpn and hold in back, k4, then p4 from dpn.
1-over-1 cross (3 sts)	Sl 2 sts to dpn and hold in front, k1, the sl the center st from dpn back to left-hand needle and knit it; k1 from dpn.	Sl 2 sts to dpn and hold in front, k1, then sl the center st from dpn back to left-hand needle and purl it; k1 from dpn.	Sl 2 sts to dpn and hold in back, k1, then sl the center st from dpn back to left-hand needle and knit it; k1 from dpn.	Sl 2 sts to dpn and hold in back, k1, then sl the center st from dpn back to left-hand needle and purl it; k1 from dpn.

80 BASIC CABLE CROSSINGS

NUMBER OF STS.	FRONT CROSS		BAC
	All Knit	*Purl Background*	*All Knit*
2-over-2 cross (5 sts)			
	Sl 3 sts to dpn and hold in front, k2, then sl the center st from dpn back to left-hand needle and knit it; k2 from dpn.	Sl 3 sts to dpn and hold in front, k2, then sl the center st from dpn back to left-hand needle and purl it; k2 from dpn.	Sl 3 sts to dpn and hold in back, k2, then sl the center st from dpn back to left-hand needle and knit it; k2 from dpn.
3-over-3 cross (7 sts)			
	Sl 4 sts to dpn and hold in front, k3, then sl the center st from dpn back to left-hand needle and knit it; k3 from dpn.	Sl 4 sts to dpn and hold in front, k3, then sl the center st from dpn back to left-hand needle and purl it; k3 from dpn.	Sl 4 sts to dpn and hold in back, k3, then sl the center st from dpn back to left-hand needle and knit it; k3 from dpn.
4-over-4 cross (9 sts)			
	Sl 5 sts to dpn and hold in front, k4, then sl the center st from dpn back to left-hand needle and knit it; k4 from dpn.	Sl 5 sts to dpn and hold in front, k4, then sl the center st from dpn back to left-hand needle and purl it; k4 from dpn.	Sl 5 sts to dpn and hold in back, k4, then sl the center st from dpn back to left-hand needle and knit it; k4 from dpn.

CROSS

Purl Background

Sl 3 sts to dpn and
hold in back, k2,
then sl the center
st from dpn back to
left-hand needle and
purl it; k2 from dpn.

Sl 4 sts to dpn and
hold in back, k3,
then sl the center
st from dpn back to
left-hand needle and
purl it; k3 from dpn.

Sl 5 sts to dpn and
hold in back, k4,
then sl the center
st from dpn back to
left-hand needle and
purl it; k4 from dpn.

Here's a useful hint for do-it-yourself designers. Remember that cables draw the fabric together very strongly, requiring a larger-than-usual number of stitches for any given width. So to work the ribbing, or some other border, for an Aran-style sweater or any article in a combination of cables, always cast on less than the number required for the cable knitting. Nine border stitches for every ten in the cable pattern is about right; or, if you want to plan it more exactly, increase one or two stitches at the base of each cable rib before starting the pattern. Similarly, when binding off, or decreasing for the ribbing in a sweater worked from the top down, work two or more stitches together in each cable rib. That way, you can be sure that your bind-off row will not have the unsightly flare that is the result of an excessive number of stitches too tightly crowded together.

Charting is especially helpful in planning cable-combination garments, where different adjacent patterns have different numbers of rows to their repeats, and might be mixed up. If the cables are neatly drawn side by side on a chart, there is never any doubt about what happens to each one on any given row. Shaping, such as that of a sleeve cap or underarm, can be handled very nicely too, because you can narrow the chart as you narrow the knitting, and still see how to keep the patterns correct without any re-counting and worrying.

Cables and cable-stitch patterns are endlessly fascinating and endlessly variable. As you work some of these originals you will discover how versatile the cabling technique can be.

LEFT: **Spliced Oval**
RIGHT: **Baroque Cable**

Example Cables:

Spliced Oval and Baroque Cable

To start you off at reading cable charts, here are two nice fancy designs that incorporate several different kinds of cable crossings, both all-knit and purl background; one of them begins with a right-side row, the other with a wrong-side row, so that you can learn to look at a chart either way. Spliced Oval has two-over-two and four-over-one crossings; the big Baroque Cable has three-over-three, three-over-two, and three-over-one. As you read the directions, follow each chart attentively and notice its way of saying the same thing in picture form.

Spliced Oval—Panel of 24 sts

Notes: FKC (Front Knit Cross)—sl 2 sts to dpn and hold in front, k2, then k2 from dpn.

BKC (Back Knit Cross)—sl 2 sts to dpn and hold in back, k2, then k2 from dpn.

FPC (Front Purl Cross)—sl 2 sts to dpn and hold in front, p2, then k2 from dpn.

BPC (Back Purl Cross)—sl 2 sts to dpn and hold in back, k2, then p2 from dpn.

4FPC (4-Stitch Front Purl Cross)—sl 4 sts to dpn and hold in front, p1, then k4 from dpn.

4BPC (4-Stitch Back Purl Cross)—sl 1 st to dpn and hold in back, k4, then p1 from dpn.

Row 1 (Right side)—P3, k4, p10, k4, p3.

Row 2 and all other wrong-side rows—Knit all knit sts and purl all purl sts.

Row 3—P3, BKC, p10, BKC, p3.

Row 5—Repeat Row 1.

Row 7—P3, 4FPC, p8, 4BPC, p3.

Row 9—P4, k2, FPC, p4, BPC, k2, p4.

Row 11—P4, (FPC) twice, (BPC) twice, p4.

Row 13—P6, FPC, FKC, BPC, p6.

Row 15—P8, (BKC) twice, p8.

Row 17—P8, k2, FKC, k2, p8.

Row 19—Repeat Row 15.

Row 21—P6, BPC, FKC, FPC, p6.

Row 23—P4, (BPC) twice, (FPC) twice, p4.
Row 25—P4, k2, BPC, p4, FPC, k2, p4.
Row 27—P3, 4BPC, p8, 4FPC, p3.
Row 28—See Row 2.
  Repeat Rows 1–28.

Baroque Cable—Panel of 42 sts

(See chart, page 68)

Notes: FKC (Front Knit Cross)—sl 3 sts to dpn and hold in front, k3, then k3 from dpn.

  BKC (Back Knit Cross)—sl 3 sts to dpn and hold in back, k3, then k3 from dpn.

  1FC (Single Front Cross)—sl 3 sts to dpn and hold in front, p1, then k3 from dpn.

  1BC (Single Back Cross)—sl 1 st to dpn and hold in back, k3, then p1 from dpn.

  2FC (Double Front Cross)—sl 3 sts to dpn and hold in front, p2, then k3 from dpn.

  2BC (Double Back Cross)—sl 2 sts to dpn and hold in back, k3, then p2 from dpn.

  3FC (Triple Front Cross)—sl 3 sts to dpn and hold in front, p3, then k3 from dpn.

  3BC (Triple Back Cross)—sl 3 sts to dpn and hold in back, k3, then p3 from dpn.

Rows 1 and 3 (Wrong side)—K3, p3, k2, p3, k7, p6, k7, p3, k2, p3, k3.

Row 2—P3, k3, p2, k3, p7, k6, p7, k3, p2, k3, p3.

Row 4—P3, 1FC, 1BC, p7, FKC, p7, 1FC, 1BC, p3.

Row 5 and all subsequent wrong-side rows—Knit all knit sts and purl all purl sts.

Row 6—P4, FKC, p6, 2BC, 2FC, p6, FKC, p4.

Row 8—P4, k3, 1FC, p3, 2BC, p4, 2FC, p3, 1BC, k3, p4.

Row 10—P4, (1FC) twice, 2BC, p8, 2FC, (1BC) twice, p4.

Row 12—P5, 1FC, BKC, p12, BKC, 1BC, p5.

Row 14—P6, FKC, 3FC, p6, 3BC, FKC, p6.

Row 16—P5, 1BC, (3FC) twice, (3BC) twice, 1FC, p5.

Row 18—P4, 1BC, p4, 3FC, FKC, 3BC, p4, 1FC, p4.

Row 20—P3, 1BC, p8, (BKC) twice, p8, 1FC, p3.

Row 22—P3, k3, p9, k3, FKC, k3, p9, k3, p3.

Row 24—P3, 1FC, p8, (BKC) twice, p8, 1BC, p3.

Row 26—P4, 1FC, p4, 3BC, FKC, 3FC, p4, 1BC, p4.

SPLICED OVAL

Panel of 24 sts.

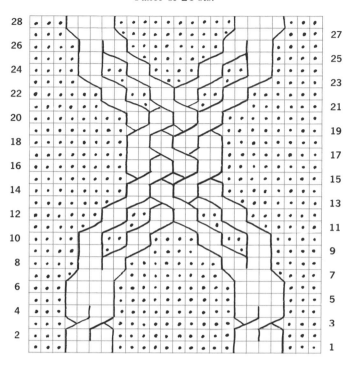

continued on page 68

BAROQUE CABLE

Panel of 42 sts.

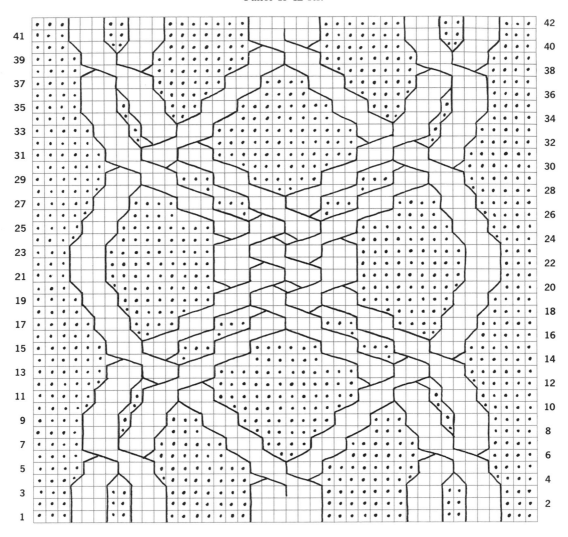

Row 28—P5, 1FC, (3BC) twice, (3FC) twice, 1BC, p5.
Row 30—P6, FKC, 3BC, p6, 3FC, FKC, p6.
Row 32—P5, 1BC, BKC, p12, BKC, 1FC, p5.
Row 34—P4, (1BC) twice, 2FC, p8, 2BC, (1FC) twice, p4.
Row 36—P4, k3, 1BC, p3, 2FC, p4, 2BC, p3, 1FC, k3, p4.
Row 38—P4, FKC, p6, 2FC, 2BC, p6, FKC, p4.
Row 40—P3, 1BC, 1FC, p7, FKC, p7, 1BC, 1FC, p3.
Row 42—Repeat Row 2.
    Repeat Rows 1–42.

CROSS-BANDED CABLE

Panel of 10 sts.

Cross-Banded Cable

LEFT: Twisted Wishbone
RIGHT: Slotted Cable

TWISTED WISHBONE

Panel of 12 sts.

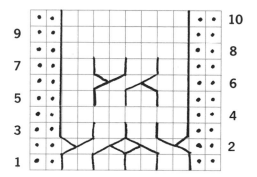

SLOTTED CABLE

Panel of 14 sts.

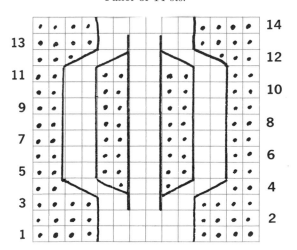

LEFT: Pretzel Cable
RIGHT: Double-Texture Cable

PRETZEL CABLE

Panel of 11 sts.

DOUBLE-TEXTURE CABLE

Panel of 12 sts.

° *Row 4*—P2, sl next 4 sts to dpn and hold in
   back, (k1, p1) twice, then k4 from dpn; p2.
° *Row 14*—P2, sl next 4 sts to dpn and hold in
   back, k4, then (k1, p1) twice from dpn; p2.

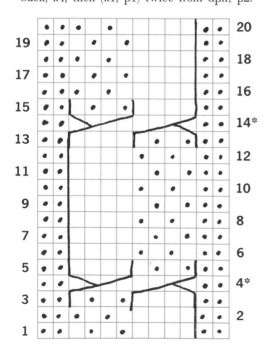

Gnarled Cable
LEFT TO RIGHT: 1. Front-Cross Gnarled Cable
2. Gnarled Wave Cable 3. Back-Cross Gnarled
Cable 4. Reverse Gnarled Wave Cable

GNARLED CABLE

Panel of 12 sts.

1. Front-cross Gnarled Cable

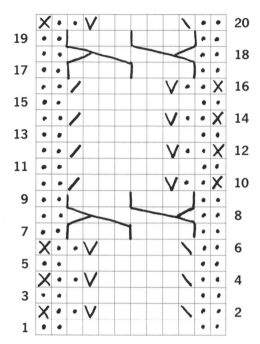

2. Gnarled Wave Cable

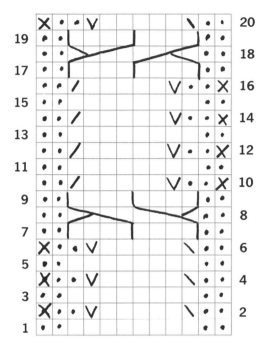

3. Back-cross Gnarled Cable

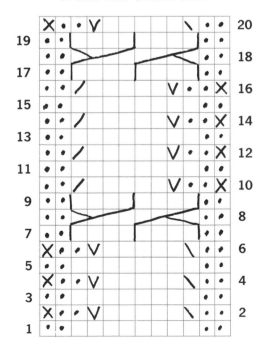

4. Reverse Gnarled Wave Cable

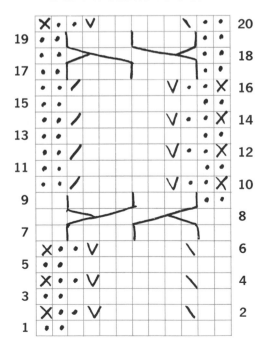

LOG CHIP CABLE

Panel of 23 sts.

° *Rows 4, 8, 12,* and *16—*◇ Make bobble as follows: (k1, yo, k1) in 1 st, turn and p3, turn and sl 1—k2 tog—psso.

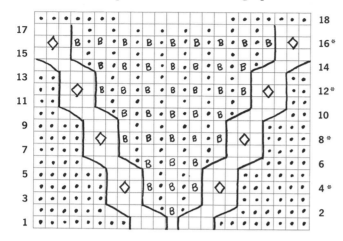

LINSMORE CABLE

Panel of 16 sts.

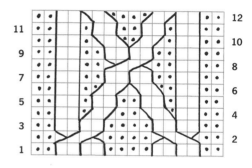

LEFT: Log Chip Cable
RIGHT: Linsmore Cable

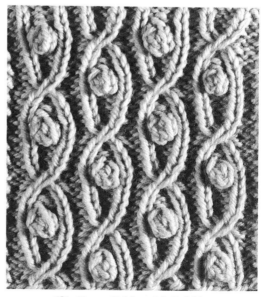

Slip-Cross Cable with Bobbles

FLAT CABLE

Panel of 14 sts.

Back Cross

° *Row 4*—P2, sl next 5 sts to dpn and hold in back, (k1 from left-hand needle, k1 from dpn) 5 times, p2.

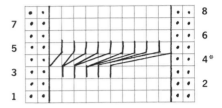

Front Cross

° *Row 4*—P2, sl next 5 sts to dpn and hold in front, (k1 from left-hand needle, k1 from dpn) 5 times, p2.

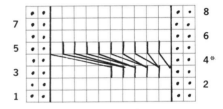

LEFT: Flat Cable, Back Cross
RIGHT: Flat Cable, Front Cross
CENTER: Rolling Braid

ROLLING BRAID

Panel of 23 sts.

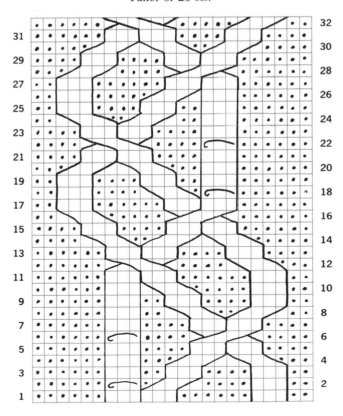

SLIP-CROSS CABLE WITH BOBBLES

Panel of 9 sts.

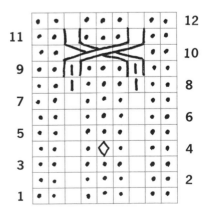

LEFT: End-Over-End Cable, Back Cross
RIGHT: End-Over-End Cable, Front Cross
CENTER: Toggle Knot

END-OVER-END CABLE, FRONT CROSS

Panel of 12 sts.

° *Row 4*—P3, sl next 6 sts to dpn and hold in front, twist dpn ½ turn clockwise, k6 from dpn, p3.

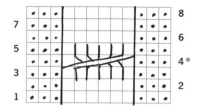

END-OVER-END CABLE, BACK CROSS

Panel of 12 sts.

° *Row 4*—P3, sl next 6 sts to dpn and hold in front, twist dpn ½ turn counterclockwise, k6 from dpn, p3.

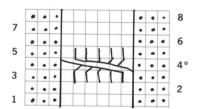

TOGGLE KNOT

Panel of 21 sts (increased to 25)

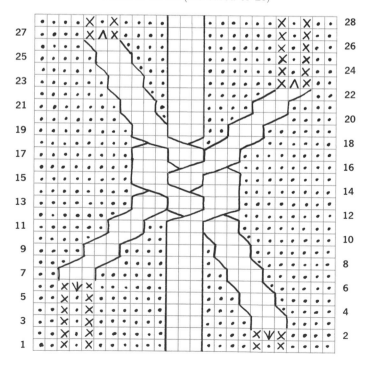

SIDE PANELS: End-Over-End Wave
CENTER PANEL: Barred and Braided Cable

END-OVER-END WAVE

Panel of 10 sts.

° *Row 4*—P2, sl next 6 sts to dpn
and hold in front, twist dpn
½ turn clockwise; p3, k3
from dpn, p2.

° *Row 12*—P2, sl next 6 sts to
dpn and hold in front, twist
dpn ½ turn counterclock-
wise; k3, p3 from dpn, p2.

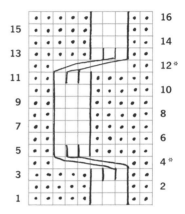

BARRED AND BRAIDED CABLE

Panel of 38 sts.

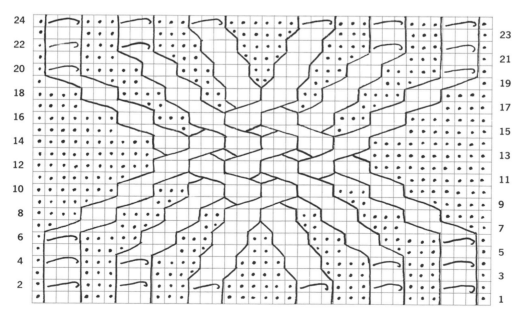

SIX-RIB KNOT CABLE I

Panel of 24 sts.

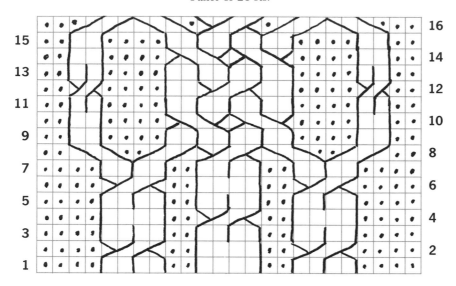

SIX-RIB KNOT CABLE II

Panel of 24 sts.

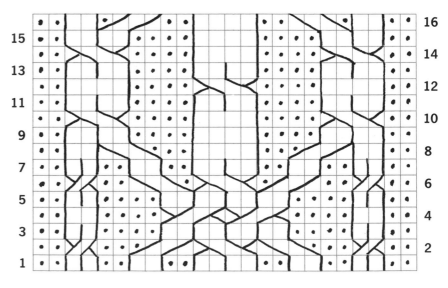

LEFT: Six-Rib Knot Cable I
RIGHT: Six-Rib Knot Cable II
CENTER: Dancing Ribbon

DANCING RIBBON

Panel of 18 sts.

° *Row 6*—work the 6 center sts as follows: sl 2 sts to dpn and hold in back; sl next 2 sts to a second dpn and hold in front. K2 from left-hand needle, k2 from front dpn, then p2 from back dpn.

° *Row 10*—work the 6 center sts as follows: sl 2 sts to dpn and hold in front, p2, k2, then k2 from dpn.

° *Row 18*—work the 6 center sts as follows: sl 4 sts to dpn and hold in front, p2; then sl 2 center sts from dpn back to left-hand needle; then pass dpn with remaining 2 sts through to back of work. K2 from left-hand needle, then k2 from dpn.

° *Row 22*—work the 6 center sts as follows: sl 4 sts to dpn and hold in back, k2, then k2, p2 from dpn.

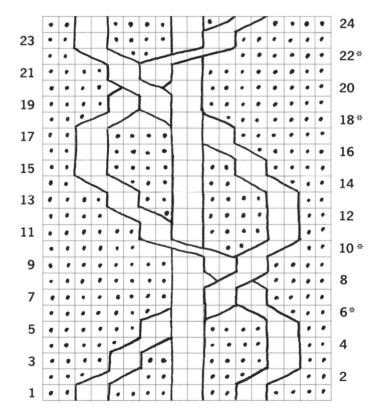

LEFT: Double Knot Cable
RIGHT: Loose Knot Cable

DOUBLE KNOT CABLE

Panel of 28 sts.

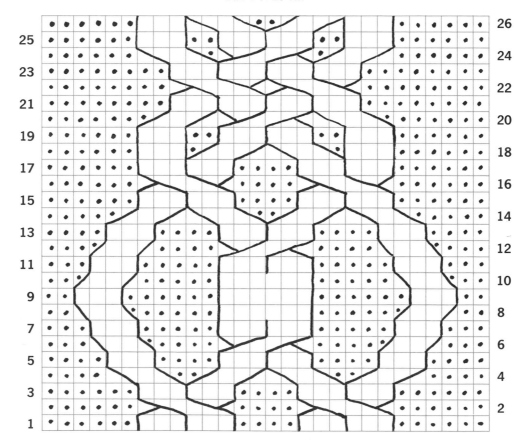

LOOSE KNOT CABLE

Panel of 28 sts.

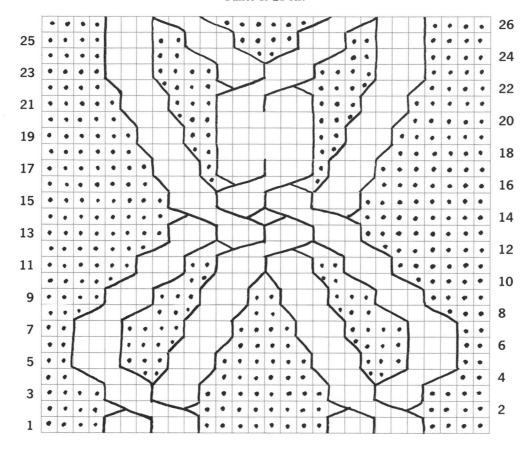

Tangled Ropes

TANGLED ROPES

Panel of 28 sts.

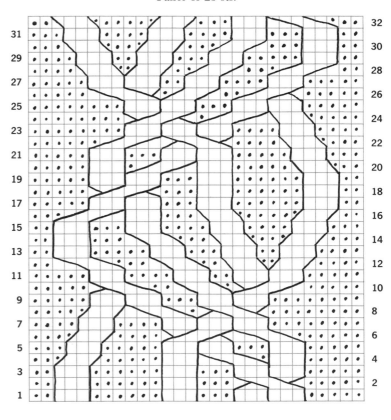

ENCLOSED CABLE, VERSION I

Panel of 24 sts.

LEFT: Enclosed Cable, Version I
RIGHT: Enclosed Cable, Version II

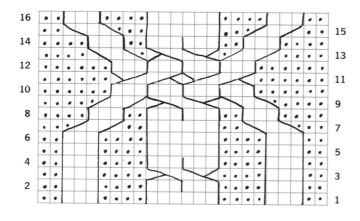

ENCLOSED CABLE, VERSION II

Panel of 24 sts.

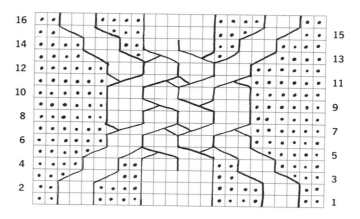

CENTER PANEL: Double X Cable
SIDE PANELS: Looping Wave

LOOPING WAVE

Panel of 23 sts.

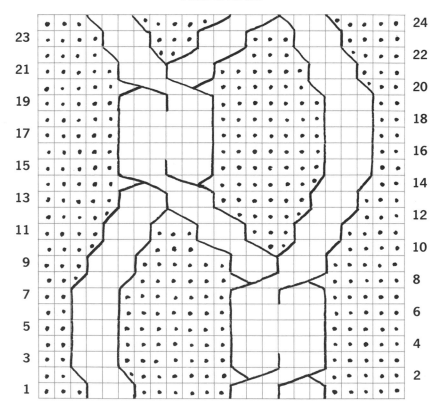

DOUBLE X CABLE

Panel of 28 sts.

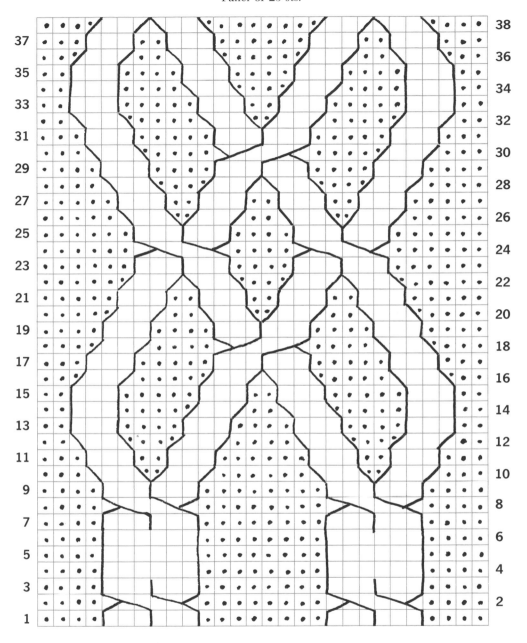

LEFT: **Branching Braid**
CENTER: **Large Enclosed Braid**
RIGHT: **Small Enclosed Braid**

BRANCHING BRAID

Panel of 24 sts.

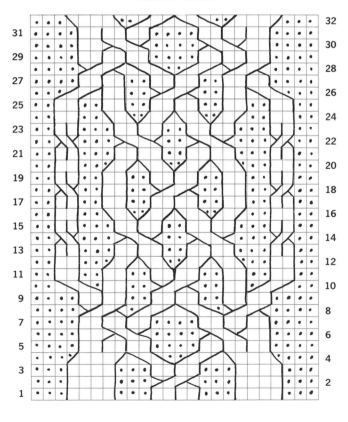

LARGE ENCLOSED BRAID

Panel of 24 sts.

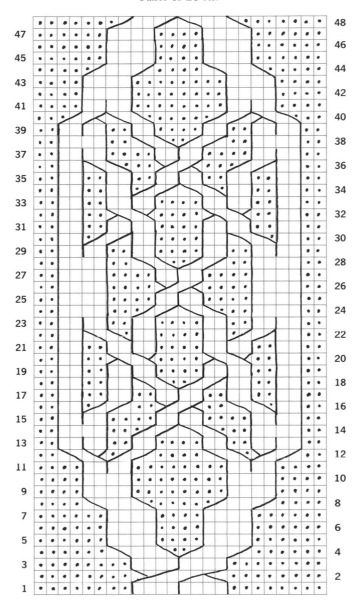

SMALL ENCLOSED BRAID

Panel of 16 sts.

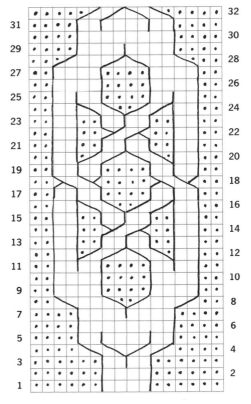

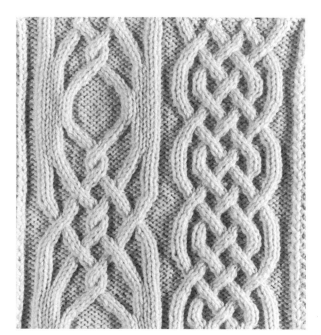

LEFT: Lancet Braid
RIGHT: Saxon Braid

SAXON BRAID

Panel of 28 sts.

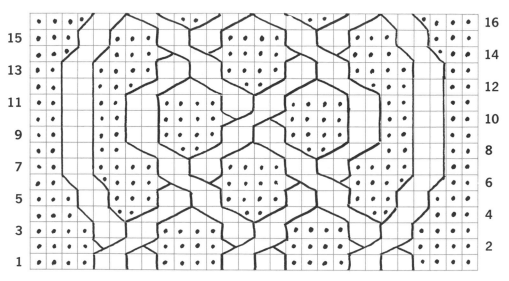

LANCET BRAID

Panel of 28 sts.

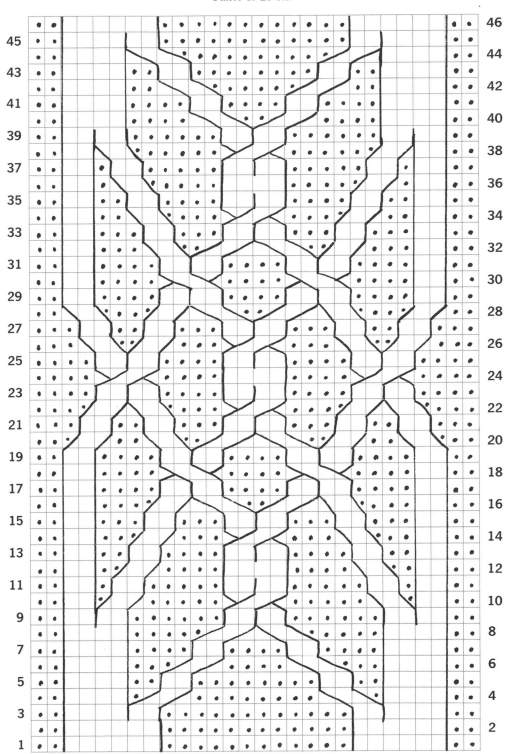

SOFT CABLE

Panel of 19 sts.

SIDE PANELS: **Soft Cable**
CENTER PANEL: **Ribbed Spindle**

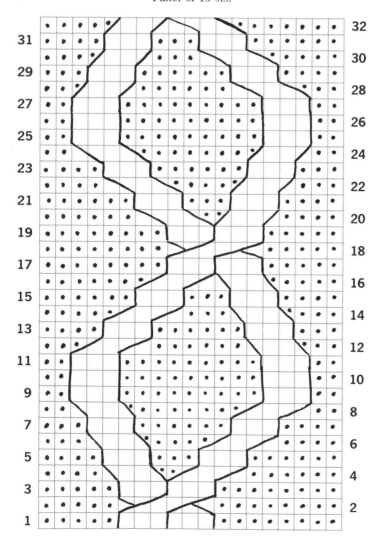

RIBBED SPINDLE

Panel of 29 sts.

° *Row 7*—P8, sl next 3 sts to dpn and hold in back, (k1-b from left-hand needle, p1 from dpn) 3 times; k1-b; sl next 3 sts to dpn and hold in front, (p1 from left-hand needle, k1-b from dpn) 3 times; p8.

° *Row 29*—P8, (sl 1 st to dpn and hold in front, p1 from left-hand needle) 3 times, then k3-b from dpn; k1-b; (sl 1 st to dpn and hold in back, k1-b from left-hand needle) 3 times, then p3 from dpn; p8.

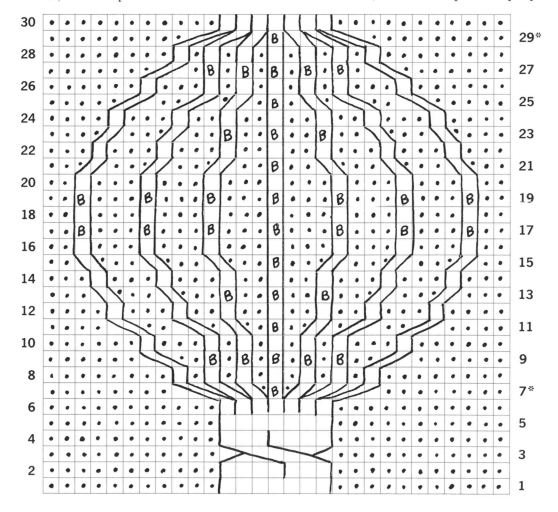

LEFT: Short Swinging Cable
RIGHT: Long Swinging Cable
CENTER: Grand Swinging Cable

LONG SWINGING CABLE

Panel of 16 sts.

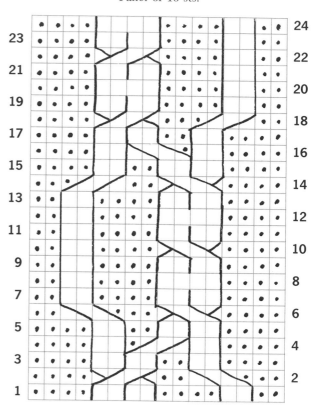

SHORT SWINGING CABLE

Panel of 18 sts.

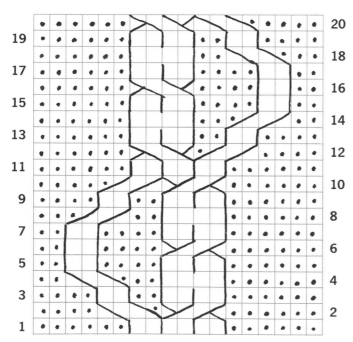

GRAND SWINGING CABLE

Panel of 25 sts.

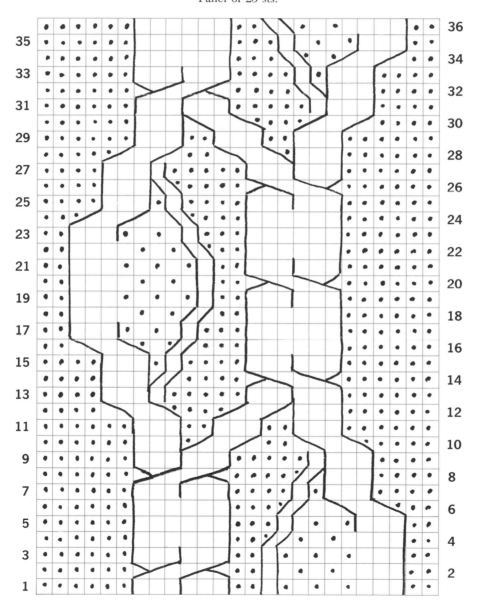

PATCHWORK CABLE I

Panel of 19 sts.

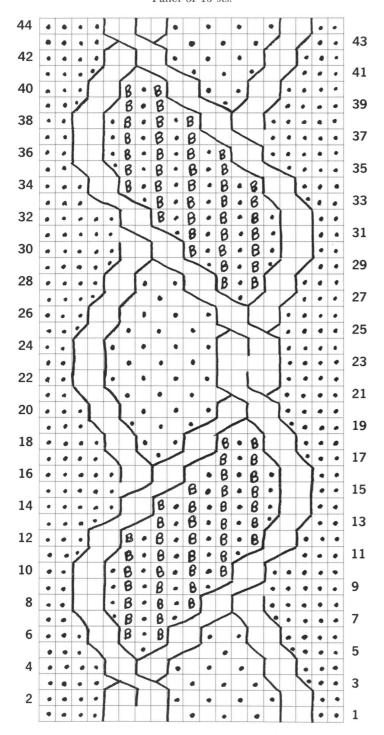

LEFT: Patchwork Cable I
RIGHT: Patchwork Cable II

PATCHWORK CABLE II

Panel of 29 sts.

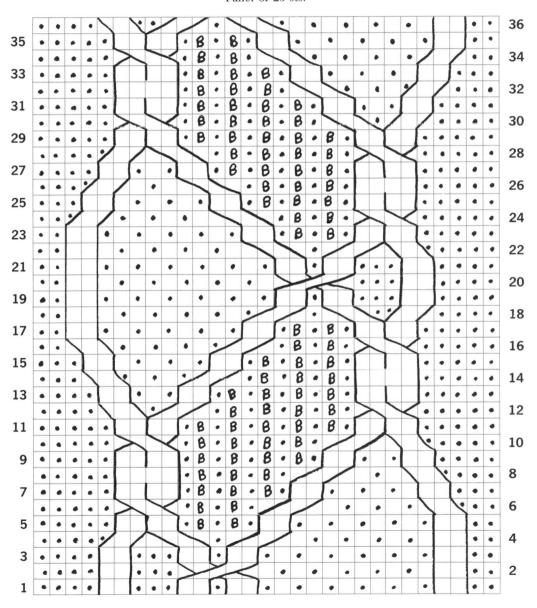

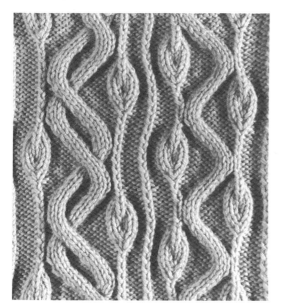

RIGHT: **Wave and Pod Cable**
LEFT: **Double Wave and Pod Cable**

WAVE AND POD CABLE

Panel of 23 sts.

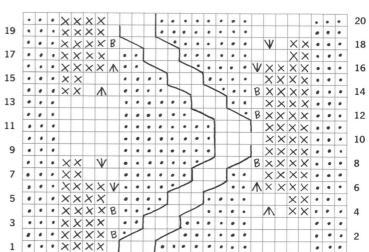

DOUBLE WAVE AND POD CABLE

Panel of 28 sts.

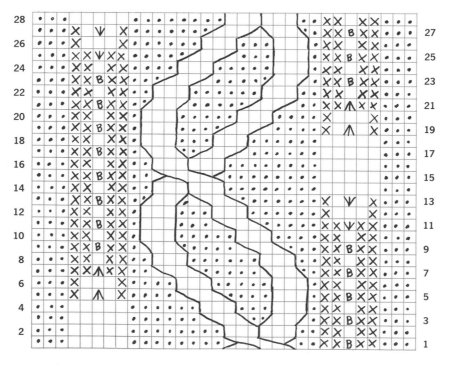

The Sands of Time

THE SANDS OF TIME

Panel of 35 sts.

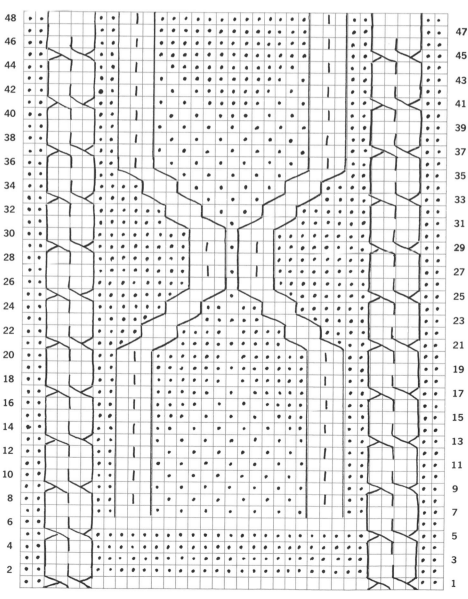

LEFT: Windblown Cable, Version I
RIGHT: Windblown Cable, Version II
CENTER: Honey Drop

LEFT: Pretzel Braid
CENTER: Pear-Shaped Cable
RIGHT: Buckle Braid

WINDBLOWN CABLE

Panel of 14 sts.

Version I

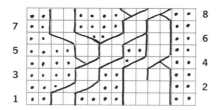

Version II

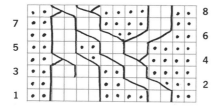

HONEY DROP

(1)—(Row 20)—k5.
(2)—(Row 21)—p2, yo, p1, yo, p2.
(3)—(Row 22)—k7.
(4)—(Row 23)—p7.
(5)—(Row 24)—ssk, k3, k2 tog.
(6)—(Row 25)—p5.
(7)—(Row 26)—ssk, k1, k2 tog.
(8)—(Row 27)—p3.

HONEY DROP

Panel of 24 sts.

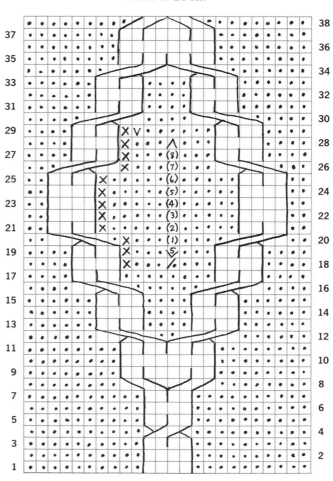

PRETZEL BRAID

Panel of 20 sts.

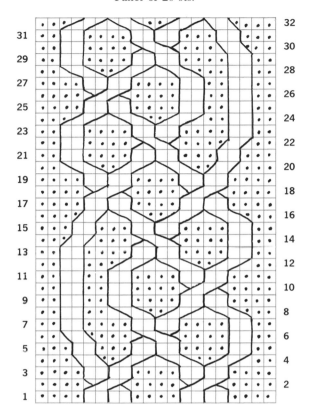

BUCKLE BRAID

Panel of 20 sts.

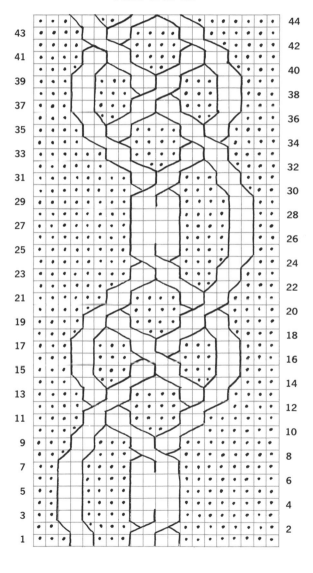

PEAR-SHAPED CABLE

Panel of 23 sts.

(1)—(Rows 9 & 11)—p5
(2)—(Row 10)—k5
(3)—(Row 12)—ssk, k1, k2 tog
(4)—(Row 13)—p3

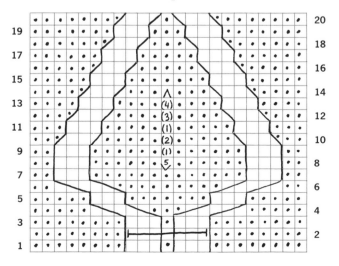

LEFT: **Latticed Spindle**
RIGHT: **Minarets**

MINARETS

Panel of 26 sts (increased to 28)

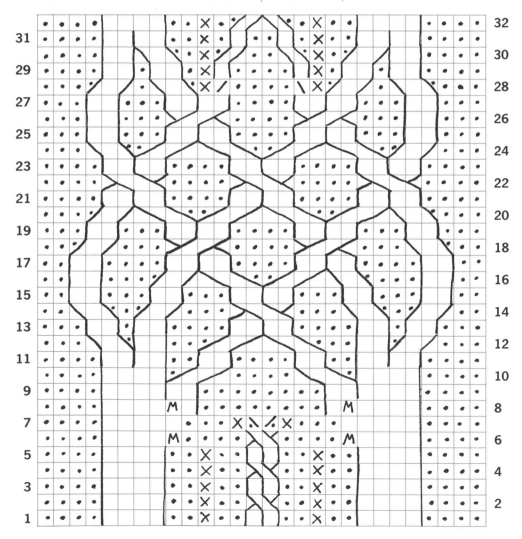

LATTICED SPINDLE

Panel of 24 sts (increased to 28)

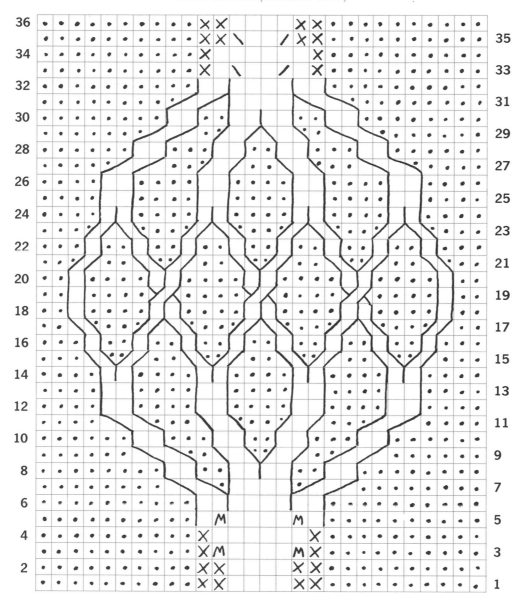

Twin Trees I

TWIN TREES I

Panel of 36 sts.

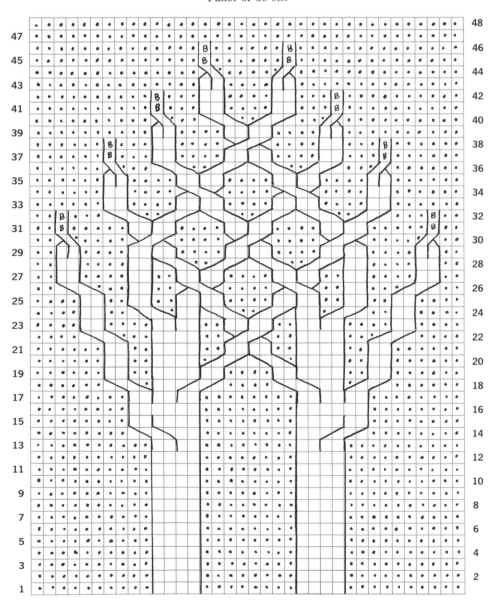

Twin Trees II

TWIN TREES II

Panel of 40 sts (increased to 48)

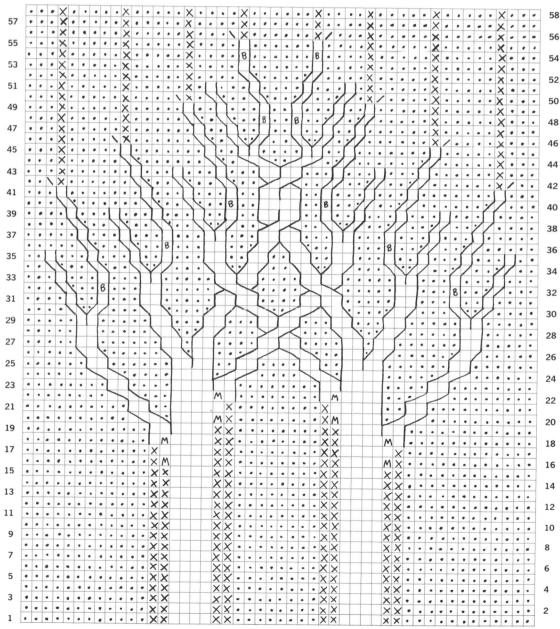

Apple Tree

APPLE TREE

Panel of 34 sts (increased to 42)

◇—MB: (k1, yo, k1, yo, k1) in one st, turn and p5, turn and ssk, k1, k2 tog, turn and p3, turn and sl 2-k1-p2sso.

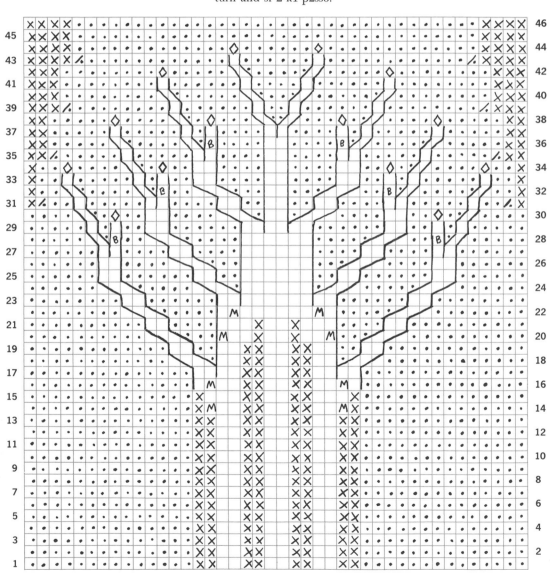

Lotus and Arch

LOTUS AND ARCH

Panel of 29 sts (increased to 39)

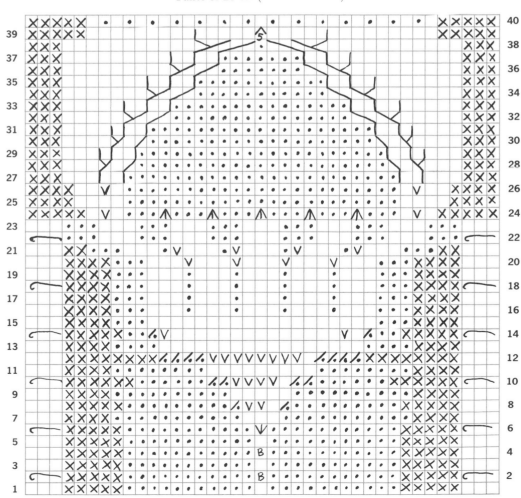

**Five-Branched
Candlestick**

FIVE-BRANCHED CANDLESTICK

Panel of 51 sts.

(1)—k1, yo, k1, yo, k1.   (5)—k2, sl 2-k1-p2sso, k2.

(2)—p5   (6)—k1, sl 1-k2 tog-psso, k1.

(3)—k2, yo, k1, yo, k2.   (7)—p3

(4)—p7

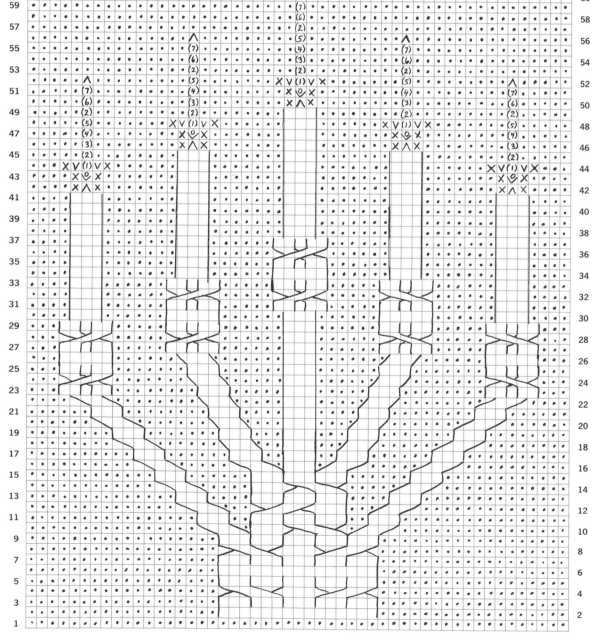

CHAPTER 4

Closed-Ring Designs in Cabling

Here are some really new ideas in cables. Special increase-and-decrease techniques make it possible, for the first time, to close the ring: to bring cabled ribs together neatly at the top and bottom of a curve. Two basic ring formations are given as examples, a small ring that opens by crossing two stitches over two at each side, and a large ring that opens by crossing three stitches over three. Subsequent patterns sometimes combine these two basics by crossing two stitches over three at the beginning of each ring or curve.

There is only one moment of acrobatic knitting in these designs, and that is the first five-stitch increase at the bottom of each ring. This is about the tightest and squinchiest little bit of knitting that you'll ever encounter. It must be so, or the increased stitches will not blend together properly. Once past this original hurdle, however, you'll find that the rest is very simple. So do persevere—muttering under your breath if you wish—in getting those first five stitches made. A rich profusion of hitherto impossible cable patterns awaits the knitter who has learned to close the ring. And remember—those "X" stitches *aren't there*!

Example A: Small Ring

Panel of 13 sts (increased to 17)

Notes: M1 (Make One)—lift running thread between the st just worked and the next st, place on left-hand needle and knit into the *back* of this thread.

1FC (Single Front Cross)—sl 2 sts to dpn and hold in front, p1, then k2 from dpn.
1BC (Single Back Cross)—sl 1 st to dpn and hold in back, k2, then p1 from dpn.
2FC (Double Front Cross)—sl 2 sts to dpn and hold in front, p2, then k2 from dpn.
2BC (Double Back Cross)—sl 2 sts to dpn and hold in back, k2, then p2 from dpn.

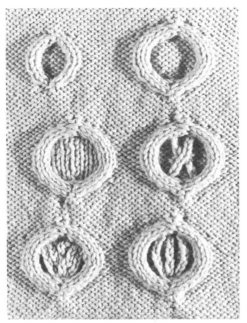

ABOVE, LEFT: Small Ring
ABOVE, RIGHT: Large Ring, Plain
CENTER, LEFT: Large Ring with Ribbing
CENTER, RIGHT: Large Ring with Two Ribs
BELOW, LEFT: Large Ring with Fan Ribs
BELOW, RIGHT: Large Ring with Three Ribs

Double increase (3 sts made from 1)—(k1-b, k1) in one st, then insert point of left-hand needle behind the vertical strand that runs downward from between the 2 sts just made, and knit into the back of this strand to form the 3rd st of the group.

Rows 1, 3, and 5 (Wrong side)—Knit.

Rows 2 and 4—Purl.

Row 6—P6, M1, double increase in center st, M1, p6.

Row 7—K6, p2, k1, p2, k6.

Row 8—P4, 2BC, p1, 2FC, p4.

Rows 9 and 15—K4, p2, k5, p2, k4.

Row 10—P3, 1BC, p5, 1FC, p3.

Rows 11 and 13—K3, p2, k7, p2, k3.

Row 12—P3, k2, p7, k2, p3.

Row 14—P3, 1FC, p5, 1BC, p3.

Row 16—P4, 2FC, p1, 2BC, p4.

Row 17—K6, decrease 5 sts down to 1 (center) st as follows: drop yarn in front, on wrong side, and leave it. Sl 3 sts to right-hand needle, then ° pass the 2nd st on right-hand needle over the first (center) st; sl the center st back to left-hand needle and pass 2nd st on left-hand needle over it; ° sl center st back to right-hand needle again, and repeat from ° to ° once more, leaving center st on left-hand needle. Pick up yarn, pass yarn to back and knit center st, completing decrease; k6.

Row 18—Purl.

Repeat Rows 1–18.

Example B: Large Ring

Panel of 19 sts (increased to 25)

Notes: M1 and double increase—same as for Example A, Small Ring.

 1FC (Single Front Cross)—sl 3 sts to dpn and hold in front, p1, then k3 from dpn.

 1BC (Single Back Cross)—sl 1 st to dpn and hold in back, k3, then p1 from dpn.

 2FC (Double Front Cross)—sl 3 sts to dpn and hold in front, p2, then k3 from dpn.

 2BC (Double Back Cross)—sl 2 sts to dpn and hold in back, k3, then p2 from dpn.

continued on page 109

EXAMPLE A: SMALL RING

Panel of 13 sts (increased to 17)

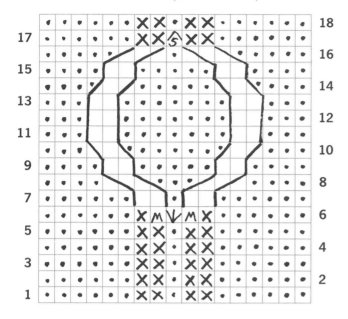

EXAMPLE B-1: LARGE RING, PLAIN

Panel of 19 sts (increased to 25)

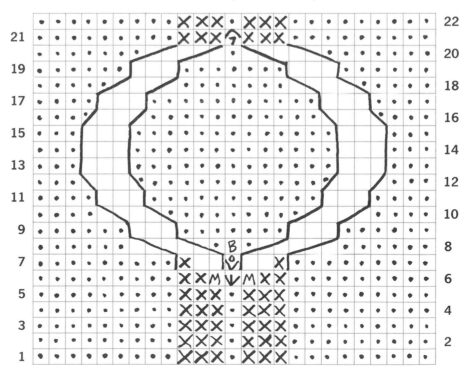

EXAMPLE B-2: LARGE RING WITH RIBBING

Panel of 19 sts (increased to 25)

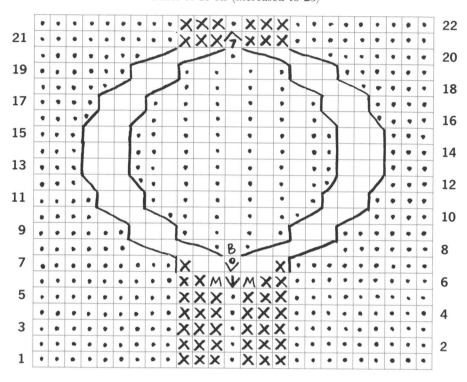

EXAMPLE B-3: LARGE RING WITH TWO RIBS

Panel of 19 sts (increased to 25)

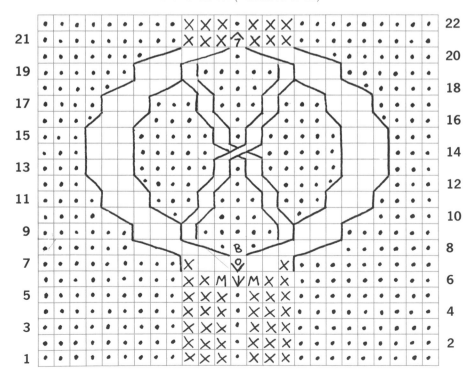

3FC (Triple Front Cross)—sl 3 sts to dpn and hold in front, p3, then k3 from dpn.
3BC (Triple Back Cross)—sl 3 sts to dpn and hold in back, k3, then p3 from dpn.

1. Large Ring, Plain

Rows 1, 3, and *5* (Wrong side)—Knit.
Rows 2 and *4*—Purl.
Row 6—P9, M1, double increase in center st, M1, p9.
Row 7—K9, p2, (p1, yo, p1) in center st, p2, k9.
Row 8—P6, 3BC, k1-b, 3FC, p6.
Rows 9 and *19*—K6, p3, k7, p3, k6.
Row 10—P4, 2BC, p7, 2FC, p4.
Rows 11 and *17*—K4, p3, k11, p3, k4.
Row 12—P3, 1BC, p11, 1FC, p3.
Rows 13 and *15*—K3, p3, k13, p3, k3.
Row 14—P3, k3, p13, k3, p3.
Row 16—P3, 1FC, p11, 1BC, p3.
Row 18—P4, 2FC, p7, 2BC, p4.
Row 20—P6, 3FC, p1, 3BC, p6.
Row 21—K9, decrease 7 sts down to 1 (center) st as follows: drop yarn in front, on wrong side, and leave it. Sl 4 sts to right-hand needle, then ° pass the 2nd st on right-hand needle over the first (center) st; sl the center st back to left-hand needle and pass 2nd st on left-hand needle over it; ° sl center st back to right-hand needle again, and repeat from ° to ° twice more, leaving center st on left-hand needle. Pick up yarn, pass yarn to back and knit center st, completing decrease; k9.
Row 22—Purl.
Repeat Rows 1–22.

2. Large Ring with Ribbing

Work the same as B-1, with the following exceptions:
Row 9 and *19*—K6, p3, (k1, p1) 3 times, k1, p3, k6.
Row 10—P4, 2BC, (p1, k1) 3 times, p1, 2FC, p4.
Rows 11 and *17*—K4, p3, (k1, p1) 5 times, k1, p3, k4.
Row 12—P3, 1BC, (p1, k1) 5 times, p1, 1FC, p3.
Rows 13 and *15*—K3, p3, k2, (p1, k1) 5 times, k1, p3, k3.
Row 14—P3, k3, p2, (k1, p1) 5 times, p1, k3, p3.
Row 16—P3, 1FC, (p1, k1) 5 times, p1, 1BC, p3.
Row 18—P4, 2FC, (p1, k1) 3 times, p1, 2BC, p4.

EXAMPLE B-4: LARGE RING WITH FAN RIBS

Panel of 19 sts (increased to 25)

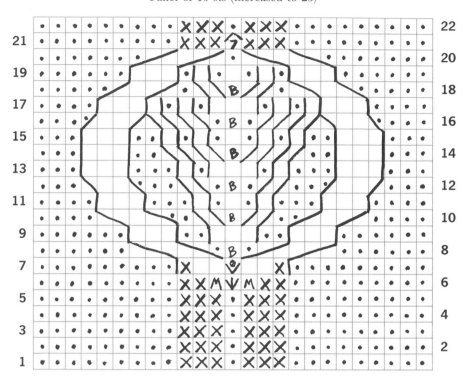

EXAMPLE B-5: LARGE RING WITH THREE RIBS

Panel of 19 sts (increased to 25)

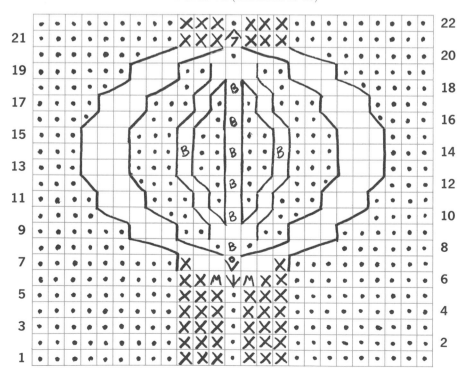

3. Large Ring with Two Ribs

Work the same as B-1, with the following exceptions:
Rows 9 and *19*—K6, p4, k5, p4, k6.
Row 10—P4, 2BC, LT, p3, RT, 2FC, p4.
Rows 11 and *17*—K4, p3, (k3, p1) twice, k3, p3, k4.
Row 12—P3, 1BC, p3, LT, p1, RT, p3, 1FC, p3.
Rows 13 and *15*—K3, p3, k5, p1, k1, p1, k5, p3, k3.
Row 14—P3, k3, p5, sl 2 sts to dpn and hold in back, k1, then sl the purl st from dpn
    back to left-hand needle and purl it, then k1 from dpn; p5, k3, p3.
Row 16—P3, 1FC, p3, RT, p1, LT, p3, 1BC, p3.
Row 18—P4, 2FC, RT, p3, LT, 2BC, p4.

4. Large Ring with Fan Ribs

Work the same as B-1, with the following exceptions:
Row 9—K6, p3, (k2, p3) twice, k6.
Row 10—P4, 2BC, p1, RT, k1-b, LT, p1, 2FC, p4.
Row 11—K4, p3, k3, (p1, k1) twice, p1, k3, p3, k4.
Row 12—P3, 1BC, p2, RT, p1, k1-b, p1, LT, p2, 1FC, p3.
Row 13—K3, p3, k3, p1, k1, p3, k1, p1, k3, p3, k3.
Row 14—P3, k3, p2, (RT) twice, k1-b, (LT) twice, p2, k3, p3.
Row 15—K3, p3, k2, (p1, k1) 4 times, p1, k2, p3, k3.
Row 16—P3, 1FC, (RT) twice, p1, k1-b, p1, (LT) twice, 1BC, p3.
Row 17—K4, p4, k1, p1, k1, p3, k1, p1, k1, p4, k4.
Row 18—P4, 2FC, p1, RT, k1-b, LT, p1, 2BC, p4.
Row 19—K6, p3, (k1, p1) 3 times, k1, p3, k6.

5. Large Ring with Three Ribs

Work the same as B-4, with the following exceptions:
Rows 13 and *15*—K3, p3, k3, (p1, k2) twice, p1, k3, p3, k3.
Row 14—P3, k3, p3, (k1-b, p2) twice, k1-b, p3, k3, p3.
Row 16—P3, 1FC, p2, LT, p1, k1-b, p1, RT, p2, 1BC, p3.
Row 17—Repeat Row 11 of B-4.
Row 18—P4, 2FC, p1, LT, k1-b, RT, p1, 2BC, p4.
Row 19—Repeat Row 9 of B-4.

Peace

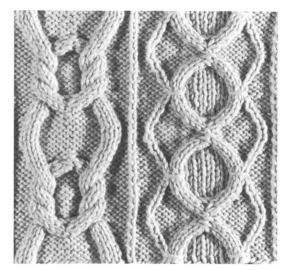

LEFT: **Reef Knot**
RIGHT: **Balanced Rings**

PEACE

Panel of 25 sts (increased to 31)

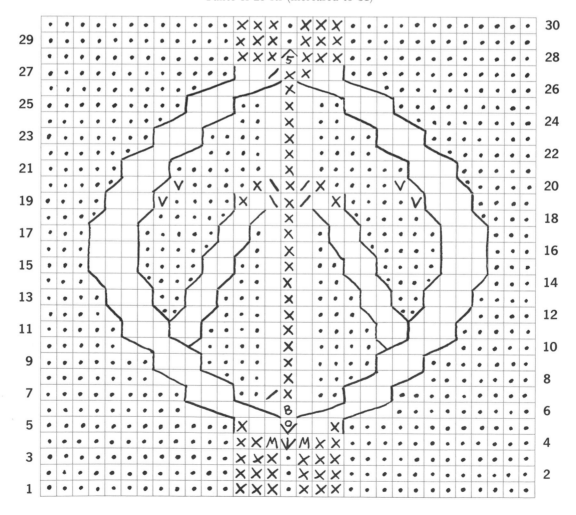

REEF KNOT

Panel of 23 sts (increased to 29)

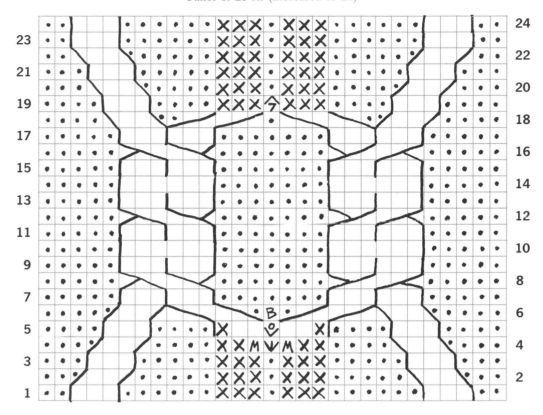

BALANCED RINGS

Panel of 31 sts.

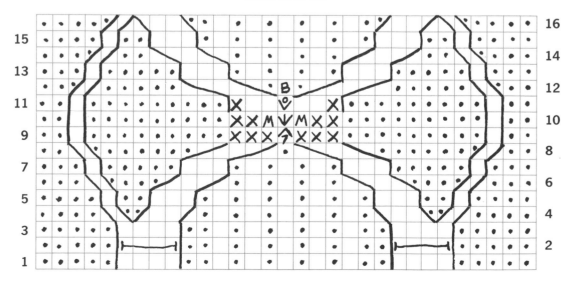

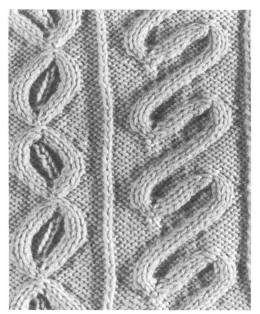

LEFT: Teetering Ovals
RIGHT: Sidewinder

TEETERING OVALS

Panel of 23 sts.

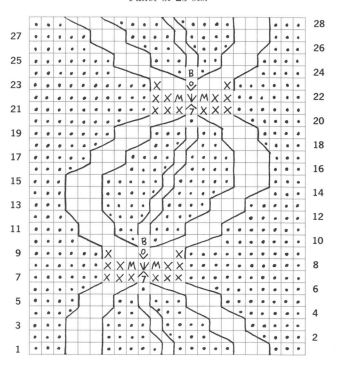

SIDEWINDER

Panel of 23 sts (increased to 29)

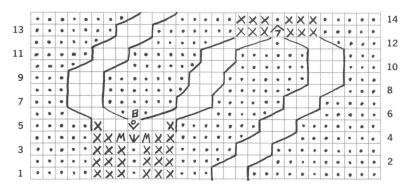

Royal Braid

LEFT: pattern begun with Row 1.

RIGHT: opposition panel—pattern begun with Row 25.

ROYAL BRAID

Panel of 32 sts (increased to 37)

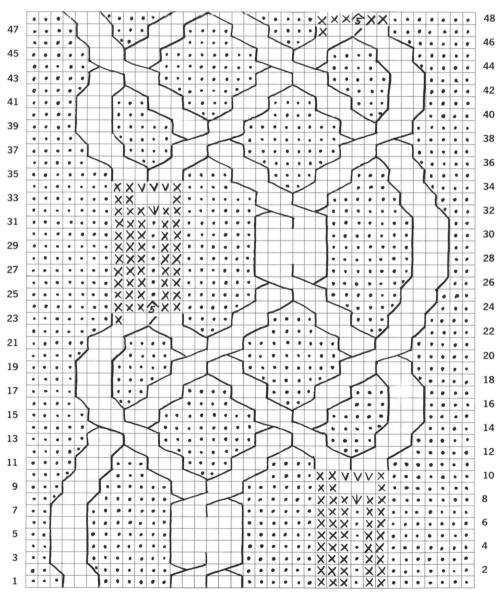

BUTTERFLY LOOP

Panel of 28 sts (increased to 36)

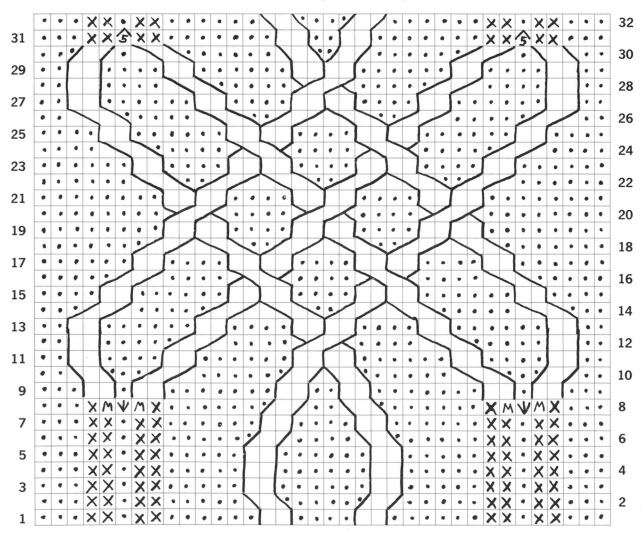

LEFT: **Butterfly Loop**
RIGHT: **Locked-Square Cable**

LOCKED-SQUARE CABLE

Panel of 25 sts (increased to 29)

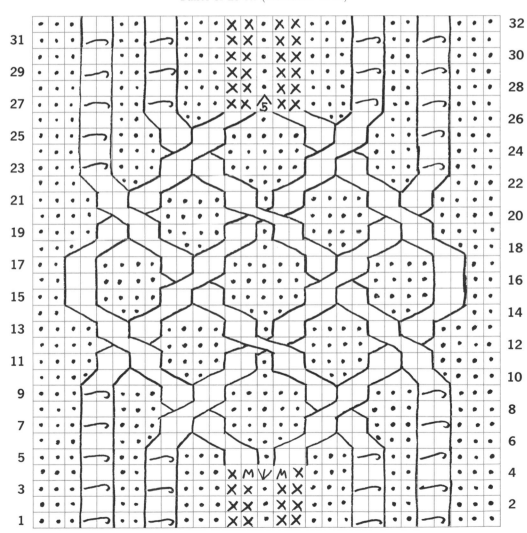

HEART STRINGS

Panel of 24 sts (increased to 32)

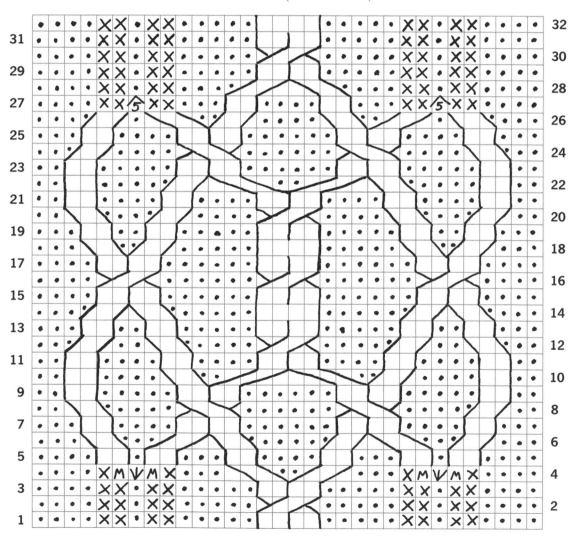

LEFT: Heart Strings
RIGHT: Loop-the-Loop

LOOP-THE-LOOP

Panel of 26 sts (increased to 30)

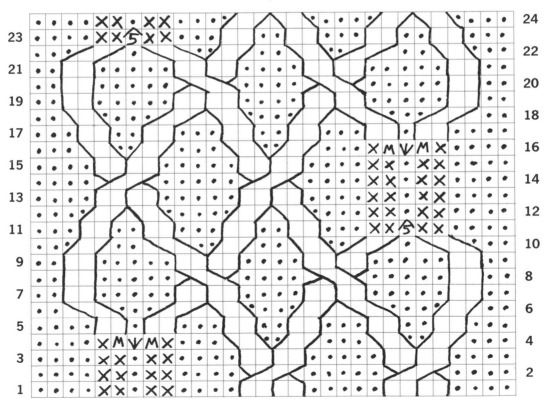

LEFT: **Long Loop I**
RIGHT: **Long Loop II**

LONG LOOP I

Panel of 42 sts (increased to 46)

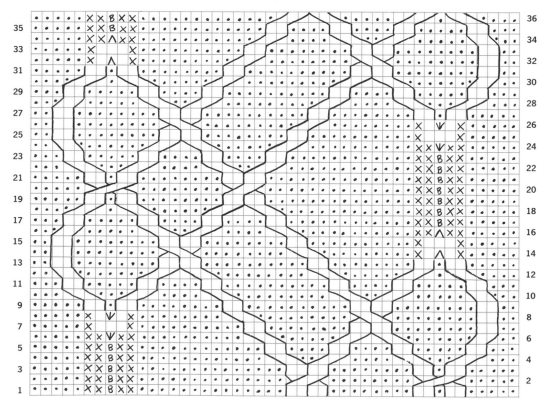

LONG LOOP II

Panel of 45 sts (increased to 50)

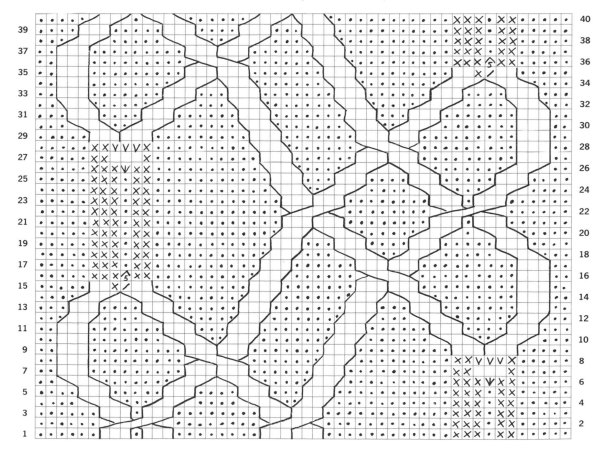

BOOTLACING CABLE

Panel of 30 sts (increased to 38)

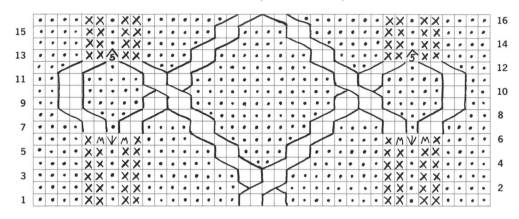

CELTIC FLOURISH

Panel of 30 sts (increased to 38)

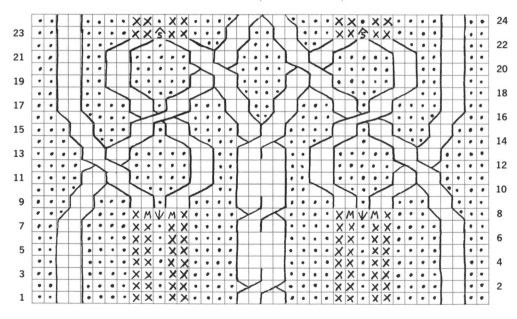

LEFT: **Bootlacing Cable**
RIGHT: **Celtic Flourish**

Fronds

FRONDS

Panel of 24 sts (increased to 32)

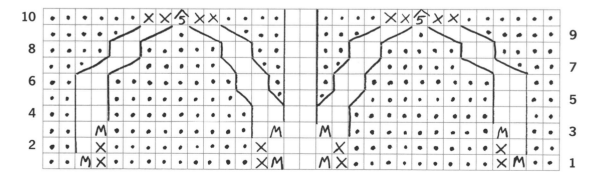

Fancy Vine

LEFT: **Curlicue**
RIGHT: **Contra Corners**

FANCY VINE

Panel of 25 sts (increased to 29)

CURLICUE

Panel of 22 sts (increased to 34)

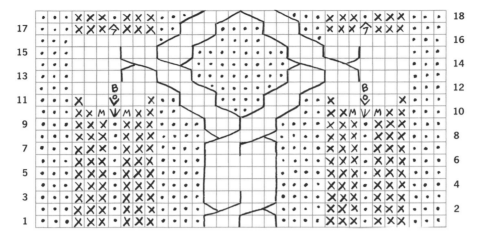

CONTRA CORNERS

Panel of 17 sts (increased to 35)

Note change of center st from k to p on Row 14, and from p to k
on Row 22.

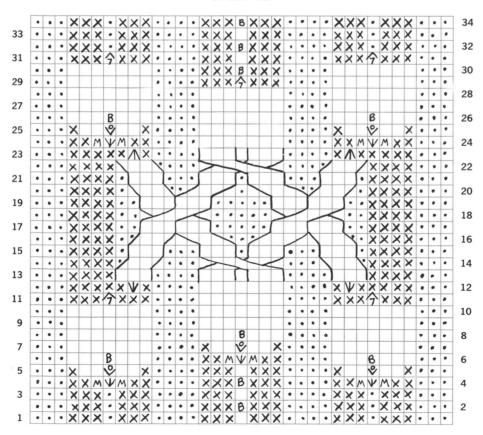

Four-Lobed Escutcheon

FOUR-LOBED ESCUTCHEON

Panel of 27 sts (increased to 31)

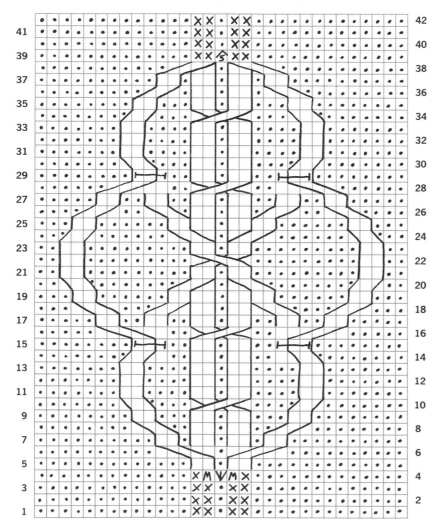

Quatrefoil with Seed Stitch

QUATREFOIL WITH SEED STITCH

Panel of 37 sts (increased to 49)

The Turtle

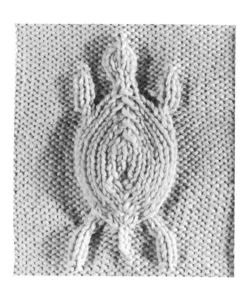

THE TURTLE

Panel of 17 sts (increased to 31)

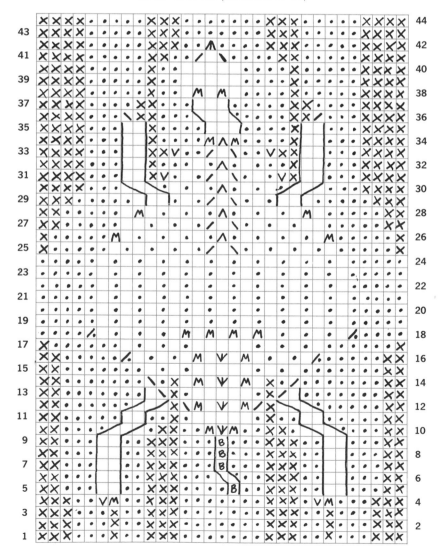

CHAPTER 5

Cable-Stitch Patterns

In this section there are patterns of several different types. Some are basically knit-purl designs, some make use of the closed-ring technique or variations of it, some have touches of openwork. All of them have just two things in common: (1) they are intended to be used all over a fabric, in many repeats rather than a single panel, and (2) they employ the cable needle. There may be a lot of cabling, or only a little touch here and there, depending on the pattern.

Needless to say, before embarking on any cable-stitch pattern you must learn all the methods for charting cables. These charts use precisely the same methods for showing each cable crossing. Refer to the introduction to Cables, and the 80 Basic Cable Crossings, to find the necessary information.

Unlike cables, however, cable-stitch patterns have repeat lines on their charts; so each chart will show some extra edge stitches that are worked only once, at the beginning and end of each row. The repeat lines are broken where the front stitches of a cable crossing pass over them, but this does not move them from their places. Sometimes, if the last repeat of a pattern is to be worked a little differently from the others, the chart will show two or more whole repeats in order to make this clear.

These designs range from very simple to very fancy, but none are really difficult to work. If you enjoy knitting fabrics with plenty of "relief"—highly embossed texture–then cable–stitch patterns are for you. They give, in a continuous, uniform design, the same rich surface that is achieved by combining various cable panels.

129

Rocking Cables

Example Cable-Stitch Pattern:

Rocking Cables

THIS is a big, bold design with some unusual cable crossings that make apparently simple cables tilt on the diagonal. It is not difficult to work, but when arranged all over a single garment (a nice bulky coat or jacket, for instance), this pattern makes a wonderful array of intricately interlocked ribs, ropes and links. For a test swatch, use at least 64 stitches (2 × 28 + 8) in order to see how the repeats join pattern lines together.

Multiple of 28 sts plus 8

Notes: FKC (Front Knit Cross)—sl 3 sts to dpn and hold in front, k3, then k3 from dpn.
BKC (Back Knit Cross)—sl 3 sts to dpn and hold in back, k3, then k3 from dpn.
FPC (Front Purl Cross)—sl 3 sts to dpn and hold in front, p2, then k3 from dpn.
BPC (Back Purl Cross)—sl 2 sts to dpn and hold in back, k3, then p2 from dpn.
8FC (8-stitch Front Cross)—sl 3 sts to dpn and hold in front, p2, k3, then k3 from dpn.
8BC (8-stitch Back Cross)—sl 5 sts to dpn and hold in back, k3, then k3, p2 from dpn.

Row 1 (Wrong side)—K1, p9, ° k16, p12; rep from °, end k16, p9, k1.
Row 2—P1, ° BKC, FPC, p12, BPC; rep from °, end BKC, p1.
Row 3 and all subsequent wrong-side rows—Knit all knit sts and purl all purl sts.
Row 4—P1, ° k6, p2, FPC, p8, BPC, p2; rep from °, end k6, p1.
Row 6—P1, ° k6, p4, FPC, p4, BPC, p4; rep from °, end k6, p1.
Row 8—P1, ° BKC, p6, FPC, BPC, p6; rep from °, end BKC, p1.
Row 10—P4, ° FPC, p6, FKC, p6, BPC; rep from °, end p4.
Row 12—P6, ° FPC, p4, k6, p4, BPC, p4; rep from °, end p2.
Row 14—P8, ° FPC, p2, k6, p2, BPC, p8; rep from °.
Row 16—P10, ° FPC, FKC, BPC, p12; rep from °, end last repeat p10.
Row 18—P10, ° 8BC, 8FC, p12; rep from °, end last repeat p10.
Rows 20 and *22*—Knit all knit sts and purl all purl sts.
Row 24—P8, ° 8BC, p4, 8FC, p8; rep from °.
Rows 26 and *28*—Knit all knit sts and purl all purl sts.

Row 30—P6, ° 8BC, p8, 8FC, p4; rep from °, end p2.

Rows 32 and *34*—Knit all knit sts and purl all purl sts.

Row 36—P4, ° 8BC, p12, 8FC; rep from °, end p4.

　　Repeat Rows 1–36.

ROCKING CABLES

Multiple of 28 sts plus 8.

° *Rows 18, 24, 30,* and *36:* Back cross—sl 5 sts to dpn and hold in back, k3, then k3, p2 from dpn.
Front cross—sl 3 sts to dpn and hold in front, p2, k3, then k3 from dpn.

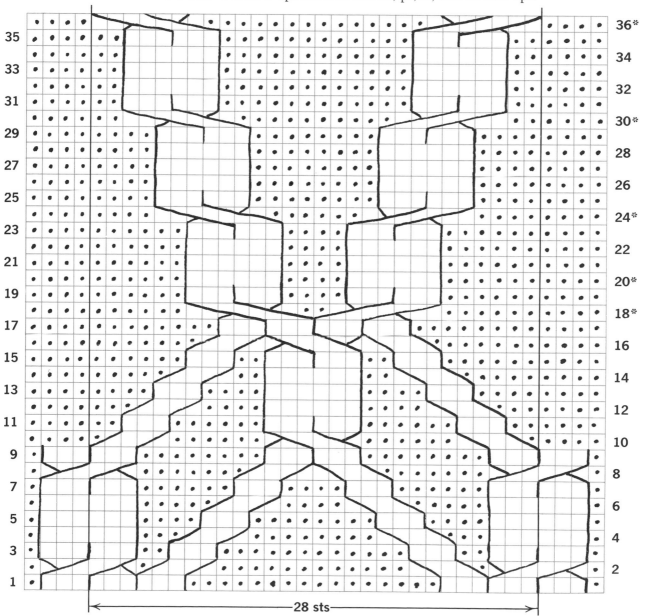

Round Link Cables

ROUND LINK CABLES

Multiple of 22 sts plus 2.

° *Rows 4* and *10*—make 9-stitch cable cross as
follows: sl 6 sts to dpn and hold in front, k3,
then sl the center 3 sts from dpn back to
left-hand needle; pass dpn with the remaining 3 sts to back of work; k3 from left-hand
needle, then k3 from dpn.

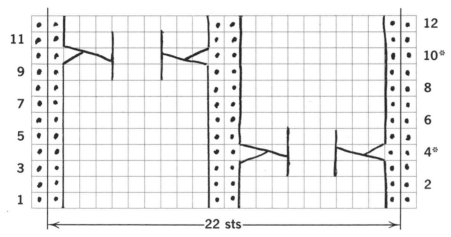

Domed Check Pattern

DOMED CHECK PATTERN

Multiple of 8 sts plus 6.

° *Row 8*—Front cross from wrong side: sl 2 sts to dpn
and hold in front, p2, then p2 from dpn.

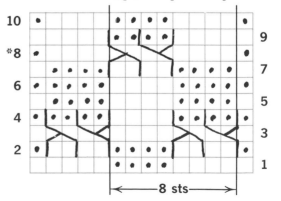

Wrung-Rib Lattice

WRUNG-RIB LATTICE

Multiple of 10 sts plus 8.

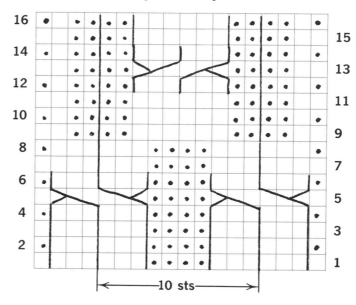

CABLE AND BAND PATTERN

Multiple of 10 sts plus 1.

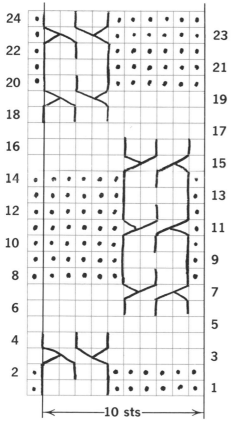

Cable and Band Pattern

MINIATURE LATTICE

Multiple of 4 sts plus 3.

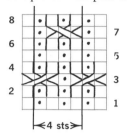

THREADED LATTICE ON SEED STITCH

Multiple of 14 sts plus 1 (29 sts minimum)

Two repeats shown

Miniature Lattice

Ornate Lattice

Threaded Lattice on Seed Stitch

ORNATE LATTICE

Multiple of 16 sts plus 6.

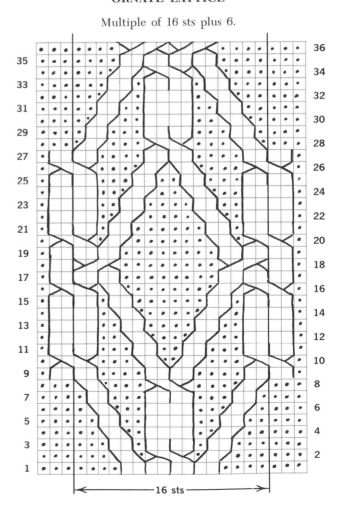

GRILLWORK LATTICE

Multiple of 8 sts (3 repeats shown)

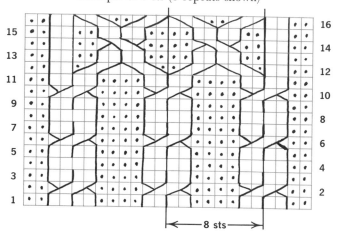

← 8 sts →

HEAVY ROPE LATTICE

Multiple of 14 sts plus 2. Two repeats shown

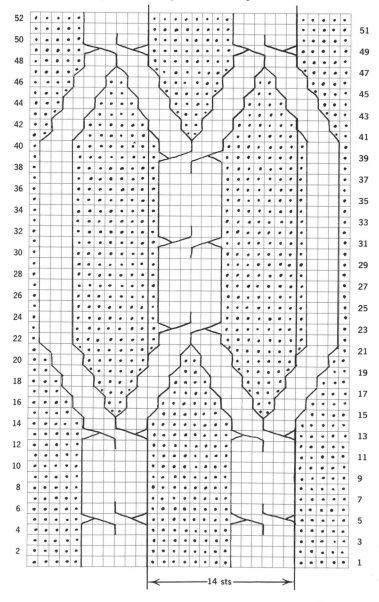

← 14 sts →

Heavy Rope Lattice

Grillwork Lattice

Interlocking Double-Twist and Single-Twist Cables

INTERLOCKING DOUBLE-TWIST AND SINGLE-TWIST CABLES

Multiple of 24 sts plus 10.

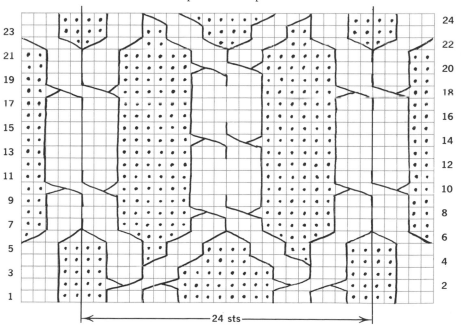

Woodgrain Pattern I

WOODGRAIN PATTERN I

Multiple of 14 sts. Two repeats shown

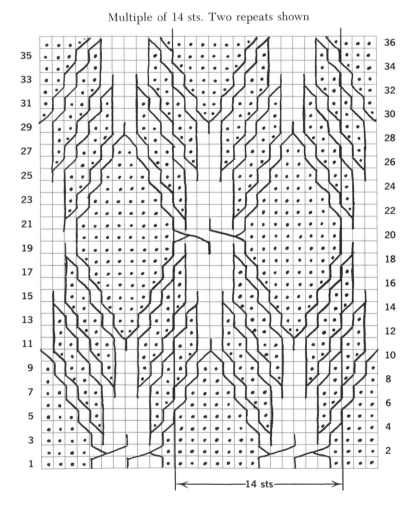

Woodgrain Pattern II

WOODGRAIN PATTERN II

Multiple of 14 sts. Two repeats shown

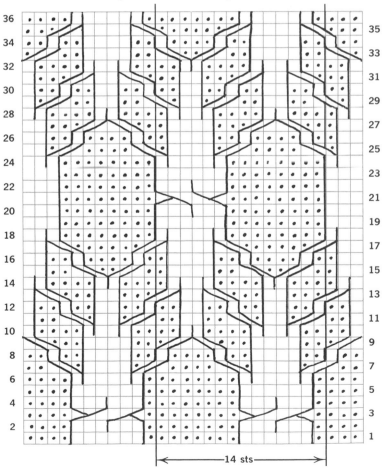

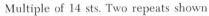

DECORATIVE LOZENGES

Multiple of 14 sts plus 3 (increased to 16 plus 3)

Two repeats shown

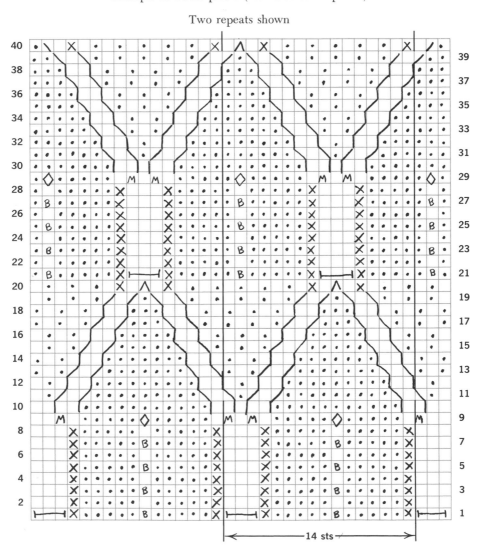

Decorative Lozenges

Garland with Pendants

GARLAND WITH PENDANTS

Multiple of 14 sts plus 3 (increased to 18 plus 3)

Two repeats shown

* *Row 1* ⌄𝟧—(k1, yo, k1, yo, k1) in one st.

° *Row 9* ◊—Make bobble as follows: (k1, p1) twice in one st, turn and p4, turn and k4, then pass 2nd, 3rd, 4th sts on right-hand needle separately over the last st made.

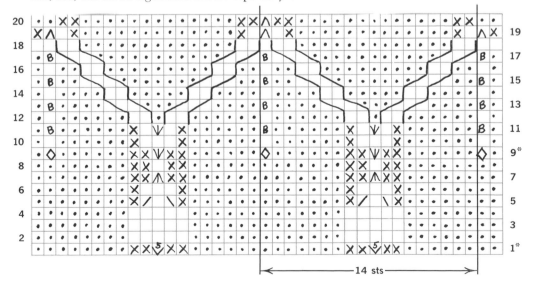

ABOVE: Pointed Arches

BELOW: Rounded Arches

Interlocking Squares

POINTED ARCHES

Multiple of 26 sts plus 14.

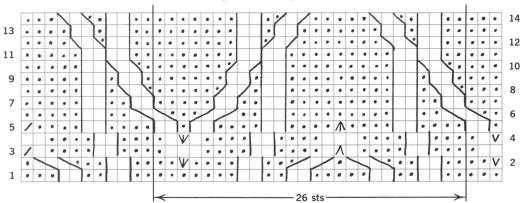

ROUNDED ARCHES

Multiple of 22 sts plus 13 (increased to 26 sts plus 17)

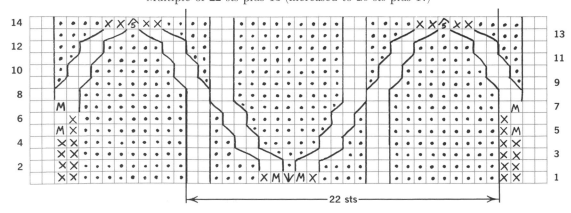

INTERLOCKING SQUARES

Multiple of 13 sts plus 1 (increased to 17 plus 1)

Two repeats shown

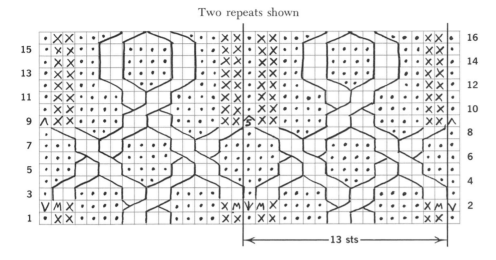

CROISSANTS

Multiple of 16 sts plus 1.

Croissants

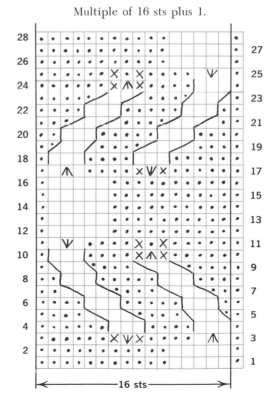

Aqueduct

Chain Link Pattern

AQUEDUCT

Multiple of 9 sts plus 2 (increased to 13 plus 2).

Two repeats shown

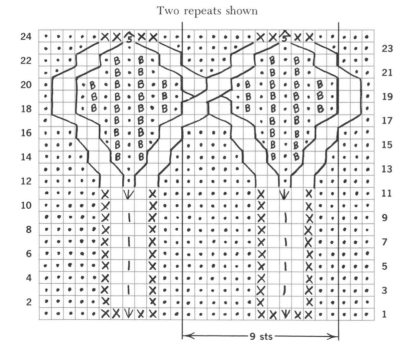

CHAIN LINK PATTERN

Multiple of 7 sts plus 10 (increased to 11 sts plus 10)

Two repeats shown

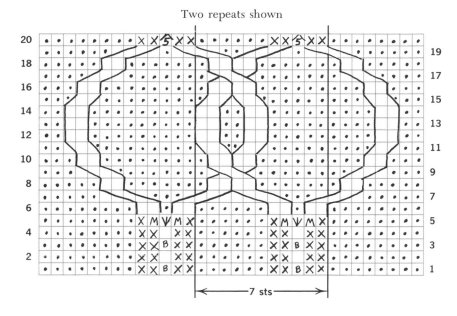

THICK-AND-THIN LATTICE

Multiple of 15 sts plus 10.

Thick-and-Thin Lattice

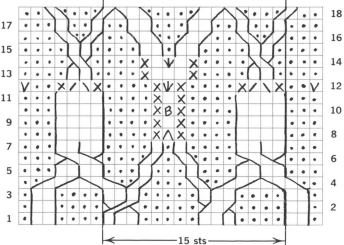

Large Lacy Cables

LARGE LACY CABLES

Multiple of 30 sts plus 9.

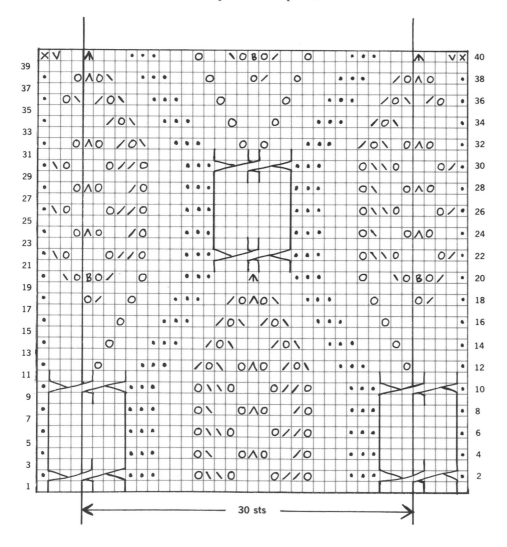

Fan Cables

FAN CABLES

Multiple of 30 sts plus 8.

(Note jog of repeat lines between Rows 16 and 17)

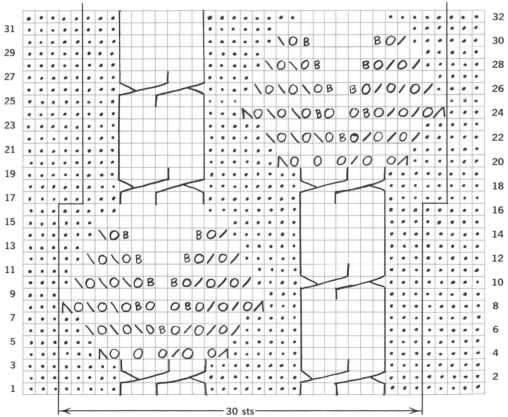

CHAPTER 6

Lace

Lace knitting is a universal favorite because it offers so much variety in shape, design, and texture, and because its results—however simple the pattern—are so lovely. Lace can be worked either all over the fabric, in multiples, or in panel formation on a fixed number of stitches. The first kind of lace is found in this chapter, the second kind in the next.

Lace patterns have been recorded in chart form for many years. Charting is especially handy for lace because the written-out directions often tend to be long, and a vertically aligned chart makes it easier for the knitter to see the positions of yarn-overs and decreases with regard to those on the row below. All sorts of symbols have been devised for charting lace. These charts use the same symbol alphabet as the other charts in preceding chapters, and are read in exactly the same way except for one small difference. On some of these charts, you will not find *all* the row numbers. You will find only right-side row numbers on the right-hand side of the chart, but no wrong-side row numbers on the left-hand side of the chart. Of course this doesn't mean that there are no wrong-side rows. It means that all the wrong-side rows are *purled* (or, in circular knitting, knitted plain). A plain purl wrong-side row would appear as a horizontal row of blank squares in this system of charting; therefore such a row can be omitted from the chart to save space. So if a pattern begins with Row 2 at the lower right-hand corner, and there are no numbers at the left, it means that the directions begin in this rather customary way: "Row 1 (wrong side) and all other wrong-side rows—Purl."

If a pattern begins with Row 1 at the lower right-hand corner, and there are no numbers at the left, it means that the first row is a right-side row and all the even-numbered rows are purled. In either case, whether the given numbers are odd or even, they are right-side row numbers only. All rows whose numbers are missing from the chart are plain purl rows—or, in circular knitting, plain knit rounds.

Naturally, if every other horizontal row is left out of a chart, the pattern picture as it appears on that chart will be somewhat shortened and broadened in comparison to its appearance in the actual knitting; but not very much. A knit stitch is not a perfect square. It is about three-quarters as high as it is wide. So a chart that shows *all* rows will distort the pattern picture the other way, making it seem a little taller and narrower than it really is.

In a few patterns, some of the wrong-side rows are omitted, but not all of them. Once in a while you will see a lonely little number or two at the left-hand side of the chart, which will indicate a row or two where something other than plain purl stitches occurs. Don't miss these lonely left-hand numbers and try to work their rows as right-side rows, from right to left. They are there to show you rows worked from left to right (unless, of course, you are working in rounds). No wrong-side row consisting of plain purl stitches is ever shown; but no wrong-side row consisting of purl stitches plus something else is ever omitted.

In many of these patterns you will see the five-stitch decrease symbol, a 5 with a little tent over it, as used in the closed-ring designs. Most of the time this decrease is best done by the second method given in the Complete List of Symbols, i.e., ssk, k3 tog, pass the ssk st over the k3-tog st. The first, or multiple slipped decrease, method can be used in lace, but usually not with the same success that attends it in embossed or cable designs. The reasons for this are (1) the multiple slipped decrease may pull downward, and obscure some of the openwork below, or (2) the multiple slipped decrease may draw the central stitch to one side and throw the pattern a bit off-center. However, these are very subtle effects which are largely dependent on the individual style of knitting. Try both ways of decreasing, and use the one that you think looks better. For the single increase (v), you may use any version of "Inc 1" that you prefer.

If you want to work lace patterns on a number of stitches other than the recommended multiple, use the chart to pair up yo's and decreases, making sure that you have equal numbers of both on any given row if you want to maintain the same stitch total. Any single decrease (ssk, k2 tog, p2 tog, or p2 tog-b) matches a single yo. Any double decrease (sl 1-k2 tog-psso, k3 tog, k3 tog-b, p3 tog, etc.) matches two yo's. Take care at the repeat lines. When edge stitches are included on the chart, a decrease or yo may appear on one side of the repeat line while its corresponding yo or decrease may appear on the other side. For example, if a row begins with a decrease outside the first repeat line, then it must always end with an increase (yo) outside the second repeat line in order to maintain the same number of stitches. Of course if you are working on a correct multiple, you don't have to worry about fine points like this; you can simply work right along and let the chart take care of such things for you. It will.

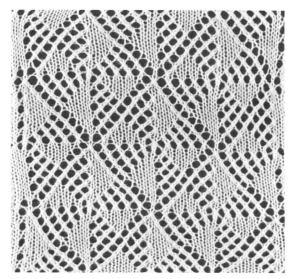

Vortex

Sunspots

Example Lace Patterns:

Vortex and Sunspots

Two pretty lace designs are given as examples, so that both ways of charting lace can be clearly demonstrated. The chart for Vortex shows right-side rows only, the wrong-side rows being plain purl rows; the chart for Sunspots shows all rows. The first of these patterns is one of the "illusion" fabrics that can be seen in several ways at once. It is an arrangement of large diamonds divided into quarters of openwork and stockinette stitch, and when looked at from this point of view it shows propellor-shaped motifs that seem to spin around a common center. Or, it may be seen as openwork butterfly shapes, half of them horizontal and half of them vertical, placed in alternating blocks. From either point of view it is interesting and graceful. The second of these two patterns is an introduction to the rounded motifs in lace knitting, quite a few of which will be encountered later. In Sunspots the rounded shapes are begun in the usual way, with a five-stitch increase; the "spots" themselves are purled, so the decreases are purled also. This highly unusual lace design is attractive on both sides of the fabric. When pressed only lightly, without much stretching, and used wrong-side out, it makes a pretty lace puff effect like coin dots surrounded by purled openwork.

I. Vortex—Multiple of 20 sts plus 5

Row 1 (Wrong side) and all other wrong-side rows—Purl.
Row 2—K1, ° yo, sl 2-k1-p2sso, yo, k6, k2 tog, yo, k1, (yo, ssk) 4 times; rep from °, end yo, sl 2-k1-p2sso, yo, k1.

Row 4—K3, ° k2 tog, yo, k4, k2 tog, yo, k3, (yo, ssk) 4 times, k1, rep from °, end k2.

Row 6—K2, ° ssk, yo, k2 tog, yo, k2, (k2 tog, yo) twice, k3, (yo, ssk) 3 times, k1; rep from °, end ssk, yo, k1.

Row 8—K3, ° (k2 tog, yo) 4 times, k5, (yo, ssk) twice, k3; rep from °, end k2.

Row 10—K2, ° ssk, yo, (k2 tog, yo) 4 times, k5, yo, ssk, k3; rep from °, end ssk, yo, k1.

Row 12—K3, ° (k2 tog, yo) 4 times, k5, (yo, ssk) twice, k3; rep from °, end k2.

Row 14—K2, ° ssk, yo, k2 tog, yo, k2, (k2 tog, yo) twice, k3, (yo, ssk) 3 times, k1; rep from °, end ssk, yo, k1.

Row 16—K3, ° k2 tog, yo, k4, k2 tog, yo, k3, (yo, ssk) 4 times, k1; rep from °, end k2.

Row 18—K1, ° yo, sl 1-k2 tog-psso, yo, k6, k2 tog, yo, k1, (yo, ssk) 4 times; rep from °, end yo, sl 1-k2 tog-psso, yo, k1.

Row 20—K2 tog, yo, ° k1, (yo, ssk) 4 times, yo, sl 2-k1-p2sso, yo, k6, k2 tog, yo; rep from °, end k1, yo, ssk.

Row 22—K4, ° (yo, ssk) 4 times, k1, k2 tog, yo, k4, k2 tog, yo, k3; rep from °, end k1.

continued on page 152

VORTEX

Multiple of 20 sts plus 5.

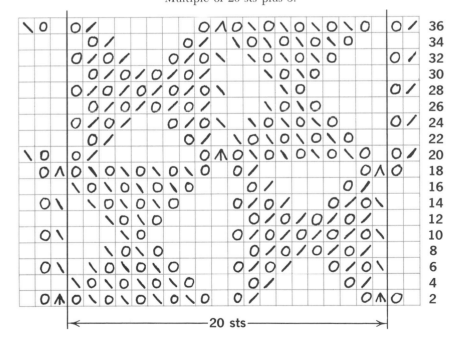

Row 24—K2 tog, yo, ° k3, (yo, ssk) 3 times, k1, ssk, yo, k2 tog, yo, k2, (k2 tog, yo) twice; rep from °, end k3.

Row 26—K6, ° (yo, ssk) twice, k3, (k2 tog, yo) 4 times, k5; rep from °, end last repeat k4.

Row 28—K2 tog, yo, ° k5, yo, ssk, k3, ssk, yo, (k2 tog, yo) 4 times; rep from °, end k3.

Row 30—K6, ° (yo, ssk) twice, k3, (k2 tog, yo) 4 times, k5; rep from °, end last repeat k4.

Row 32—K2 tog, yo, ° k3, (yo, ssk) 3 times, k1, ssk, yo, k2 tog, yo, k2, (k2 tog, yo) twice; rep from °, end k3.

Row 34—K4, ° (yo, ssk) 4 times, k1, k2 tog, yo, k4, k2 tog, yo, k3; rep from °, end k1.

Row 36—K2 tog, yo, ° k1, (yo, ssk) 4 times, yo, sl 1-k2 tog-psso, yo, k6, k2 tog, yo; rep from °, end k1, yo, ssk.

Repeat Rows 1–36.

II. Sunspots—Multiple of 12 sts plus 3

Notes: Double inc: (k1-b, k1) in one stitch, then insert left-hand needle point behind the vertical strand that runs downward from between the 2 sts just made, and k1-b into this strand to make the 3rd st of the group.

Inc 1: insert needle downward into the back of the st in the row below the first st on left-hand needle, and knit; then knit the st on needle.

Row 1 (Right side)—K1, k2 tog, ° yo, k2 tog, yo, p5, yo, ssk, yo, sl 1-k2 tog-psso; rep from °, end last repeat ssk, k1 instead of sl 1-k2 tog-psso.

Row 2—P5, ° k5, p7; rep from °, end k5, p5.

Row 3—K1, ° yo, k3 tog, yo, p7, yo, ssk; rep from °, end yo, k2 tog.

Rows 4, 6, and *8*—P4, ° k7, p5; rep from °, end k7, p4.

Row 5—Ssk, yo, ° ssk, yo, p7, yo, sl 2-k1-p2sso, yo; rep from °, end k1.

Row 7—K1, ° yo, sl 2-k1-p2sso, yo, p7, yo, k2 tog; rep from °, end yo, k2 tog.

Row 9—K1, inc 1, ° yo, ssk, yo, p2 tog, p3 tog, p2 tog, yo, k2 tog, yo, double inc; rep from °, end last repeat inc 1, k1 instead of double inc.

Row 10—P6, ° k3 tog, p9; rep from °, end k3 tog, p6.

Row 11—K1, inc 1, ° (yo, ssk) twice, p1, (k2 tog, yo) twice, double inc; rep from °, end last repeat inc 1, k1 instead of double inc.

Row 12—P7, ° k1, p11; rep from °, end k1, p7.

Row 13—K1, p3, ° yo, ssk, yo, sl 1-k2 tog-psso, yo, k2 tog, yo, p5; rep from °, end last repeat p3, k1 instead of p5.

Row 14—P1, k3, ° p7, k5; rep from °, end p7, k3, p1.

Row 15—K1, p4, ° yo, ssk, yo, k3 tog, yo, p7; rep from °, end last repeat p4, k1 instead of p7.

Rows 16, 18, and *20*—P1, k4, ° p5, k7; rep from °, end p5, k4, p1.

Row 17—K1, p4, ° yo, sl 2-k1-p2sso, yo, ssk, yo, p7; rep from °, end last repeat p4, k1 instead of p7.

Row 19—K1, p4, ° yo, k2 tog, yo, sl 2-k1-p2sso, yo, p7; rep from °, end last repeat p4, k1 instead of p7.

Row 21—K1, p2 tog, ° p2 tog, yo, k2 tog, yo, double inc, yo, ssk, yo, p2 tog, p3 tog; rep from °, end last repeat p2 tog, k1 instead of p3 tog.

Row 22—P1, k2 tog, ° p9, k3 tog; rep from °, end p9, k2 tog, p1.

Row 23—K1, p1, ° (k2 tog, yo) twice, double inc. (yo, ssk) twice, p1; rep from °, end k1.

Row 24—P1, k1, ° p11, k1; rep from °, end p1.

Repeat Rows 1–24.

SUNSPOTS

Multiple of 12 sts plus 3. Two repeats shown

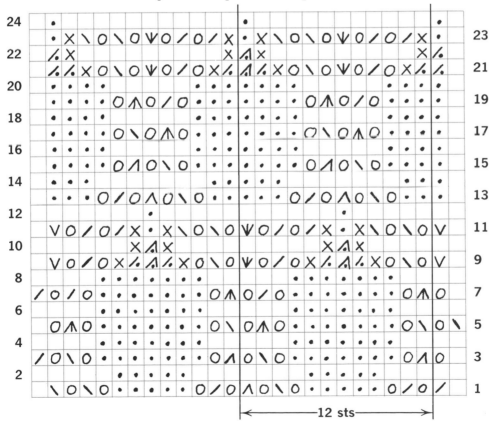

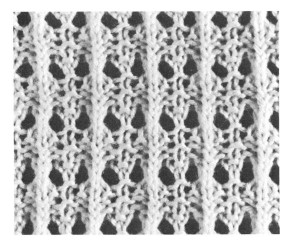

Eyelet Bar Stitch

EYELET BAR STITCH

Multiple of 4 sts plus 1.

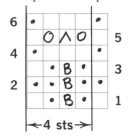

IVY PATTERN

Multiple of 7 sts plus 3.

(Note jog of repeat line)

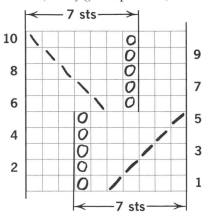

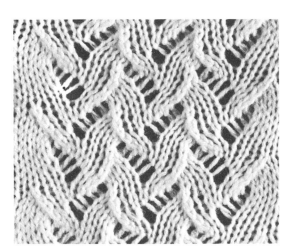

Ivy Pattern

ALSATIAN PATTERN

Multiple of 12 sts plus 1

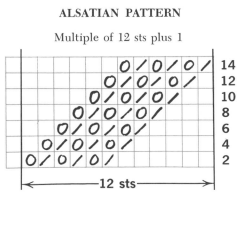

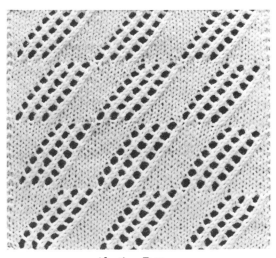

Alsatian Pattern

BUMBLEBEE PATTERN

Multiple of 8 sts plus 2. Two repeats shown

All wrong-side rows—Purl, working (k1, p1) into every double yo.

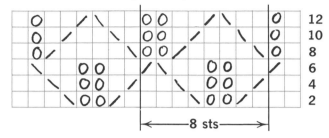

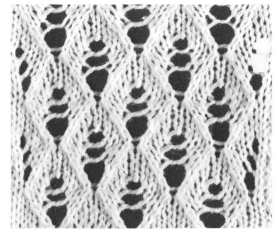

Bumblebee Pattern

FAGGOTING AND FANCY RIB

Multiple of 8 sts plus 4.

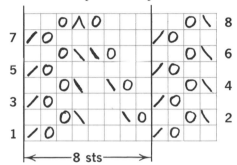

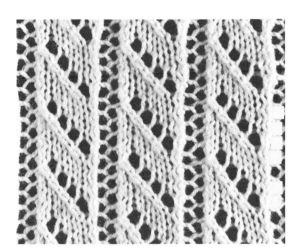

Faggoting and Fancy Rib

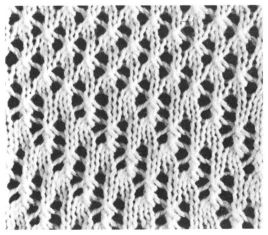

ABOVE: Petite Lace Pattern
BELOW: Variation

PETITE LACE PATTERN

Multiple of 6 sts plus 1.

Two repeats shown

For Variation, work each pattern row twice, making 12 rows in all.

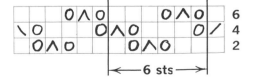

Eyelet and Bead Pattern

EYELET AND BEAD PATTERN

Multiple of 8 sts plus 1.

Two repeats shown

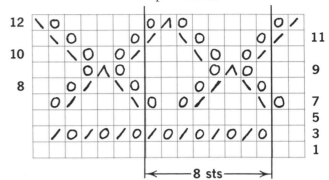

Bleeding Hearts

BLEEDING HEARTS

Multiple of 12 sts plus 1.

Two repeats shown

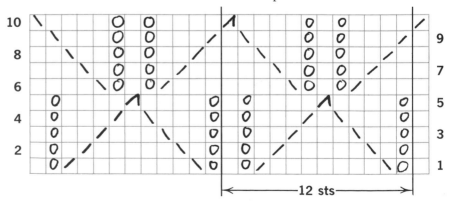

VANDYKE LACE

Multiple of 4 sts plus 1. Two repeats shown

Vandyke Lace

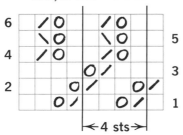

←4 sts→

Vandyke Lace Variation

←4 sts→

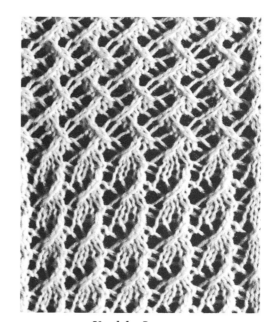

ABOVE: **Vandyke Lace**
BELOW: **Vandyke Lace Variation**

PARACHUTE PATTERN

Multiple of 6 sts plus 1.

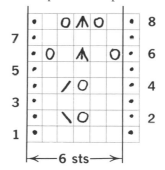

←6 sts→

LITTLE PARACHUTE

Multiple of 14 sts plus 2.

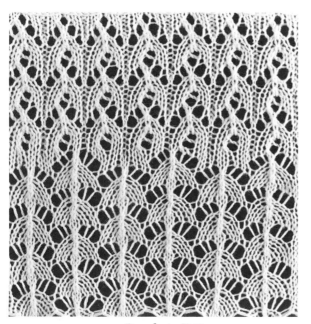

ABOVE: **Parachute Pattern**
BELOW: **Little Parachute**

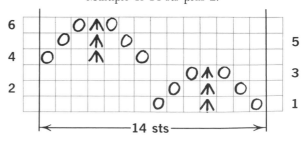

←14 sts→

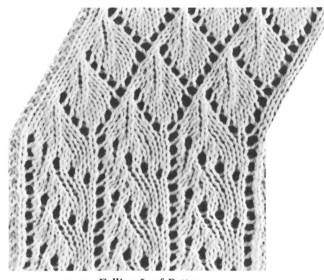

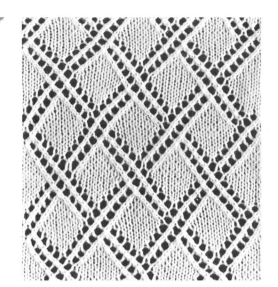

ABOVE: **Falling Leaf Pattern**
BELOW: **Falling Leaf Variation**

Lace Lattice

FALLING LEAF PATTERN (BIAS FABRIC)

Multiple of 9 sts plus 1.

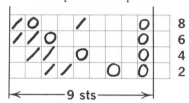

FALLING LEAF VARIATION (STRAIGHT FABRIC)

Multiple of 9 sts plus 3.

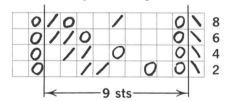

LACE LATTICE

Multiple of 12 sts plus 4. Two repeats shown

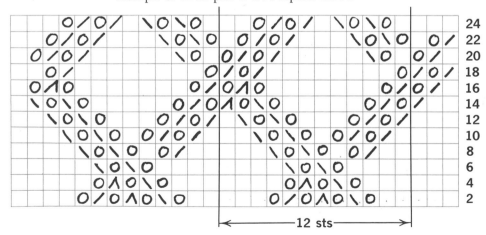

Butterfly Eyelet

Tuxedo Lace

BUTTERFLY EYELET

Multiple of 16 sts plus 4.

NOTE: on all wrong-side rows, purl, working (k1, p1) into each double yo.

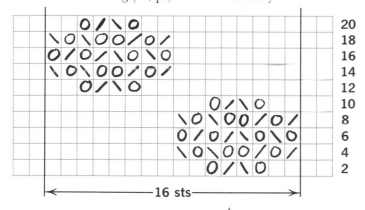

├─────── 16 sts ───────┤

TUXEDO LACE

Multiple of 10 sts plus 3. Two repeats shown

NOTE: on all wrong-side rows, purl working (k1, p1, k1) into each triple yo.

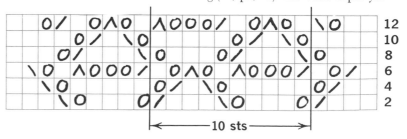

├─────── 10 sts ───────┤

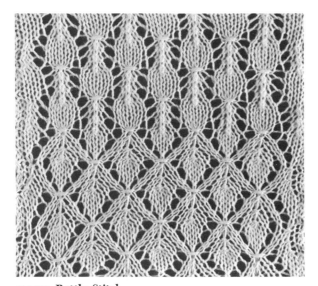

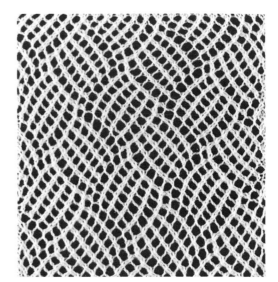

ABOVE: **Bottle Stitch**
BELOW: **Smocked Lace**

Subtle Mesh

BOTTLE STITCH

Multiple of 10 sts plus 1. Two repeats shown

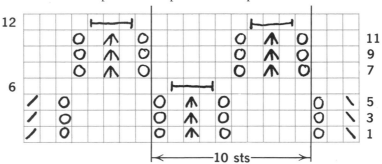

SMOCKED LACE

Multiple of 10 sts plus 1. Two repeats shown

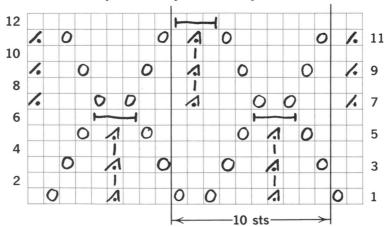

SUBTLE MESH

Multiple of 12 sts plus 4.

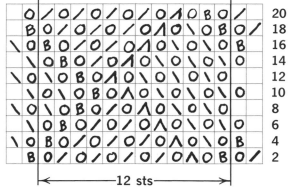

DIAMOND FANTASIA

Diamond Fantasia

Multiple of 16 sts plus 1. Two repeats shown

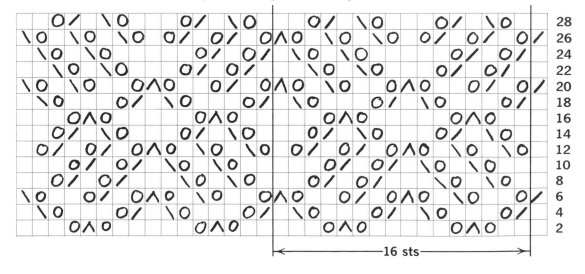

Hexagon Fern

Interlocking Arrowheads

HEXAGON FERN

Multiple of 18 sts plus 1.

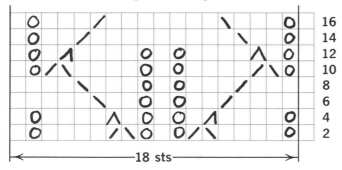

INTERLOCKING ARROWHEADS

Multiple of 18 sts plus 5.

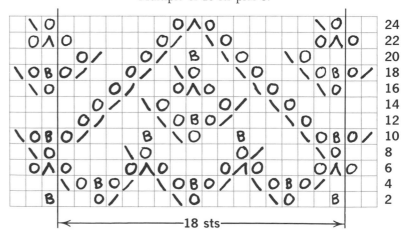

WIDE-WEAVE LACE (TWO VERSIONS)

Multiple of 16 sts plus 5.

I. Trellis version

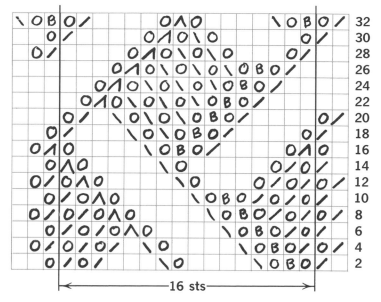

16 sts

Wide-Weave Lace
ABOVE: **Trellis version**
BELOW: **Eyelet version**

II. Eyelet version

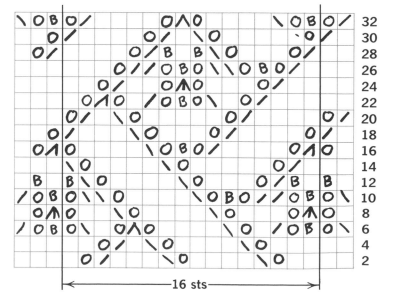

16 sts

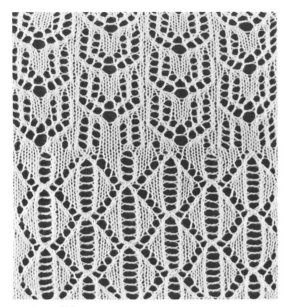

ABOVE: **Elkhorn**
BELOW: **Laddered Diamonds**

ELKHORN

Multiple of 24 sts.

NOTE: All wrong-side rows—purl, working (k1, p1) into each double yo.

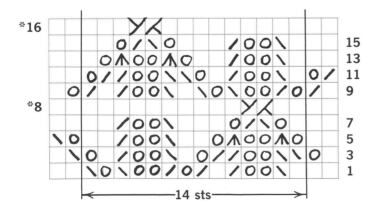

LADDERED DIAMONDS

Multiple of 14 sts plus 4.

NOTE: All wrong-side rows except Rows 8 and 16—purl, working (k1, p1) into every double yo.

° *Rows* 8 and *16*—⅄Ⲭ—P2 tog, leave on needle; insert right-hand needle between the 2 sts just purled tog, and purl the first st again; then sl both sts from needle together.

Chatelaine

CHATELAINE

Multiple of 24 sts plus 5.

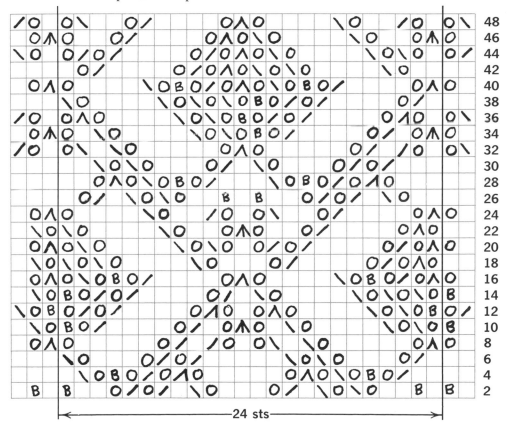

24 sts

Cherry Stitch

CHERRY STITCH

Multiple of 8 sts plus 1. Two repeats shown

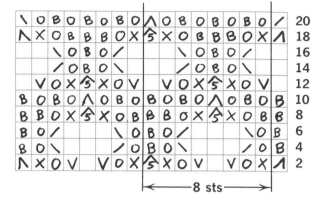

← 8 sts →

Wave Peaks

WAVE PEAKS

Multiple of 22 sts plus 1. Two repeats shown

← 22 sts →

COGWHEEL PATTERN

Multiple of 8 sts plus 5. Two repeats shown

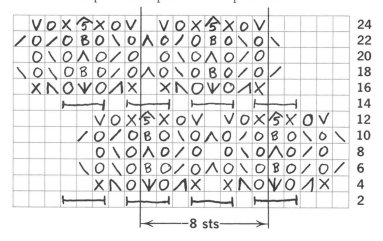

Cogwheel Pattern

Grand Ovals

GRAND OVALS

Multiple of 24 sts plus 3. Two repeats shown

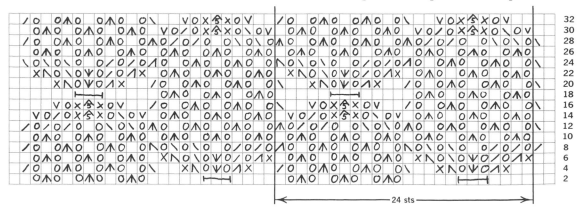

Grand Gothic Border

GRAND GOTHIC BORDER

Multiple of 24 sts plus 3. Two repeats shown

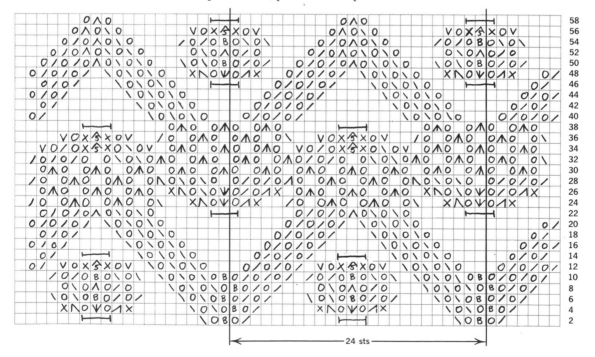

CHAPTER 7

Lace Panels

The distinction between lace panels and lace is the same as the distinction between cables and cable-stitch patterns. In both cases, the former are worked on a fixed number of stitches, which can be delineated by two markers in the midst of a knitted piece, while the latter are worked on multiples of stitches all the way across the piece. Therefore lace panels, like cables, lack repeat lines. But if you are especially fond of a particular lace panel, there is no rule that says you must work it only once. You may work it as many times as you wish across each row, and make an allover pattern of it if this seems good to you. Alternatively, you may combine two, three, or more lace panels in the same piece of knitting, just as cables are combined in a fisherman sweater.

One way to convert lace panels into allover lace patterns is the half-drop method, shown, for example, in the illustration for Wheel Web. In this method, the pattern rows are divided in half, and the first half worked in one panel along with the second half in an adjacent panel. The half-drop method usually makes very pleasing designs; but if it seems too much trouble, you may work the same row on every panel that you have. Why not? After all, it's your knitting. You can do with it whatever you most enjoy doing.

Like any other lace pattern, a panel pattern can be simple or fancy, or anything in between. Patterns of all degrees of complexity are represented here. The larger and more striking ones are well suited for use as single-panel accents in an otherwise solid fabric, and may be placed, for instance, in the center of a sleeve or a garment front without altering the rest of the directions for making the garment. Some of the panels that form a complete design in one repeat of the pattern rows, such as the Heart Motif, Reflected Scroll, Little Hobbyhorse, Cabbage-Rose Design, Cleopatra's Collar, Persian Jar, etc., can be worked just once as a lace accent somewhere in a garment, or in the center of a table mat or cushion or handbag. The last two articles are greatly enhanced by a fabric lining in a color that contrasts strongly with the color of the lace yarn. Combinations of panels will make attractive runners, curtains, stoles, tablecloths or shawls.

Charts for lace panels follow all the same rules that apply to lace knitting in general, so before trying these patterns, read the introduction to the lace chapter if you haven't already done so. Then, mix-and-match lace panels and have fun.

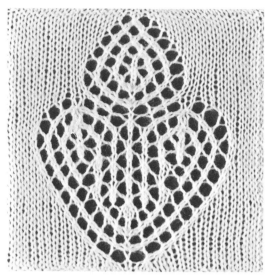

Flacon

Example Lace Panel:

Flacon

A LITTLE heart-shaped perfume flask with a teardrop stopper makes a pretty design in lace. This pattern can be repeated in a vertical panel, or its 40 rows can be worked only once for a spot accent, or several panels can be worked side by side as a border. Though more complicated than the majority of lace panels, it gives a good example because it demonstrates all the techniques used in the wheel-shaped designs, and variations thereof, that are found later in this chapter.

Notice that the X's appearing in Rows 2, 4, 24, and 26 of this pattern do not represent any reduction in the total number of stitches, which remains at 27 throughout every row. The X's only fill in spaces on the chart that are left by the multiple-decrease symbols. Notice also that many of the O's (yarn-overs) are arranged in vertical columns on the chart even though most of them do not come out so in the lace itself. This shows that increases and decreases sometimes necessitate a somewhat non-graphic alignment, since to draw these yarn-overs in their correct diagonal relationship would destroy the usefulness of the chart as a set of directions.

Panel of 27 sts

Notes: Double inc: (k1-b, k1) in one stitch, then insert left-hand needle point behind the vertical strand that runs downward from between the 2 sts just made, and k1-b into this strand to make the 3rd st of the group.

Inc 1: insert needle downward into the back of the st in the row below the first st on left-hand needle, and knit; then knit the st on needle.

5 tog: ssk, k3 tog, then pass the ssk st over the k3-tog st.

Row 1 (Wrong side) and all other wrong-side rows—Purl.

Row 2—K10, k3 tog, yo, double inc, yo, k3 tog-b, k10.

Row 4—K8, k3 tog, yo, k2 tog, yo, double inc, yo, ssk, yo, k3 tog-b, k8.

Row 6—K7, (k2 tog, yo) 3 times, k1, (yo, ssk) 3 times, k7.

Row 8—K6, (k2 tog, yo) 3 times, k3, (yo, ssk) 3 times, k6.

Row 10—K5, (k2 tog, yo) 3 times, k1-b, yo, sl 1-k2 tog-psso, yo, k1-b, (yo, ssk) 3 times, k5.

Row 12—K4, (k2 tog, yo) twice, k2, (yo, sl 2-k1-p2sso, yo, k1) twice, k1, (yo, ssk) twice, k4.

Row 14—K3, (k2 tog, yo) twice, (k1, yo, sl 2-k1-p2sso, yo) 3 times, k1, (yo, ssk) twice, k3.

Row 16—K2, (k2 tog, yo) 3 times, k2, (yo, sl 2-k1-p2sso, yo, k1) twice, k1, (yo, ssk) 3 times, k2.

Row 18—K1, (k2 tog, yo) 3 times, k1-b, (yo, sl 2-k1-p2sso, yo, k1) twice, yo, sl 2-k1-p2sso, yo, k1-b, (yo, ssk) 3 times, k1.

Row 20—K2, yo, (k2 tog, yo) twice, sl 2-k1-p2sso, (yo, ssk) twice, yo, k1, yo, (k2 tog, yo) twice, sl 2-k1-p2sso, (yo, ssk) twice, yo, k2.

Row 22—K1, (ssk, yo) 3 times, k1, (yo, k2 tog) twice, yo, sl 2-k1-p2sso, yo, (ssk, yo) twice, k1, (yo, k2 tog) 3 times, k1.

Row 24—K3, yo, ssk, yo, 5 tog, yo, k2 tog, yo, k1-b, yo, double inc. yo, k1-b, yo, ssk, yo, 5 tog, yo, k2 tog, yo, k3.

Row 26—K3, inc 1, yo, 5 tog, yo, (k2 tog, yo) twice, double inc, (yo, ssk) twice, yo, 5 tog, yo, inc 1, k3.

Row 28—K7, (k2 tog, yo) 3 times, k1, (yo, ssk) 3 times, k7.

Row 30—K8, yo, (k2 tog, yo) twice, sl 2-k1-p2sso, (yo, ssk) twice, yo, k8.

Row 32—K7, (ssk, yo) 3 times, k1, (yo, k2 tog) 3 times, k7.

Row 34—K9, yo, ssk, yo, sl 1-k2 tog-psso, yo, (k2 tog, yo) twice, k9.

Row 36—K10, yo, ssk, yo, sl 1-k2 tog-psso, yo, k2 tog, yo, k10.

Row 38—K11, yo, sl 1-k2 tog-psso, yo, k2 tog, yo, k11.

Row 40—K12, yo, sl 1-k2 tog-psso, yo, k12.

FLACON

Panel of 27 sts.

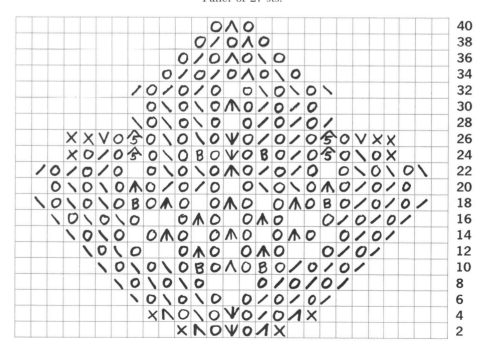

Cable-Twist Lace Pattern
LEFT: **Left Cable-Twist**
CENTER: **Right Cable-Twist**
RIGHT: **Re-Crossing or Wave Cable-Twist**

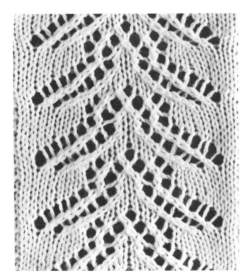

Pagoda Pattern

CABLE-TWIST LACE PATTERN

Panel of 15 sts.

Left Cable-Twist

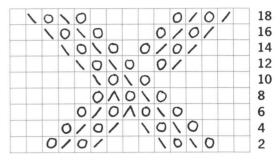

Right Cable-Twist

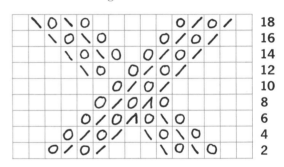

NOTE: for 3rd variation, Re-Crossing or Wave Cable-Twist, work Left and Right versions alternately.

PAGODA PATTERN

Panel of 23 sts.

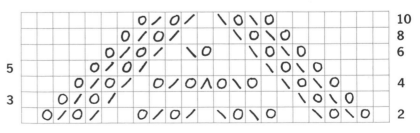

BATWING LACE

Panel of 12 sts.

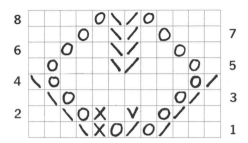

QUADRUPLE DIAMOND

Panel of 17 sts.

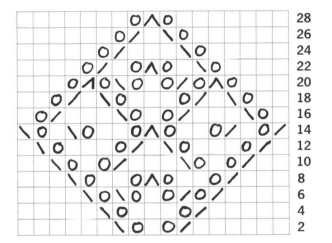

CENTER PANEL: Quadruple Diamond
SIDE PANELS: Batwing Lace

WHEEL WEB

Panel of 15 sts.

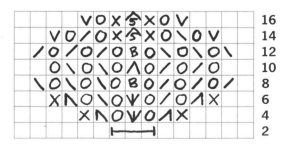

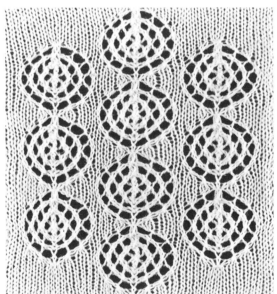

Wheel Web

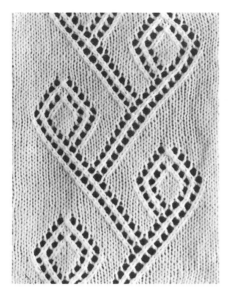

Budding Branch

Lobed Leaf Pattern

BUDDING BRANCH

Panel of 30 sts.

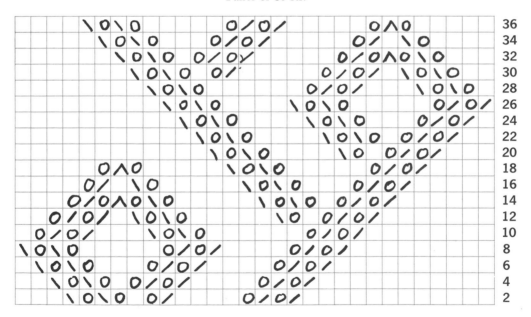

LOBED LEAF PATTERN

Panel of 27 sts.

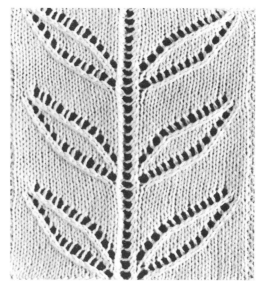

Ladder and Leaf

LADDER AND LEAF

Panel of 34 sts.

NOTE: Chart shows 33 sts because each right-side row decreases 1 st. On each wrong-side row, increase (**v**) by working (k1, p1) into the central yo, restoring 34 sts.

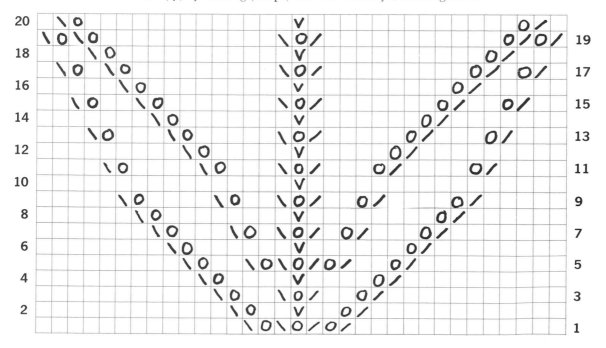

LEFT: Milady's Fan
RIGHT: Inverted Fan

MILADY'S FAN

Panel of 23 sts.

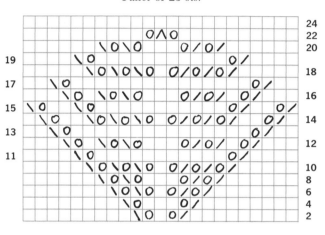

INVERTED FAN

Panel of 23 sts.

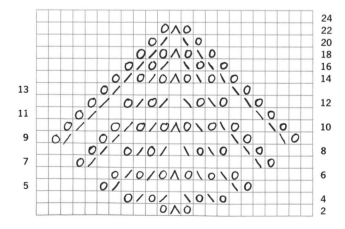

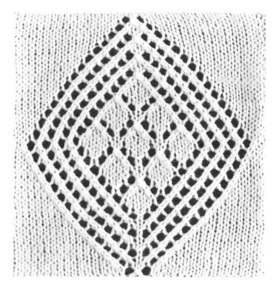

Fancy Medallion

FANCY MEDALLION

Panel of 35 sts.

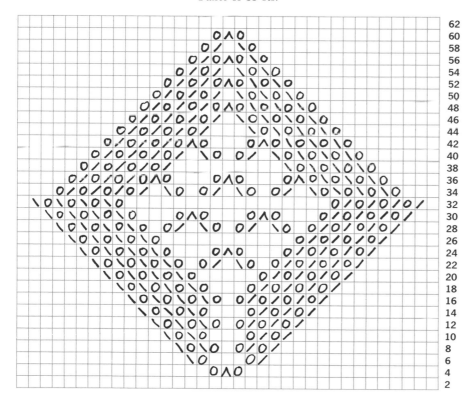

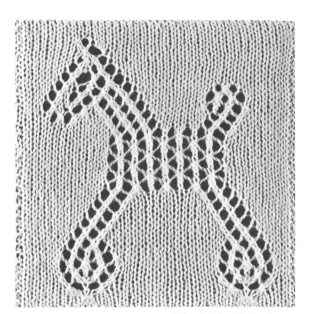

The Little Hobbyhorse

Reverse Curve

The Bat

REVERSE CURVE

Panel of 22 sts.

O	⋏	O	⁄	O				⟍	O	⟍	O	⟍	O		O	⁄	O	⁄	O	⁄	28
O	⟍	O	⋏	O					×	⋏	O	⟍	O	⩔	O	⁄	O	⋏	×		26
O	⋏	O	⁄	O						×	⋏	O	⩔	O	⋏	×					24
O	⟍	O	⋏	O							⊢			⊣							22
O	⋏	O	⁄	O					V	O	×	⑤	×	O	V						20
O	⟍	O	⋏	O			V	O	⁄	O	×	⑤	×	O	⟍	O	V				18
⟍	O	⟍	O	⟍	O			O	⁄	O	⁄	O	⋏	O	⟍	O	⟍	O			16
⟍	O	⟍	O	⟍	O		O	⁄	O	⁄	O	⁄		O	⟍	O	⋏	O			14
×	⋏	O	⟍	O	⩔	O	⁄	O	⁄	⟍	×		O	⋏	O	⁄	O				12
	×	⋏	O	⩔	O	⋏	×						O	⟍	O	⋏	O				10
			⊢			⊣							O	⋏	O	⁄	O				8
	V	O	×	⑤	×	O	V						O	⟍	O	⋏	O				6
V	O	⁄	O	×	⑤	×	O	⟍	O	V			O	⋏	O	⁄	O				4
O	⁄	O	⁄	O	⋏	O	⟍	O	⟍	O			O	⁄	O	⁄	O	⁄			2

THE LITTLE HOBBYHORSE

Panel of 36 sts.

On Row 47 (wrong side), work (k1, p1) into the double yo of Row 46.

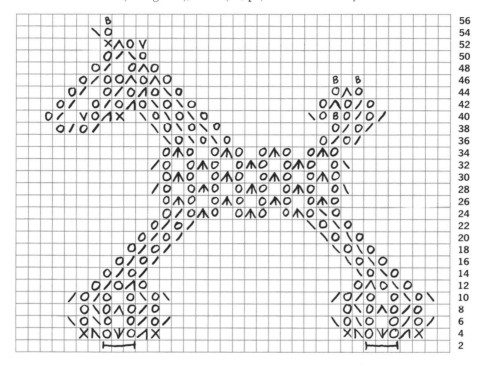

THE BAT

Panel of 33 sts.

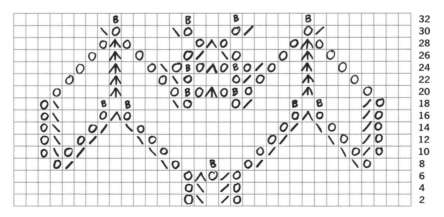

CENTER PANEL, ABOVE: Heart Motif
CENTER PANEL, BELOW: Double-Eight Motif
SIDE PANELS: Lightning

LIGHTNING

Panel of 11 sts.

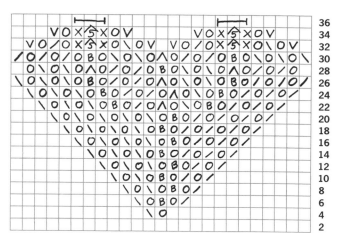

HEART MOTIF

Panel of 25 sts.

DOUBLE-EIGHT MOTIF

Panel of 25 sts.

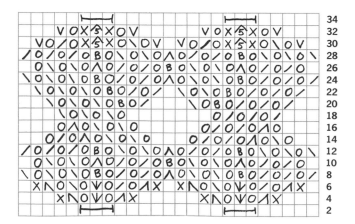

LEFT SIDE PANEL: Little Figure-Eight Scroll,
Right-Twist Version
RIGHT SIDE PANEL: Little Figure-Eight Scroll,
Left-Twist Version
CENTER PANEL: Reflected Scroll

LITTLE FIGURE-EIGHT SCROLL (TWO VERSIONS)

Panel of 9 sts.

Left-Twist Version

V	O	X	ꟷ	X	O	V			24
╱	O	╱	O	B	O	╲	O	╲	22
	O	╲	O	╱	O	╱	O		20
╲	O	╲	O	B	O	╱	O	╱	18
	╲	O	╲	O	B	O	╱		16
		╲	O	╲	O				14
		O	╱	O	╲	O			12
╱	O	╱	O	B	O	╲	O	╲	10
	O	╲	O	╱	O	╱	O		8
╲	O	╲	O	B	O	╱	O	╱	6
	X	╱	O	ꟷ	O	╲	X		4
			┣━┫						2

Right-Twist Version

V	O	X	ꟷ	X	O	V			24
╱	O	╱	O	B	O	╲	O	╲	22
	O	╲	O	╱	O	╱	O		20
╲	O	╲	O	B	O	╱	O	╱	18
	╲	O	B	O	╱	O	╱		16
		O	╱	O	╱				14
		O	╱	O	╲	O			12
╱	O	╱	O	B	O	╲	O	╲	10
	O	╲	O	╱	O	╱	O		8
╲	O	╲	O	B	O	╱	O	╱	6
	X	╱	O	ꟷ	O	╲	X		4
			┣━┫						2

REFLECTED SCROLL

Panel of 27 sts.

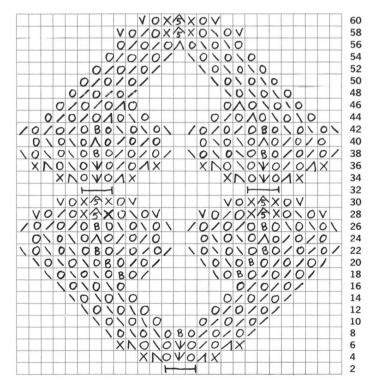

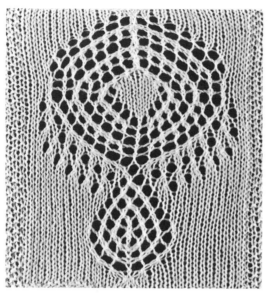

Cleopatra's Collar

CLEOPATRA'S COLLAR

Panel of 31 sts.

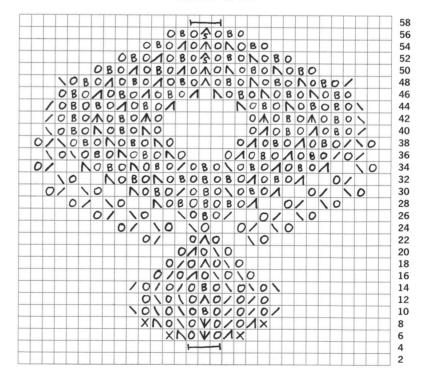

BUD AND DIAMOND

Panel of 13 sts.

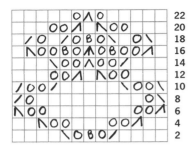

SIDE PANELS: **Bud and Diamond**
CENTER PANEL: **Cabbage-Rose Design**

Note for both patterns:

All wrong-side (odd-numbered) rows: Purl, working (k1, p1) into every double yo.

CABBAGE-ROSE DESIGN

Panel of 39 sts.

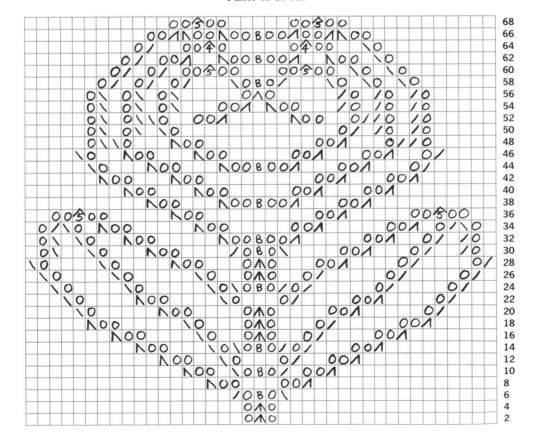

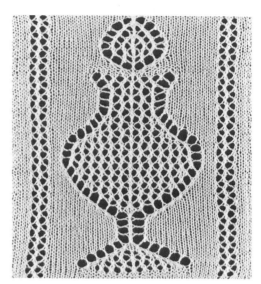

PERSIAN JAR

Panel of 35 sts.

All wrong-side rows except Rows 1 and 65—
Purl, working (k1, p1) into every double yo.

Persian Jar

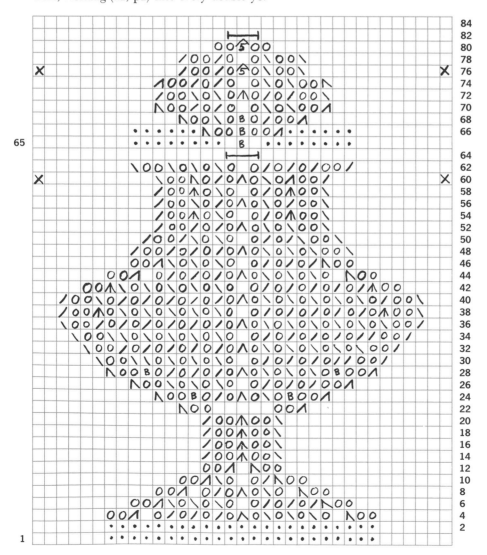

CHAPTER 8

Mosaic Patterns

Mosaic patterns are slip-stitch designs in two colors. Two different strands are used, one at a time. They are changed at the beginning of each right-side row. So a mosaic pattern is made by working one right-side row and one wrong-side row with Color A, then dropping Color A at the right-hand edge, picking up Color B, and working the next two rows with Color B—and so on.

This is an easy way to make color designs, because the knitter never has to handle both strands at once. Also, it admits of greater flexibility in the fabric texture, because the wrong-side rows can be worked with either knit or purl stitches, or a combination of them.

The two primary principles of mosaic patterns are: (1) every slip-stitch is slipped with yarn in *back* on all right-side rows, and with yarn in *front* on all wrong-side rows (that is, with the yarn held always to the wrong side); and (2) every wrong-side row is just like the preceding right-side row, with the same stitches being worked, and the same stitches being slipped. The second principle is the source of that peculiar advantage of mosaics, that they may be worked on any number of stitches; the multiple given for a mosaic pattern can be ignored if you want to work that pattern on more or fewer stitches. In such a case, the pattern motifs may be slightly off center; but the wrong-side rows cannot be started wrong, because the colors themselves tell you which stitches to work and which to slip on every wrong-side row. For instance, if you have just worked a right-side row with Color A, and ended it somewhere in the midst of an odd multiple, simply turn the work and look at the wrong side. All the A stitches that you have just worked are now on the left-hand needle, interspersed with the B stitches that you have just slipped. So, on the return row, you work all those A stitches again, and slip all those B stitches again, this time slipping with yarn in front. The wrong-side row copies the right-side row exactly, whether it has ended on a correct multiple or not.

Because wrong-side rows are the same as the preceding right-side rows, each mosaic pattern chart compresses the two rows into one for the sake of convenience. Therefore each single horizontal row of squares represents *two* rows of knitting, one going from right to left (right side), and the other from left to right (wrong side). So you will see the odd row

185

numbers, which always designate right-side rows, to the right of the chart, and the even row numbers, which always designate the following wrong-side rows, to the left. Each pair of numbers (1 and 2, 3 and 4, etc.) will be on the *same* row of squares.

The two colors are shown by black and white squares, as in the usual sort of chart for Fair Isle knitting. But these charts are read quite differently. Here's how you do it:

First of all, always cast on with the color corresponding to the white squares, and knit or purl one row with this color. Then tie on the color corresponding to the black squares. Now you are ready to begin reading the chart. Lay your ruler, or other straight edge, so that it covers the second horizontal row on the chart, and look only at the first row. On every chart, the first square of Row 1, in the lower right-hand corner, is a black square. This means: knit the first stitch with black (or whatever color you are using as black—it could be white, or red, or yellow, or green, or what have you). Now look along the row. Some squares are black, some white. You must *knit* all the stitches represented by black squares, and *slip*—with yarn in back—all the stitches represented by white squares. Work back and forth between the two repeat lines, as usual, always going from right to left, until you come to the final edge stitches. The very last stitch on the row, like the first one, will be shown as a black square. These first and last squares on each row will tell you which color to knit with.

Now turn the work, and still using your black yarn, work back across the row, either knitting or purling all the same black stitches that you worked before, and slipping all the same white stitches with yarn in front. You don't have to look at the chart to work wrong-side rows. If the preceding right-side row was counted correctly, then the wrong-side row will be correct too.

You have progressed to Row 3, which always begins and ends with a white square. Move the ruler up to expose the second row of the chart. Drop the black yarn in front, toward you, and pick up the white yarn behind it. Leaving the black yarn hanging, knit the first stitch, corresponding to the first square, with white. Now—here's the trick—you must *reverse* the reading of the black and white squares; you knit all the stitches represented by *white* squares, and slip—with yarn in back—all the stitches represented by *black* squares. The slip-stitches will always be black stitches that were made on the preceding row. If you find yourself slipping white stitches on a white row, or black stitches on a black row, you've miscounted. Of course, if all the squares on a row are the same color, there are no slip-stitches on that row; so you just knit straight across.

After working the white right-side row, turn and go back on the wrong side as before, knitting or purling the same stitches that you knitted on Row 3, and slipping the same slip-stitches with yarn in front. Then pick up the black yarn again and work Row 5, which begins and ends with black, the same as Row 1: knitting blacks, slipping whites. The pattern is done this way throughout, with the colors changing every other row, and the knits and slips changing color with them.

So the rule for reading mosaic charts is as follows: on every row that begins and ends with a black square, all black stitches are knitted, all white stitches slipped. On every row that begins and ends with a white square, all white stitches are knitted, all black stitches slipped. Now that's a simple rule, one that you can get used to in next to no time.

Every chart begins with a black row, so remember always to cast on with the white yarn and work one preparatory row before starting the chart; or else you won't have any white stitches to slip on Row 1. Remember also that if you should end a pattern repeat in the middle, because of having a different number of stitches than the given multiple, always knit the very last stitch with whatever color you are using at the moment, even if the chart tells you to slip it. That way, you can keep the left-hand edge of the knitting alternating, the same as the right-hand edge. And a third thing to remember: on these charts, "black" and "white" are just arbitrary ways of designating the two colors. You can always work the black squares with a light-colored yarn and the white squares with a dark-colored one, if you wish; there is no rule that says your colors can't be opposite to the way they are shown on the chart.

To work a mosaic pattern in circular knitting, cast on with white as usual, using the correct multiple, *minus* the edge stitches. Join, and knit one round. Then tie in black, and begin Round 1 of the pattern with the first stitch *inside* the first (right-hand) repeat line. If this first stitch is shown by a white square, then the first stitch of Round 1—a black round—is slipped. If this first stitch is shown by a black square, then the first stitch of Round 1 is knitted. Continue to work the round from the first repeat line to the second (left-hand) repeat line, slipping all slip-stitches with yarn in back as usual, and never crossing the second repeat line at all. If you have the correct multiple of stitches on the needle, the last stitch of the round will be the last square *inside* the second repeat line.

The second, or "wrong-side," round will be identical with the first. You still work with the same color, still slipping the same slip-stitches again with yarn in *back*. For a stockinette-stitch fabric, knit all the second-round stitches again, as before; for a garter-stitch fabric, purl all the second-round stitches, still slipping the same slip-stitches with yarn in *back*. In circular knitting all slip-stitches are always slipped with yarn in back, on all rounds, because you are always working on the right side. On the third round, of course, pick up the white yarn again and follow Row 3 of the chart, inside the repeat lines from right to left. The fourth round is worked with white again, either knitting or purling. You may, if you wish, knit all the second rounds of one color, and purl all the second rounds of the other, for contrast. (See Texture and Shape in Mosaic Patterns.) When picking up new strands for the odd-numbered rounds, be sure you pick them up all the same way, either to the right or to the left of the old strands. It doesn't matter which, but to make a neat spiral of strands on the wrong side it must be done the same way each time.

If your circular knitting is not going to be divided at any point, but will continue in rounds to the very end—like a tubular scarf, or the leg portion of a sock, or a totally seamless sweater, or a long stocking-cap—you may work only one round of each color, in which case you will complete the pattern in only half the number of rows. But if the knitting must be divided and worked in rows for a while, you'll need two rounds of each color in order to have the "row" portion of the article look the same as the "round" portion.

The basic technique of mosaic knitting is simple enough so that even a beginner can use it to achieve exciting designs in two colors. The success of the knitting does not depend on careful regulation of tension, as it does in Fair Isle knitting. Forming designs with slip-stitches eliminates the need to strand the second color across the back of the fabric, which sometimes causes unsightly lumpiness if the tension is not exact. Of course, these same charts can be used to work the patterns by the Fair Isle method, just by treating each row of the chart as a single row, and working all the white stitches with white, the black stitches with black. However, some mosaic patterns are only indifferently suited to Fair Isle knitting because they have long stretches—7, 8, 9 or more stitches—worked in the same color, which means that the opposite color would have to be hooked on the back to prevent over-long strands. These patterns are designed for mosaic knitting, and are most effective when worked in that way.

You can use mosaic patterns for almost any purpose; they do well as borders, as allover designs, in panels, or in combination with each other. Marvelously colorful knitwear can be made of different mosaic patterns worked in different colors in consecutive horizontal bands; or, using the same background color throughout, you can change the second color as you change from one pattern to the next. You never have to worry about matching multiples, because a dozen or more different patterns can be worked on the same number of stitches, all the way up. Neither do you have to worry about a change in pattern making a change in gauge. As long as you use the same type of yarn and the same needles, every mosaic pattern will produce the same gauge as every other. Few knitting techniques give so much scope for pattern variation within any one particular stitch gauge. And the combination of mosaics in horizontal bands makes for fascinating knitting, because after you have worked three or four inches of one pattern and are beginning to get tired of it, you can change to another. There are plenty of interesting designs to choose from. You could even make a multicolored afghan, and use them all!

Example Mosaic:

Magic Squares

Magic Squares

THE motifs in this pattern interlock in an interesting way, with fret-like spirals that turn always counterclockwise, but from all four directions. Squares, crosses and rectangles make it a strictly rectilinear design, but the pull of the slipped stitches imparts a slight wave to the horizontal lines, so that the actual knitting gives a somewhat softer effect than the design reproduced on the chart. Use 39 stitches, or more, for a test swatch, so that the alternate motifs will be shown.

Multiple of 18 sts plus 3. Colors A and B

Note: On all right-side (odd-numbered) rows, slip all sl-sts with yarn in back. Cast on with Color A and knit one row.

Row 1 (Right side)—With B, k1, ° (sl 1, k1) twice, sl 2, k7, sl 2, k1, sl 1, k1; rep from °, end sl 1, k1.

Row 2 and all other wrong-side rows—With same color as previous row, knit (or purl) all the same sts worked on previous row; slip all the same sl-sts with yarn in front.

continued on page 190

MAGIC SQUARES

Multiple of 18 sts plus 3.

←——————18 sts——————→

Row 3—With A, k2, ° sl 1, k1, sl 1, k2, sl 1, k5, sl 1, k2, (sl 1, k1) twice; rep from °, end k1.

Row 5—With B, k3, ° sl 1, k4, sl 1, k3; rep from °.

Row 7—With A, k4, ° sl 1, k2, (sl 1, k1) 3 times, sl 1, k2, sl 1, k5; rep from °, end last repeat k4.

Row 9—With B, k5, ° sl 2, (k1, sl 1) 3 times, k1, sl 2, k7; rep from °, end last repeat k5.

Row 11—With A, k7, ° sl 1, k1, sl 1, k3, sl 1, k11; rep from °, end last repeat k7.

Row 13—With B, k8, ° sl 1, k17; rep from °, end last repeat k12.

Row 15—With A, k1, ° sl 1, k5, sl 1, k11; rep from °, end sl 1, k1.

Row 17—With B, k2, ° sl 1, k3, sl 1, (k1, sl 1) 3 times, k5, sl 1, k1; rep from °, end k1.

Row 19—With A, k1, ° sl 1, k1, sl 1, k3, sl 1, k5, sl 1, k3, sl 1, k1; rep from °, end sl 1, k1.

Row 21—With B, k2, ° sl 1, k5, (sl 1, k1) 3 times, sl 1, k3, sl 1, k1; rep from °, end k1.

Row 23—With A, k1, ° sl 1, k11, sl 1, k5; rep from °, end sl 1, k1.

Row 25—With B, k12, ° sl 1, k17; rep from °, end last repeat k8.

Row 27—With A, k7, ° sl 1, k3, sl 1, k1, sl 1, k11; rep from °, end last repeat k7.

Row 29—With B, repeat Row 9.

Row 31—With A, repeat Row 7.

Row 33—With B, repeat Row 5.

Row 35—With A, repeat Row 3.

Row 37—With B, repeat Row 1.

Row 39—With A, k4, ° sl 1, k11, sl 1, k1, sl 1, k3; rep from °, end last repeat k2.

Row 41—With B, ° k17, sl 1; rep from °, end k3.

Row 43—With A, k10, ° sl 1, k5, sl 1, k11; rep from °, end last repeat k4.

Row 45—With B, k1, ° sl 1, k1, sl 1, k5, sl 1, k1, sl 1, k3, (sl 1, k1) twice; rep from °, end sl 1, k1.

Row 47—With A, k4, ° sl 1, k3, (sl 1, k1) twice, sl 1, k3, sl 1, k5; rep from °, end last repeat k4.

Row 49—With B, k1, ° (sl 1, k1) twice, sl 1, k3, sl 1, k1, sl 1, k5, sl 1, k1; rep from °, end sl 1 , k1.

Row 51—With A, k4, ° sl 1, k5, sl 1, k11; rep from °, end last repeat k10.

Row 53—With B, k3, ° sl 1, k17; rep from °.

Row 55—With A, k2, ° sl 1, k1, sl 1, k11, sl 1, k3; rep from °, end k1.

Row 56—See Row 2.

Repeat Rows 1–56.

Texture and Shape in Mosaic Patterns:

Tongue-and-Groove Stripe, and Double Key Pattern

THESE two patterns illustrate some of the possibilities for varying the texture of the fabric and the shapes of the designs in mosaic knitting. In the first (Vertical) arrangement of Tongue-and-Groove Stripe, a smooth stockinette-stitch fabric is achieved by purling all the stitches that are not slipped, on all wrong-side rows. In the second (Horizontal) arrangement, a nubby garter-stitch fabric is obtained by knitting all the worked stitches on all wrong-side rows. The difference in the direction of the stripes is created by the simple expedient of turning the chart of one version on its side, and working the second version from this angle. You can try all three of these operations on any mosaic pattern; or you can try a fourth by purling the wrong-side rows of one color, and knitting the wrong-side rows of the other, to make a contrast in texture as well as in color.

Another possibility for variation in texture is shown by the Double Key Pattern. Here, all the wrong-side stitches of some repeats are purled, while all the wrong-side stitches of other repeats are knitted. Notice the apparent waviness of the horizontal bands in the illustration. This is due to the natural tendency of the stockinette-stitch fabric to lengthen and narrow, and of the garter-stitch fabric to shorten and broaden. In both cases the charted pattern is identical, having the same number of stitches and rows to each repeat. But the way in which you elect to work wrong-side rows will make a difference in the

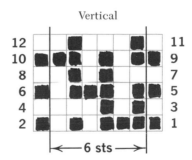

Tongue-and-Groove Stripe
ABOVE: **Vertical (wrong-side rows purled)**
BELOW: **Horizontal (wrong-side rows knit)**

TEXTURE AND SHAPE IN MOSAIC PATTERNS:

TONGUE-AND-GROOVE STRIPE

Multiple of 6 sts plus 2.

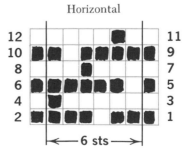

Vertical

Horizontal

DOUBLE KEY PATTERN

Multiple of 15 sts.

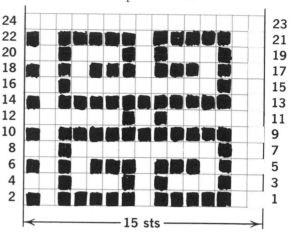

← 15 sts →

Double Key Pattern

FROM TOP—1ST AND 3RD BANDS: Stockinette-stitch fabric on 1st and 3rd repeats; garter-stitch fabric on 2nd and 4th repeats

2ND AND 4TH BANDS: Garter-stitch fabric on 1st and 3rd repeats; stockinette-stitch fabric on 2nd and 4th repeats

proportions of your knitted piece. An all-stockinette version of any mosaic pattern will be slightly longer and narrower than an all-garter-stitch version of the same thing; and you may combine the two versions in the same fabric just as was done in the case of the Double Key.

In circular knitting, of course, a mosaic pattern would be worked on the same principle as a plain stockinette or garter-stitch fabric; that is, for stockinette stitch you would *knit* all the alternate rounds (the *second* round of each color), whereas for garter stitch you would *purl* the same alternate rounds, slipping all the slip-stitches with yarn in *back* at all times. The first rounds of each color would be always knitted, just as is usual in flat knitting.

The Double Key Pattern shows you still another way to vary your mosaic, that is, by alternating the colors. The same pattern is worked first with light-on-dark motifs, then with dark-on-light. This is done very simply by exchanging the positions of the "A" and "B" yarn. If a chart is given with black squares forming motifs on a white background, that doesn't mean you have to work it that way. You can reverse it, using a light-colored yarn to work the black rows and a dark-colored yarn to work the white ones. You might like it better than the way it is shown on the chart.

All these possibilities for variation in texture and shape apply to all mosaic patterns, so you must keep them in mind when looking over the illustrations for all patterns in this section. Swatches are shown sometimes in the garter-stitch version, sometimes in the stockinette-stitch version, or sometimes in combinations of the two; but it is never necessary for you to make your own test swatch exactly like the illustration for that pattern. You can purl or knit wrong-side rows (or rounds) as you choose; you can alternate colors as you will. Each mosaic pattern really has half a dozen different variations to be worked from the same chart, so that all of these patterns are enormously flexible. Just remember the basic principles: start each row with the color of the first square, slip all slip-stitches with yarn to the wrong side of the fabric, and keep the pattern correct by working strictly between the vertical repeat lines until you come to the end of the row. A world of pattern excitement is yours to play with in the colorful realm of mosaics.

Evolution of a Mosaic Pattern:

Nine Variations on the Four-Armed Square

THE following series of patterns shows how a simple motif—a little three-stitch square with arms proceeding from its corners—can be enlarged and placed in different arrangements to form new designs. Charting is not only the method by which these patterns are presented; it is also the method by which they are created. Working the pattern on paper, before knitting, is the quickest and easiest way to design a mosaic. It eliminates a good many false starts and rippings-out.

The basic four-armed square is shown in the first variation with one angle, or bend, to each arm. Here the motifs are placed in a simple half-drop arrangement: that is to say, the upper half of each motif occupies the same rows as the lower half of the adjoining motif. In the second variation, the arms have two bends, and the squares are vertically aligned instead of placed in a half-drop design. The intervening spaces are filled by plain squares. There are two versions of the third variation, where the arms have three bends; in the first,

Four-Armed Square with arms bent once

EVOLUTION OF A MOSAIC PATTERN:

I. FOUR-ARMED SQUARE WITH ARMS BENT ONCE

Multiple of 12 sts plus 3.

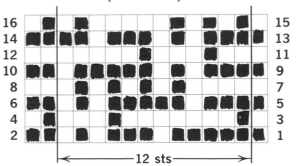

Four-Armed Square with arms bent twice

II. FOUR-ARMED SQUARE WITH ARMS BENT TWICE

Multiple of 10 sts plus 3.

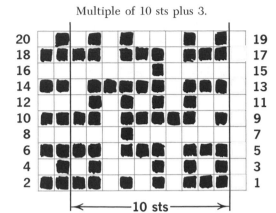

III. FOUR-ARMED SQUARE WITH ARMS BENT THREE TIMES

Multiple of 12 sts plus 3.

Version 1: half-drop formation
with separate motifs

Version 2: half-drop formation
with joined motifs

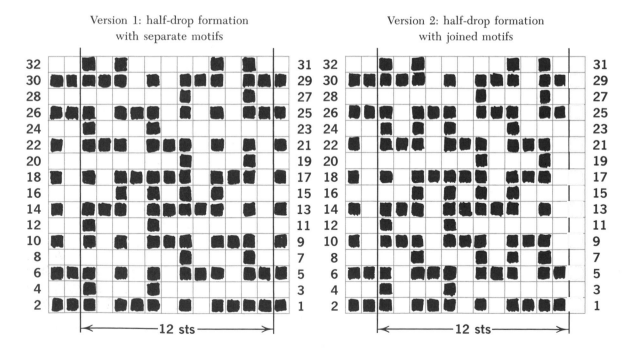

the motifs are separate, and in the second they are joined together. Here again the arrangement is a half-drop in both cases. The fourth variation shows four bends to each arm, with motifs vertically aligned. The fifth, sixth, seventh, and eighth variations all show the half-drop formation, with the arms growing ever longer, sometimes coiled, sometimes extended. The seventh variation has an additional sub-pattern in the form of an off-center cross, while the fifth variation has each arm coiled back on itself to make more little squares surrounding the original ones.

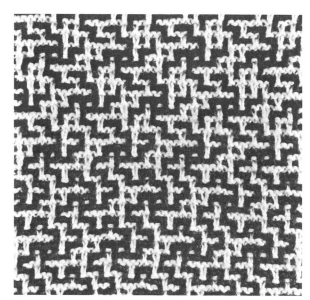

Four-Armed Square with arms bent three times
ABOVE: Version 1, separated motifs
BELOW: Version 2, joined motifs

Four-Armed Square with arms bent four times

IV. FOUR-ARMED SQUARE WITH ARMS BENT FOUR TIMES

Multiple of 10 sts plus 3.

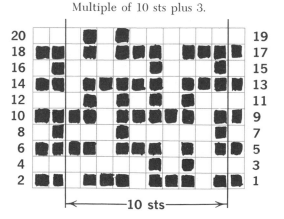

None of these designs represent the only possibility for arrangement of any given motif. On the contrary, they are arbitrary selections from an infinite number of possibilities. Patterns similar to, or incorporating, the basic four-armed square will be found elsewhere in this section. Once you have studied these charts and worked these patterns, you may want to try designing your own. Designing mosaics is an easy matter if you remember that, since the colors are alternated on every right-side row, each slipped stitch must have a stitch

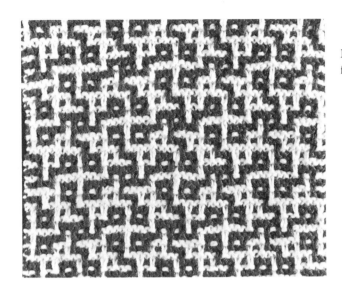

Four-Armed Square with arms bent five times

V. FOUR-ARMED SQUARE WITH ARMS BENT FIVE TIMES

Multiple of 16 sts plus 3.

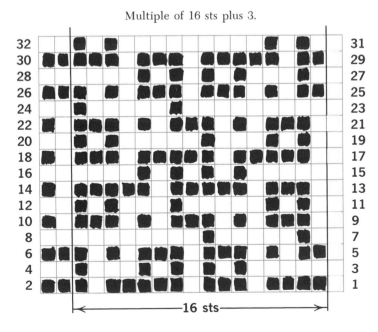

of the same color immediately beneath it, and preferably above it too. Therefore the vertical lines of your design will usually run in threes, i.e., six rows: two rows to establish the stitch, two rows of the other color to slip it, and two rows of the first color to catch it again. With this principle in mind you can plan almost any shape on paper before casting on the first stitch.

Four-Armed Square with arms bent six times

VI. FOUR-ARMED SQUARE WITH ARMS BENT SIX TIMES

Multiple of 20 sts plus 3.

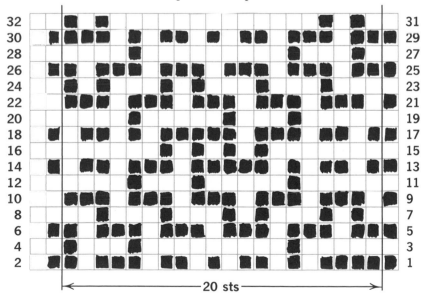

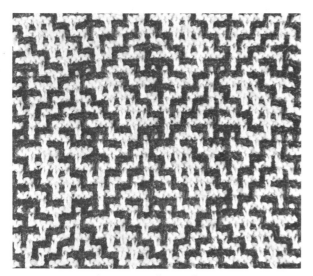

Four-Armed Square with arms bent seven times

VII. FOUR-ARMED SQUARE WITH ARMS BENT SEVEN TIMES

Multiple of 24 sts plus 5.

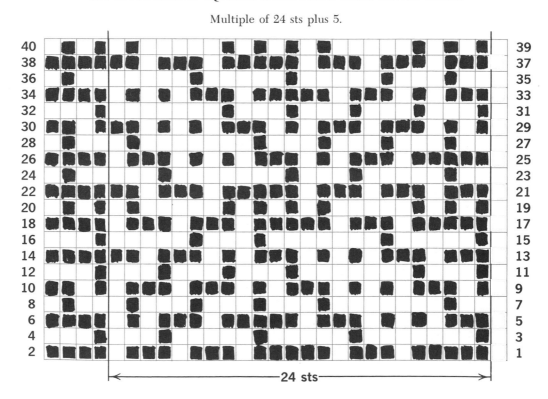

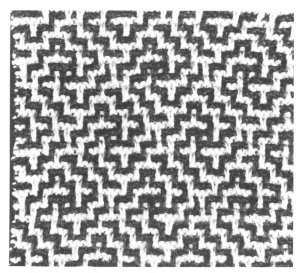

Four-Armed Square with arms bent eight times

VIII. FOUR-ARMED SQUARE WITH ARMS
BENT EIGHT TIMES

Multiple of 16 sts plus 3.

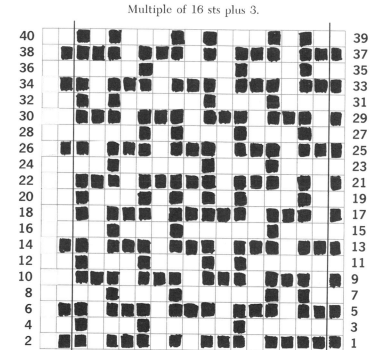

Stepped Fret

STEPPED FRET

Multiple of 10 sts plus 3.

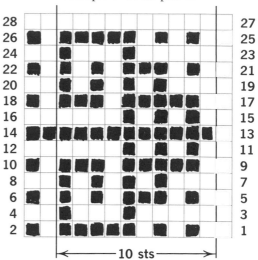

10 sts

SPEARHEAD

Multiple of 14 sts plus 3.

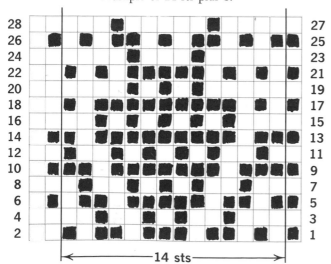

14 sts

Spearhead

JERUSALEM CROSS

Multiple of 12 sts plus 3.

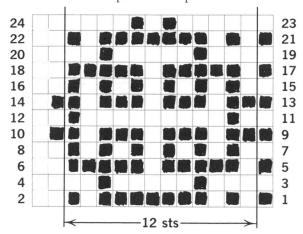

Jerusalem Cross

Albani Pattern

ALBANI PATTERN

Multiple of 8 sts plus 3.

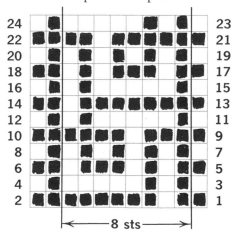

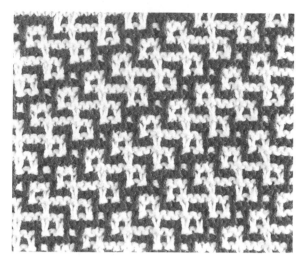

Running Chain

Long Zigzag

RUNNING CHAIN

Multiple of 20 sts plus 3.

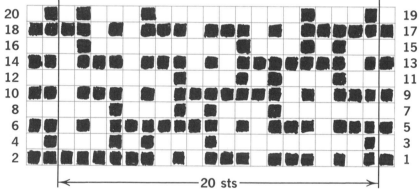

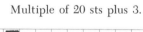

20 sts

LONG ZIGZAG

Multiple of 8 sts plus 2.

8 sts

BLOCK AND CROSS CHECK PATTERN

Multiple of 12 sts plus 2.

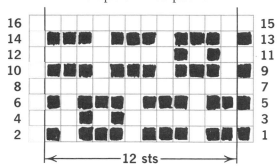

— 12 sts —

PHARAOH'S CHECK

Multiple of 14 sts plus 2.

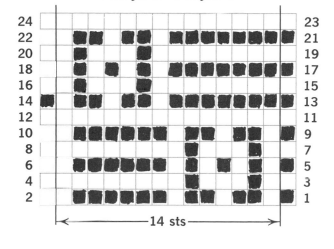

— 14 sts —

CRUSADER'S CHECK

Multiple of 14 sts plus 2.

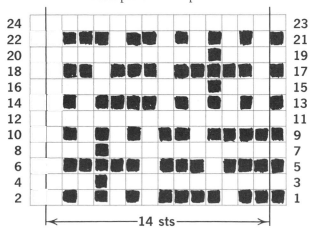

— 14 sts —

Block and Cross Check Pattern

ABOVE: Pharaoh's Check
BELOW: Crusader's Check

Alternating Key

ALTERNATING KEY

Multiple of 14 sts plus 3.

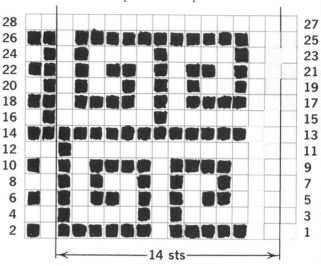

← 14 sts →

CAESAR'S CHECK

Multiple of 16 sts plus 1.

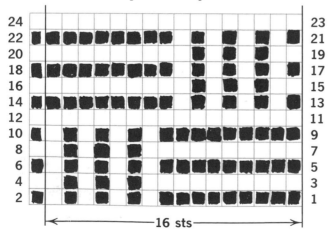

← 16 sts →

Caesar's Check

CURLED CROSS

Multiple of 10 sts plus 3.

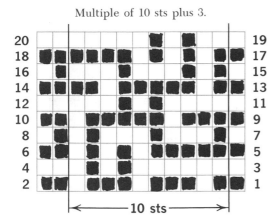

Curled Cross

TEMPLE OF ZEUS

Multiple of 16 sts plus 2.

Temple of Zeus

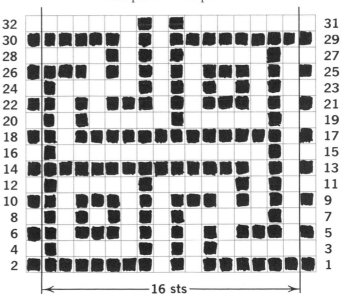

Ionian Key

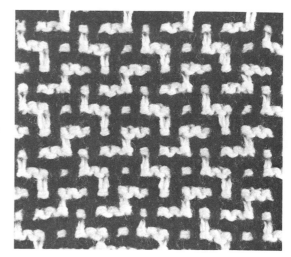

Moroccan Pattern

IONIAN KEY

Multiple of 24 sts plus 3.

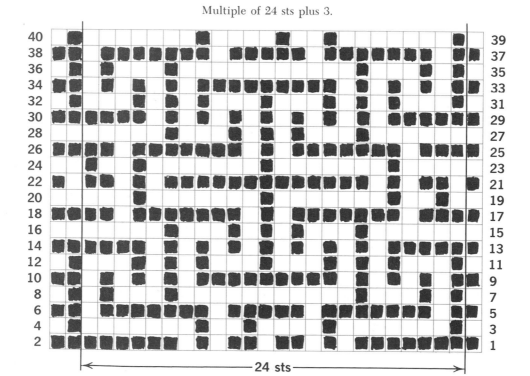

MOROCCAN PATTERN

Multiple of 6 sts plus 5.

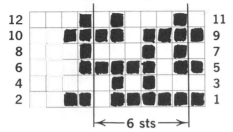

← 6 sts →

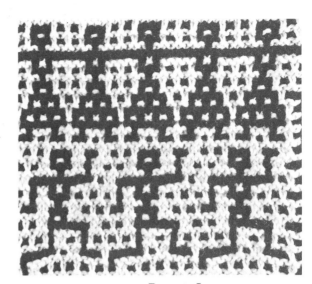

PUPPETS I

Multiple of 8 sts plus 3.

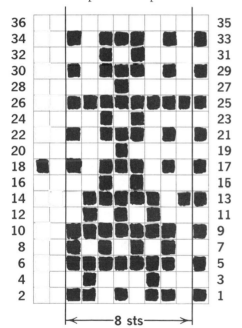

← 8 sts →

PUPPETS II

Multiple of 13 sts plus 3.

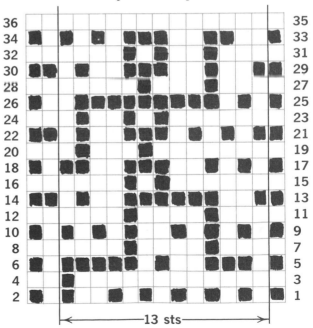

← 13 sts →

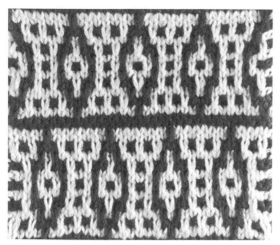

Pillared Band

PILLARED BAND

Multiple of 8 sts plus 3.

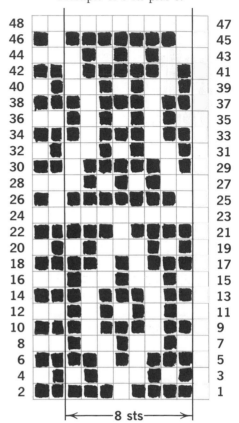

8 sts

CROSS AND DIAMOND

Multiple of 12 sts plus 3.

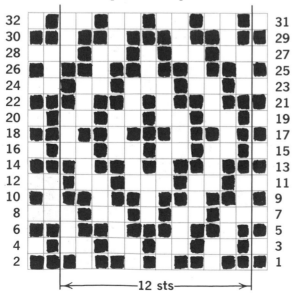

12 sts

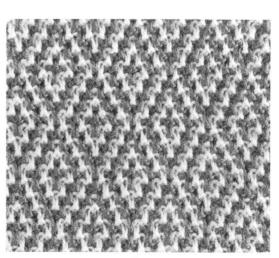

Cross and Diamond

T-SQUARE

Multiple of 10 sts plus 2.

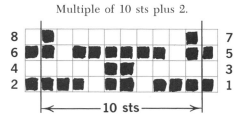

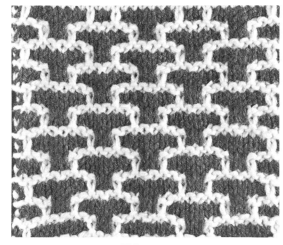

T-Square

Trend

TREND

Multiple of 18 sts plus 2.

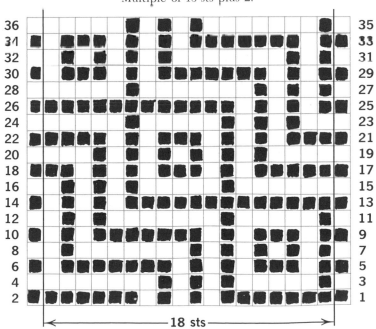

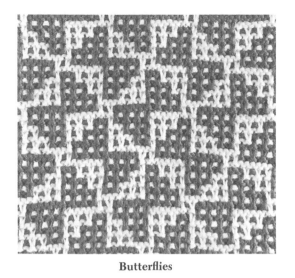

Butterflies

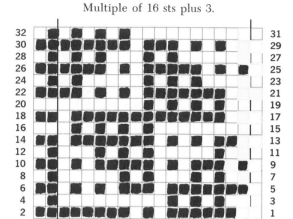

BUTTERFLIES

Multiple of 16 sts plus 3.

Ten-Stitch Chevron

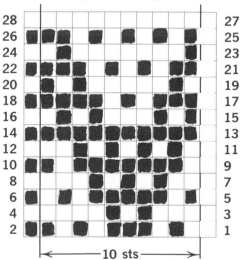

TEN-STITCH CHEVRON

Multiple of 10 sts plus 2.

SHAMROCK

Multiple of 14 sts plus 2.

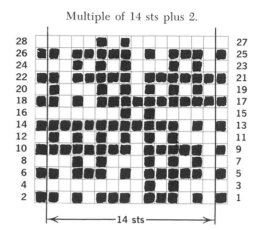

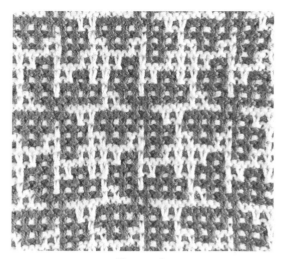

Shamrock

TILTED SWASTIKA AND VINE

Multiple of 18 sts plus 3.

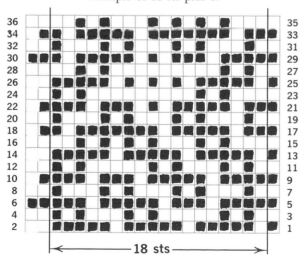

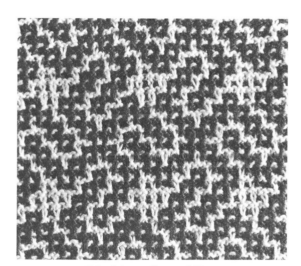

Tilted Swastika and Vine

Doric Key

DORIC KEY

Multiple of 22 sts plus 3.

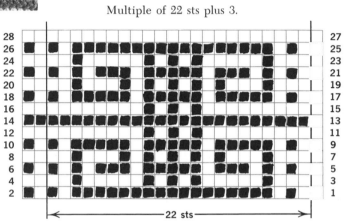

22 sts

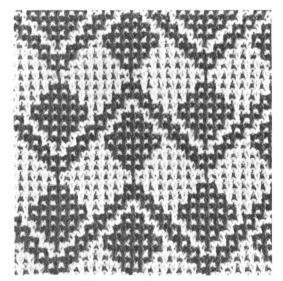

Chevron and Pendants

Solar Square

CHEVRON AND PENDANTS

Multiple of 32 sts plus 3.

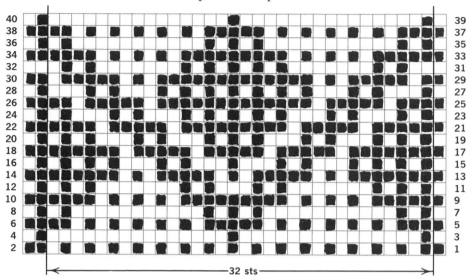

32 sts

SOLAR SQUARE

Multiple of 26 sts plus 3.

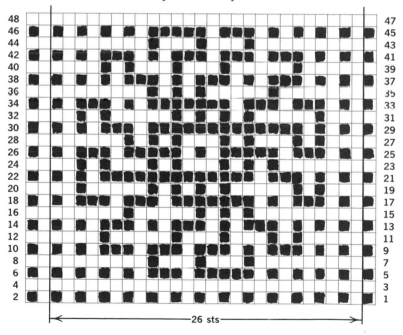

26 sts

OVALS AND SPIRALS

Multiple of 13 sts plus 2.

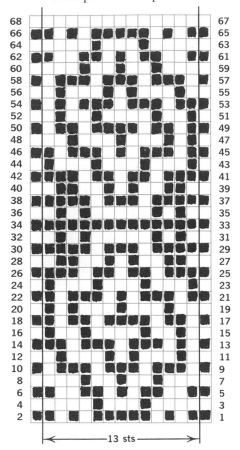

13 sts

Ovals and Spirals

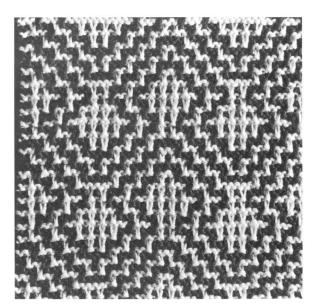

Inverted Chevron

Scarab Pattern

SCARAB PATTERN

Multiple of 16 sts plus 3.

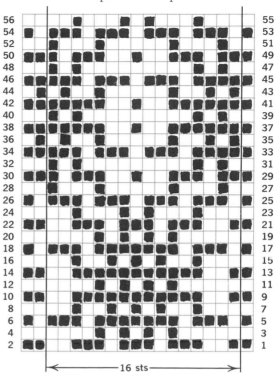

INVERTED CHEVRON

Multiple of 24 sts plus 3.

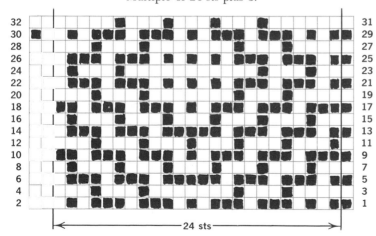

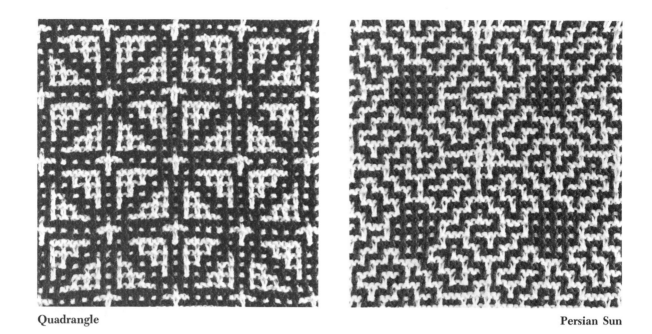

Quadrangle

Persian Sun

QUADRANGLE

Multiple of 24 sts plus 3.

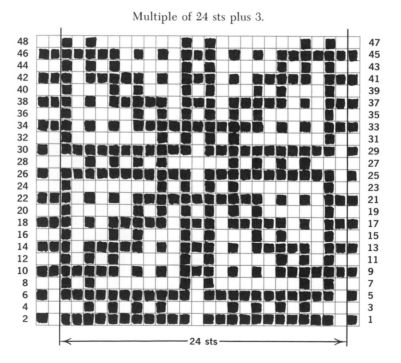

Double Spiral

DOUBLE SPIRAL

Multiple of 14 sts plus 2.

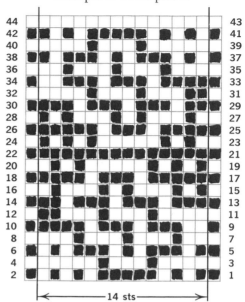

14 sts

PERSIAN SUN

Multiple of 24 sts plus 3.

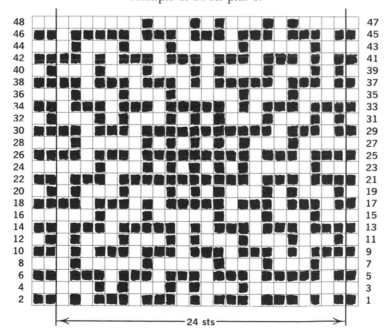

24 sts

WALLPAPER LATTICE

Multiple of 16 sts plus 3.

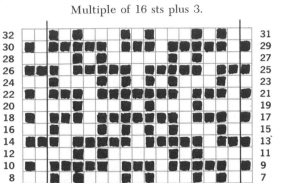

Wallpaper Lattice

WALKING SQUARE

Multiple of 20 sts plus 3.

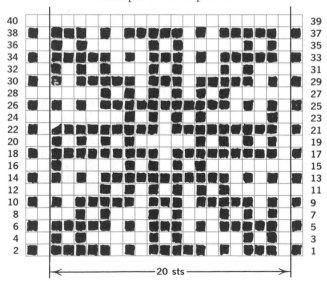

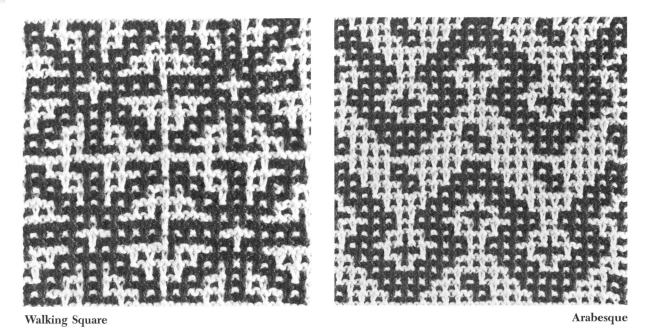

Walking Square   **Arabesque**

ARABESQUE

Multiple of 24 sts plus 3.

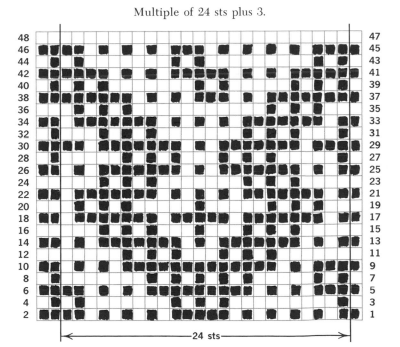

FOUR-WAY SPIRAL

Multiple of 26 sts plus 3.

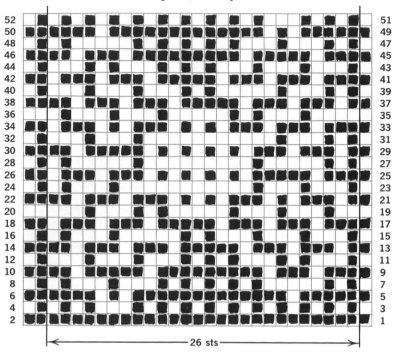

Four-Way Spiral

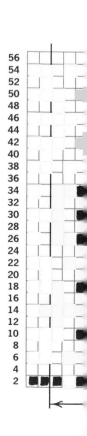

Vibrant Diamond

Colors reversed in second repeat.

VIBRANT DIAMOND

Multiple of 56 sts plus 3.

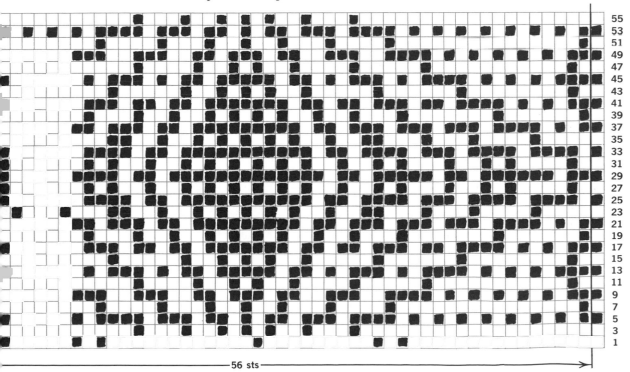

55
53
51
49
47
45
43
41
39
37
35
33
31
29
27
25
23
21
19
17
15
13
11
9
7
5
3
1

◀—— **56 sts** ——▶

Crown of Candles

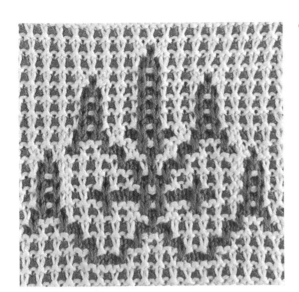

CROWN OF CANDLES

Panel of 39 sts.

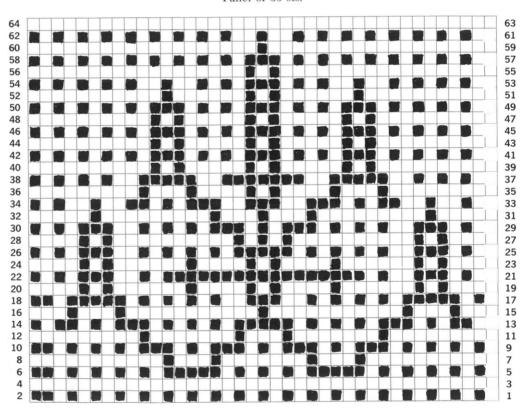

SYNCOPATION I

Multiple of 10 sts plus 3.

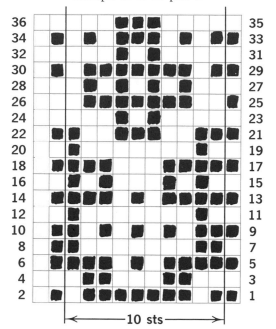

Syncopation I

SYNCOPATION II

Multiple of 14 sts plus 3.

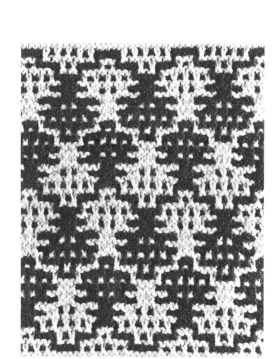

Syncopation II

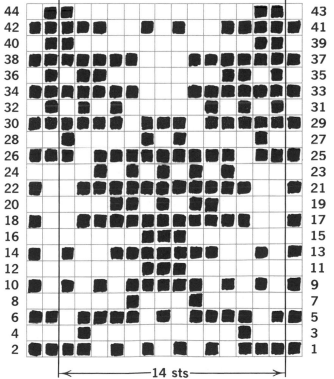

AZTEC ORCHARD

Multiple of 14 sts plus 3.

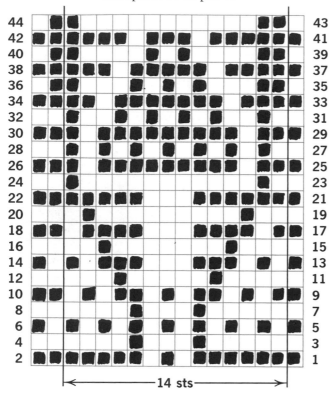

Simulated Basketweave

Aztec Orchard

SIMULATED BASKETWEAVE

Multiple of 10 sts plus 5.

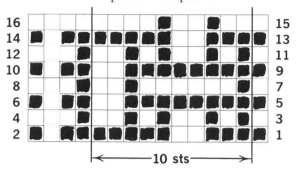

KNOBBED FRET

Multiple of 11 sts plus 2.

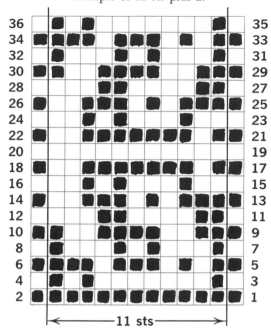

NARROW FRET

Multiple of 6 sts plus 2.

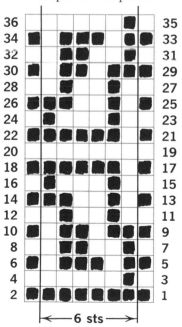

LEFT: Narrow Fret
RIGHT: Knobbed Fret

CHAPTER 9

Color Patterns

Charts for color patterns in general are less successful, as pictures, than charts for mosaic patterns, because they can't show the colors. They are too busy showing the positions of slip-stitches and other knitting operations. The colors, which give life to these patterns, are quite left out of things. They are reduced to cold black-and-white A's, B's, and C's. Each row number has a letter beside it, to indicate that the *entire row* is worked with the color designated by that letter. Other colors are left dangling for the moment. These are all slip-stitch patterns, so all of them achieve their effects by using just one color at a time. To know which color is being used on which row, you must look at the letter beside the row number. Although the charts may look a bit drab in their colorless condition, their patterns surely are not.

Since they show slip-stitch designs, these charts will have many short vertical or horizontal lines. The short vertical lines mean "sl 1 wyib" on the right-side rows, and "sl 1 wyif" on the wrong-side rows. The short horizontal lines mean "sl 1 wyif" on the right-side rows, and "sl 1 wyib" on the wrong-side rows. When you work these patterns in circular knitting, of course all rounds are right-side "rows," worked from right to left between the repeat lines, and the slip-stitches are slipped as on right-side rows only.

When either kind of slip-stitch symbol is found right next to one or more symbols of the same kind, it shows that you must slip two or more stitches together in the same way. There is a separate symbol for each stitch that is slipped.

Color patterns of this type tend to be small, with comparatively few stitches and rows to each repeat; so they are easily learned by novice knitters. Beginners are usually delighted by the dazzling fabrics that can be easily obtained with color patterns. Before using such patterns in a garment, however, the knitter is cautioned to make test swatches and check their gauge carefully. The fabrics are inclined to be dense, requiring more stitches for each inch of width than an average stockinette-type pattern would need.

Tweeds and other slip-stitch color patterns make excellent coats, suits, jackets, winter sports wear, cushion covers, and blankets. A sampler of different patterns worked in different color combinations makes a lovely afghan—so save your test swatches.

226

Example Color Pattern:

Raspberries and Cream

Raspberries and Cream

THIS pattern makes a nice thick, cosy fabric with little nubby "berries" peeking through a layer of gracefully slanted knit stitches. It is a good Example because there are quite a few different symbols on its chart—knit and purl stitches, decreases, increases, and no-stitch X's to be ignored. It's an easy and satisfying pattern to work, and practical for heavy sweaters, mittens, winter-weight baby blankets and the like. At least 3 repeats (13 stitches)—preferably more—must be used for a test swatch.

Multiple of 4 sts plus 1. Colors A and B

Row 1 (Right side)—With A, knit.

Row 2—With A, purl.

Row 3—With B, k1, ° sl 3 wyib, (k1, yo, k1) in next st; rep from °, end sl 3 wyib, k1.

Row 4—With B, k1, ° sl 3 wyif, k3; rep from °, end sl 3 wyif, k1.

Row 5—With A, k1, ° sl 1-k2 tog-psso, sl 3 wyib; rep from °, end sl 1-k2 tog-psso, k1.

Row 6—With A, k1, ° (p1, yo, p1) in next st, sl 3 wyif; rep from °, end (p1, yo, p1) in next st, k1.

Row 7—With B, k1, ° sl 3 wyib, p3; rep from °, end sl 3 wyib, k1.

Row 8—With B, k1, ° sl 3 wyif, p3 tog; rep from °, end sl 3 wyif, k1.

continued on page 228

RASPBERRIES AND CREAM

Multiple of 4 sts plus 1 (13 sts minimum). Colors A and B.

Three repeats shown

← 4 sts →

Rows 9 and *10*—With A, repeat Rows 1 and 2.

Row 11—With B, k3, ° sl 3 wyib, (k1, yo, k1) in next st; rep from °, end sl 3 wyib, k3.

Row 12—With B, k3, ° sl 3 wyif, k3; rep from °.

Row 13—With A, k3, ° sl 1-k2 tog-psso, sl 3 wyib; rep from °, end sl 1-k2 tog-psso, k3.

Row 14—With A, p3, ° (p1, yo, p1) in next st, sl 3 wyif; rep from °, end (p1, yo, p1) in next st, p3.

Row 15—With B, k3, ° sl 3 wyib, p3; rep from °, end sl 3 wyib, k3.

Row 16—With B, k3, ° sl 3 wyif, p3 tog; rep from °, end sl 3 wyif, k3.

Repeat Rows 1–16.

Nubby Tweed

NUBBY TWEED

Even number of sts.

Colors A and B.

Two-Color Fabric Stitch

TWO-COLOR FABRIC STITCH

Even number of sts.

Colors A and B.

Cast on with Color A and purl
one row.

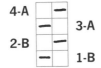

SCOTTIE TWEED

Multiple of 3 sts plus 1.
Colors A and B.

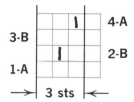

SCOTTIE TWEED, 3-COLOR VARIATION

Multiple of 3 sts plus 1.
Colors A, B, and C.

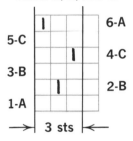

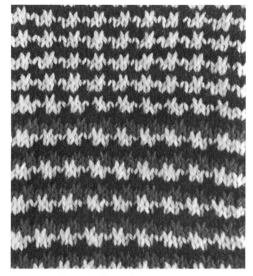

ABOVE: Scottie Tweed
BELOW: Scottie Tweed, 3-Color Variation

FLECKED TWEED

Multiple of 4 sts plus 3. Colors A, B, and C.
Cast on with Color A and knit one row.

NOTE: for Variation (Two-Color Flecked Tweed), work the 1st 4 rows only, Rows 1 & 2 in Color B, Rows 3 & 4 in Color A

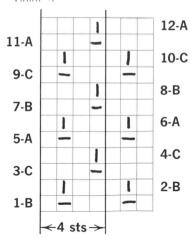

ABOVE: Flecked Tweed
BELOW: Variation (Two-Color Flecked Tweed)

Moorland Tweed

MOORLAND TWEED

Multiple of 4 sts plus 1.
Colors A and B.

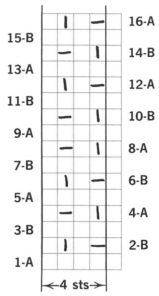

EMBROIDERY PATTERN

Multiple of 10 sts plus 7. Colors A and B.
M—inc 1 st by knitting under running thread
between the st just worked and the next st.

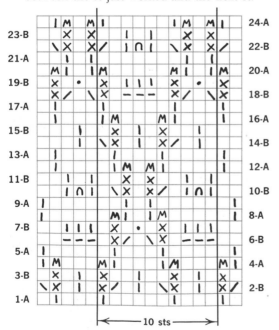

Embroidery Pattern

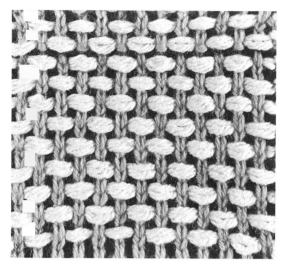

Thick Woven Coating Fabric

THICK WOVEN COATING FABRIC

Multiple of 4 sts plus 5.
Colors A, B, and C. Cast
on with Color A and purl
one row.

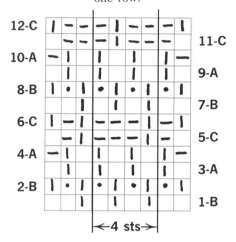

THICK-AND-THIN CHECK

Multiple of 6 sts plus 2.
Colors A and B.

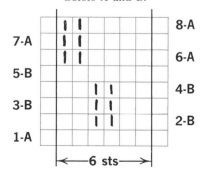

Thick-and-Thin Check

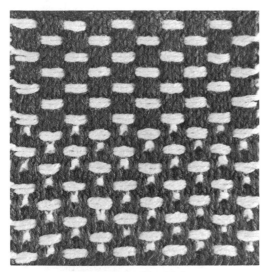

ABOVE: **Triple-Slip, Plain**
BELOW: **Triple-Slip, Dotted**

TRIPLE-SLIP, PLAIN

Multiple of 6 sts plus 2.
Colors A and B.

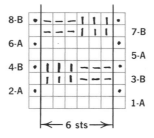

TRIPLE-SLIP, DOTTED

Multiple of 6 sts plus 2.
Colors A and B.

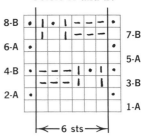

TRIPLE-SLIP TWEED

Multiple of 4 sts plus 3.
Colors A and B.
Cast on with Color A
and purl one row.

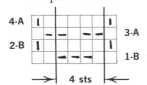

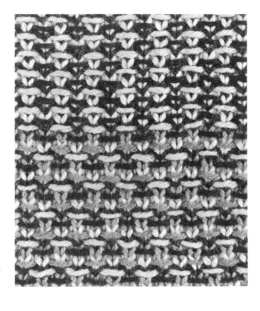

ABOVE: **Triple-Slip Tweed**
BELOW: **Triple-Slip Tweed,**
3-Color Variation

TRIPLE-SLIP TWEED, THREE-COLOR VARIATION

Multiple of 4 sts plus 3.
Colors A, B, and C.
Cast on with Color A
and purl one row.

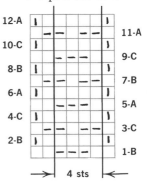

TRIPLE-SLIP, BASKETWEAVE STYLE

Multiple of 4 sts plus 3.
Colors A and B.

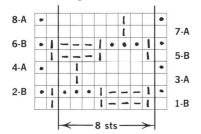

ABOVE: **Triple-Slip, Basketweave Style**
BELOW: **Triple-Slip, Rib Style**

TRIPLE-SLIP, RIB STYLE

Multiple of 8 sts plus 3.
Colors A and B.
Cast on with Color A
and purl one row.

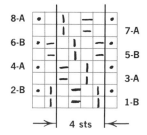

DIAGONAL RIPPLE

Multiple of 4 sts plus 3.
Colors A and B.
Cast on with Color A
and purl one row.

Diagonal Ripple

Wildcat Stripes

Belt-Buckle Stripes

WILDCAT STRIPES

Multiple of 18 sts plus 3. Colors A and B.
Cast on with Color A and purl one row.

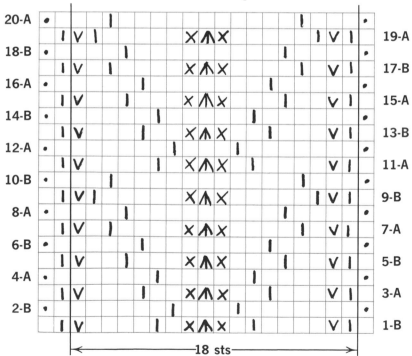

BELT-BUCKLE STRIPES

Multiple of 30 sts. Colors A and B.

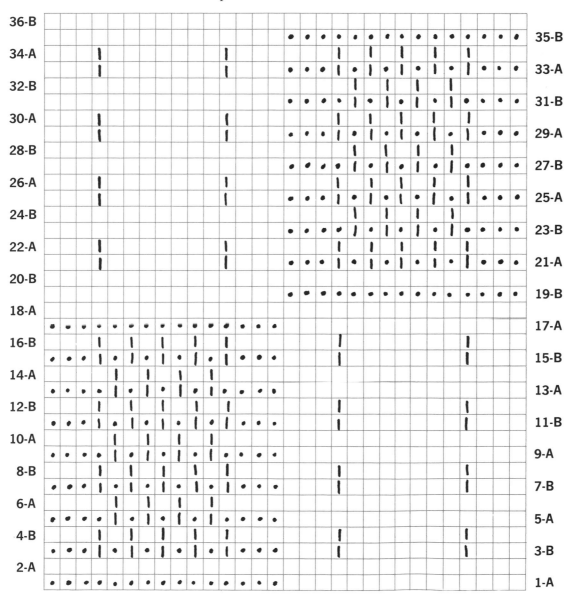

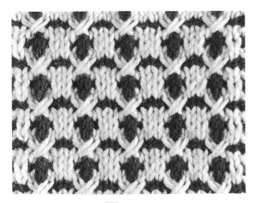

Waycross

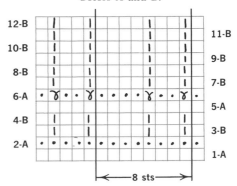

WAYCROSS

Multiple of 6 sts plus 2. Colors A and B.
Cast on with Color A and purl one row. Two repeats shown

° *Row 5*—With B, k2, ° drop next st off needle to front of work, sl 2 wyib, drop next st off needle
to front of work; pick up first dropped st onto left-hand needle, sl the same 2 Color A sts
back to left-hand needle, then with right-hand needle pick up second dropped st and place it
on left-hand needle; k1, sl 2 wyib, k3; rep from °.

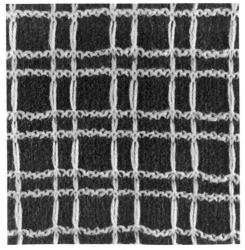

Instant Plaid

INSTANT PLAID

Multiple of 8 sts plus 6.
Colors A and B.

POLKADOT POPCORNS

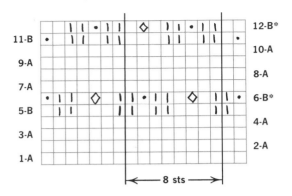

Polkadot Popcorns

Multiple of 8 sts plus 1. Colors A and B. Two repeats shown

° ◇ —To make popcorns in Rows 6 and 12, work to popcorn stitch, then ° insert right-hand needle from front between 1st (popcorn st) and 2nd sts on left-hand needle; draw through a loop and place this loop on left-hand needle to make a new first st; rep from ° 3 times more; then draw through a 5th and last loop from between the last 2 sts made, pass yarn to front, place last loop on left-hand needle, pass yarn to back, k6; then pass the 2nd, 3rd, 4th, 5th, and 6th sts on right-hand needle one at a time over the first st, completing popcorn.

DAISY LATTICE

Multiple of 4 sts plus 1.
Colors A and B. Cast on with Color
A and purl one row.
Two repeats shown

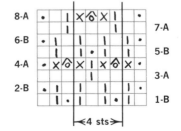

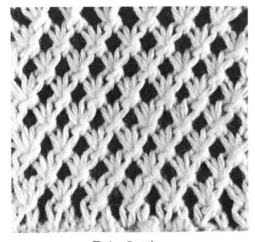

Daisy Lattice

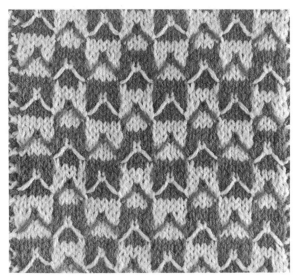

Dutch Tiles

DUTCH TILES

Multiple of 10 sts plus 2.
Colors A and B.

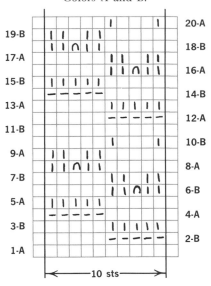

SCALE QUILTING

Multiple of 6 sts plus 1. Colors A and B.
Cast on with Color B and purl one row.
Two repeats shown
NOTE: Preparation Row (0) not to be repeated.

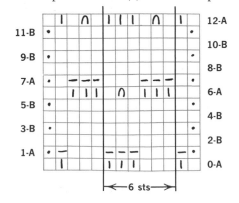

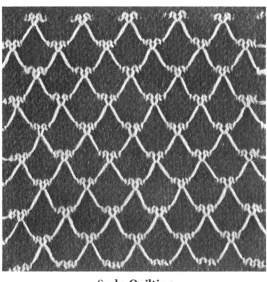

Scale Quilting

DOTTED QUILTING

Multiple of 10 sts plus 7. Colors A and B.
Cast on with Color A and purl one row.
NOTE: Preparation Row (0) not to be repeated.

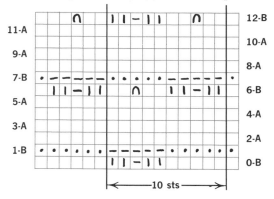

Dotted Quilting

IMPERIAL QUILTING

Multiple of 12 sts plus 5. Colors A and B.
Cast on with Color A and purl one row.
NOTE: Preparation Row (0) not to be repeated.

Imperial Quilting

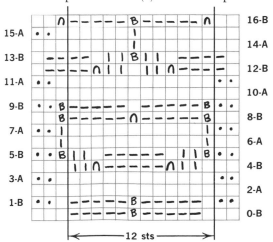

SEAGULL QUILTING

Multiple of 24 sts plus 3. Colors A and B.
Cast on with Color A and purl one row.
NOTE: Preparation Row (0) not to be repeated.

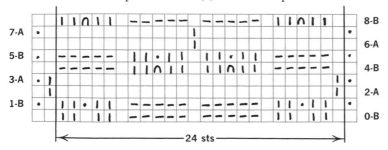

FANCY QUILTING

Multiple of 16 sts plus 5. Colors A and B.
Cast on with Color A and purl one row.

NOTE: Preparation Row (0) not to be repeated.
∩—K1 under *top* strand only of the 2 loose strands below.

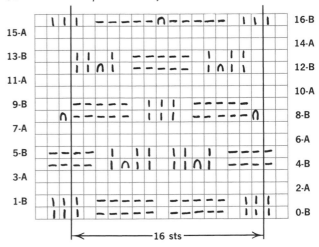

ABOVE: **Seagull Quilting**
BELOW: **Fancy Quilting**

Lattice with Striped Background

LATTICE WITH STRIPED BACKGROUND

Multiple of 12 sts plus 3 (27 minimum)
Two repeats shown. Colors A and B.
Cast on with Color A and knit one row.

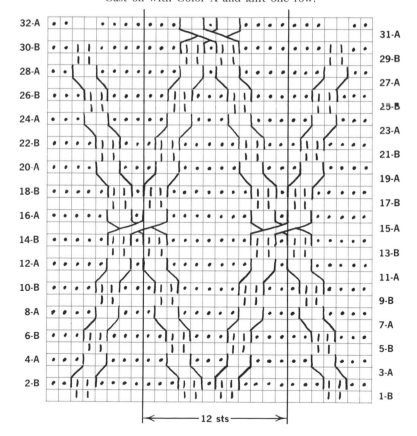

32-A
31-A
30-B
29-B
28-A
27-A
26-B
25-B
24-A
23-A
22-B
21-B
20-A
19-A
18-B
17-B
16-A
15-A
14-B
13-B
12-A
11-A
10-B
9-B
8-A
7-A
6-B
5-B
4-A
3-A
2-B
1-B

12 sts

Open Cables on Dotted Background

OPEN CABLES ON DOTTED BACKGROUND

Multiple of 12 sts plus 3.
Colors A and B.
Cast on with Color A and
knit one row.

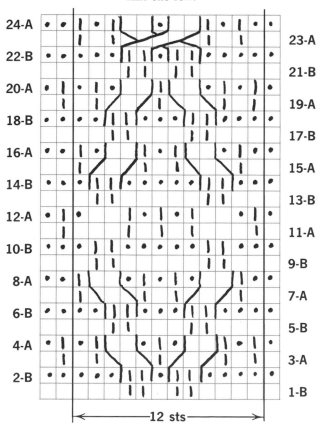

CHAPTER 10

Uncharted Miscellany

The patterns in this section are little ones, with directions either too brief to bother charting, or too unique and specialized to bother inventing symbols for them. This sounds as though the patterns are poor relations, without any particular flair or interest to distinguish them. But such is not the case. The little patterns can display some perfectly fascinating techniques within their small multiples and few rows. They make various kinds of fancy fabrics—textures, meshes, or spot-patterns—that are intended for use all over the garment or other knitted article.

Mesh patterns are good for summer-weight sweaters, scarves, dresses and openwork vests; solid fabrics illustrated here are good for coats, suits and jackets. Any of these patterns are good for the purpose of extending the knitter's skill. Many of them do things with yarn that you probably never thought of doing before; so it can only be to your advantage to try them. These patterns also offer an advantage to the beginner: because their directions are so short, they can be learned very quickly. After they have been learned, they can be worked quite mechanically, without making too many demands on the knitter's attention.

Except for the brevity common to all of them, these patterns cannot be classified in any other way, since they use a broad assortment of knitting techniques. Each one has its own individual quality, and some may have a little trick or two that will surprise you, and—I hope—delight you as well.

Triple-Stitch Knot

Triple-Stitch Knot
ABOVE: Purl Version
BELOW: Knit Version

HERE are two different methods of working a simple allover texture pattern, which produce two quite different results. The purl version forms crescent-shaped ribs twisting to the right; the knit version, which is easier to work, makes a nubby crochet-like fabric with open spaces between the fanned-out stitches. Each is pretty in its own way, and either can be used in almost any type of yarn.

Multiple of 3 sts

I. Purl Version

Rows 1 and *3* (Right side)—Knit.
Row 2— ° P3 tog, leave on needle; yarn to back between needles and knit first st of the 3 just purled tog; sl this st from needle, then knit the 2nd st and sl the 2nd and 3rd sts from needle; rep from °.
Row 4—Purl.
Repeat Rows 1–4.

II. Knit Version

Row 1 (Wrong side)—Knit.
Row 2—° K3 tog, leave on needle; then knit the first of the 3 sts again, then k2 tog (the 2nd and 3rd sts); rep from °.
Row 3—Purl.
Row 4—Knit.
Repeat Rows 1–4.

ABOVE: Caliper Cables
BELOW: Elongated-Stitch Herringbone

Caliper Cables

THIS is a somewhat unusual variation on the double cable. These cables can be used in any way that an ordinary cable might be used; but their effect is one of indentation into the fabric rather than one of a strongly embossed pattern.

Multiple of 13 sts plus 3. (Or, panel of 16)

Row 1 (Wrong side)—K3, ° p1 wrapping yarn twice, p8, p1 wrapping yarn twice, k3; rep
from °.
Row 2—P3, ° drop elongated st off needle to front of work, k4, pick up dropped st and
knit it; sl 4 wyib, drop second elongated st off needle to front of work, sl the same
4 sts back to left-hand needle, pick up dropped st and knit it, k4, p3; rep from °.
Rows 3 and *4*—Repeat Rows 1 and 2.
Row 5—K3, ° p10, k3; rep from °.
Row 6—P3, ° k10, p3; rep from °.
Repeat Rows 1–6.

Variation: Elongated-Stitch Herringbone

Repeat Rows 1 and 2 of the above pattern
only.

Pebble Stitch

ABOVE: Pebble Stitch
BELOW: Variation

FOR a man's outdoor sweater, a tweed suit, a
casual jacket, or any other article where a
nubby, rough texture is wanted, this easy
pattern is excellent for a beginner to use.

Multiple of 4 sts plus 2

Rows 1 and *3* (Right side)—Knit.
Row 2—P2, ° yo, k2, pass the yo over the 2 knit sts, p2; rep from °.
Row 4—Yo, k2, pass the yo over the 2 knit sts, ° p2, yo, k2, pass the yo over the 2 knit
sts; rep from °.
Repeat Rows 1–4.

Variation

Pebble Stitch is attractive when the pattern rows are doubled, so that there are 8 rows
to the pattern instead of 4. Knit all right-side rows, work Rows 2 and 4 the same as Row
2, above; work Rows 6 and 8 the same as Row 4, above.

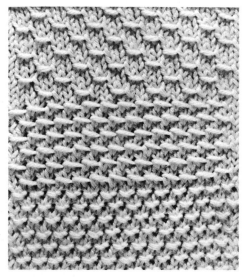

ABOVE: **Miniature Smocking Stitch**
CENTER: **Horizontal Bar Pattern**
BELOW: **Fish-Scale Pattern**

Miniature Smocking Stitch

BOTH this pattern and its variations, below, give a handsome texture and are almost ridiculously easy to knit—good examples of how a "different" effect can be obtained by any beginner, without complex knitting operations.

Multiple of 4 sts plus 2

Rows 1 and *3* (Wrong side)—Purl.
Row 2—K2, ° yo, k2, pass the yo over the 2 knit sts, k2; rep from °.
Row 4—K4, ° yo, k2, pass the yo over the 2 knit sts, k2; rep from °, end k2.
Repeat Rows 1–4.

Variation: Horizontal Bar Pattern—Even number of sts

Rows 1 and *3* (Wrong side)—Purl.
Row 2—K1, ° yo, k2, pass the yo over the 2 knit sts; rep from °, end k1.
Row 4—K2, ° yo, k2, pass the yo over the 2 knit sts; rep from °, end k2.
Repeat Rows 1–4.

Variation: Fish-Scale Pattern—Odd number of sts

Rows 1 and *3* (Wrong side)—Purl.
Row 2—K1, ° yo in reverse (i.e., bring yarn over needle from back to front), k2, pass the yo over the 2 knit sts; rep from °.
Row 4—° Yo in reverse, k2, pass the yo over the 2 knit sts; rep from °, end k1.
Repeat Rows 1–4.

Two Coating Fabrics:

Textured Plait Stitch and Fancy Herringbone

Textured Plait Stitch

THESE are interesting texture stitches for medium to heavy yarn, especially attractive in coats, jackets, and other outdoor garments. Textured Plait Stitch makes a firm, close fabric. Fancy Herringbone, using a yarn-over-and-slip-stitch technique, is a little looser and more flexible. Both are examples of the knits with a not-knit look, resembling woven cloth of an unusual design. The fabric is flat and free of curl.

Textured Plait Stitch—Multiple of 3 sts plus 1

Row 1 (Right side)—K1, ° insert needle as if to purl *through* the next st, and knit the second st on left-hand needle; then knit the first st in back loop and sl both sts from needle together; k1; rep from °.

Row 2—P1, ° p1, p2 tog and leave on needle; insert right-hand needle between the two sts just purled together, and purl the first st again; then sl both sts from needle together; rep from °.

Repeat Rows 1 and 2.

Fancy Herringbone— Multiple of 3 sts plus 1

Row 1 (Right side)—K1, ° yo, sl 1 wyib, k2, pass sl-st over the 2 knit sts; rep from °.

Row 2—P1, ° yo, sl 1 wyif, p2, pass sl-st over the 2 purl sts; rep from °.

Repeat Rows 1 and 2.

Note: To bind off Fancy Herringbone firmly, omit the yo's from the last row, then bind off the resulting reduced number of sts.

Fancy Herringbone

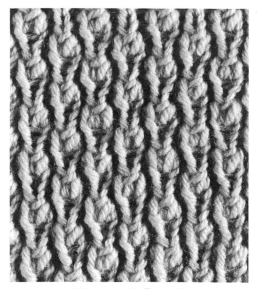

Miniature Puff Stitch

Miniature Puff Stitch

THIS pattern makes a lovely deep texture resembling small waved and knotted ribs. It is attractive in suits, sweaters, mittens or jackets.

Multiple of 4 sts plus 1

Row 1 (Right side)—P1, ° (k1, yo, k1, yo, k1) in next st, making 5 sts from one; p1, k1, p1; rep from °.

Row 2—° K1, p1, k1, p2 tog, p3 tog, pass the first of the last 2 sts over the second, decreasing 5 sts back to one; rep from °, end k1.

Row 3—° P1, k1, p1, (k1, yo, k1, yo, k1) in next st; rep from °, end p1.

Row 4—K1, ° p2 tog, p3 tog, pass 1st of the last 2 sts over 2nd, k1, p1, k1; rep from °. Repeat Rows 1–4.

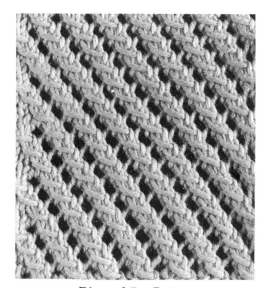

Diagonal Bar Pattern

Two Semi-Open Mesh Patterns:

Diagonal Bar Pattern and Semi-Smocked Mesh

THESE are handsome all-purpose patterns for summer sweaters, scarves, stoles and mesh vests. The knitting style of some knitters may produce a slight bias tendency in the fabrics, but this is not so pronounced that it cannot be blocked out.

I. Diagonal Bar Pattern—Multiple of 3 sts plus 1

Row 1 (Wrong side) and all other wrong-side rows—Purl.
Row 2—K1, ° yo, sl 1, k2, psso the 2 knit sts; rep from °.
Row 4—K2, ° yo, sl 1, k2, psso the 2 knit sts; rep from °, end k2.
Row 6—K3, ° yo, sl 1, k2, psso the 2 knit sts; rep from °, end k1.
Repeat Rows 1–6.

II. Semi-Smocked Mesh— Multiple of 3 sts plus 1

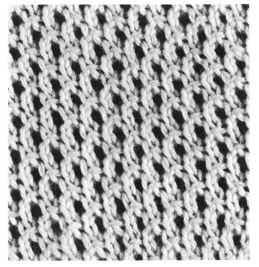

Semi-Smocked Mesh

Rows 1 and 3 (Wrong side)—Purl.
Row 2—K2, ° yo, k1, yo, sl 1, k1, pass the sl-st and the preceding yo together over the last knit st; rep from °, end k2.
Row 4—K2, ° yo, sl 1, k1, pass the sl-st and the preceding yo together over the last knit st, yo, k1; rep from °, end k2.
Repeat Rows 1–4.

Honeycomb Cluster

Honeycomb Cluster

THIS pretty fabric is a kind of smocking, which leaves lace-like holes without the aid of yarn-overs. The cluster strands bind the stitches together, four at a time, alternating every right-side row.

Multiple of 4 sts plus 2

Rows 1 and 3 (Wrong side)—Purl.
Row 2—K1, ° skip 4 sts, insert needle from front between 4th and 5th sts on left-hand

needle and draw through a loop; knit the 4 skipped sts, then pass the front strand of loop over these 4 sts; rep from °, end k1.

Row 4—K3, rep from ° of Row 2, end k3.

Repeat Rows 1–4.

Honeycomb Lace

ON the wrong-side rows of this mesh, the first "p2 tog" takes up a stitch and the first loop of the following double yarn-over; the next "p2 tog" takes up the second loop of the same double yarn-over, plus the following stitch. Take care that the second loop of the double yarn-over does not fall off the needle before it is caught with the stitch. If it should fall off, it can be picked up easily and put back on the needle; but you must keep looking at the work, to make sure. So don't try to knit this lace while reading or watching television!

Multiple of 3 sts plus 1

Row 1 (Right side)—° K2, (yo) twice; rep from °, end k1.

Row 2—° P2 tog; rep from °, end p1.

Row 3—K1, ° (yo) twice, k2; rep from °.

Row 4—P1, ° p2 tog; rep from °.

Repeat Rows 1–4.

Little Honeycomb Lace

Multiple of 3 sts plus 1

Row 1 (Wrong side)—P1, ° k1, p2; rep from °.

Row 2—K1, ° yo, k1, k2 tog; rep from °.

Row 3—° P2, k1; rep from °, end p1.

Row 4—K1, ° k2 tog, yo, k1; rep from °.

Repeat Rows 1–4.

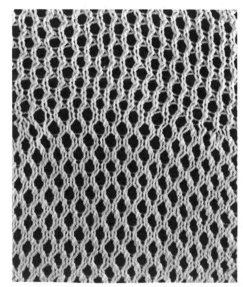

ABOVE: Little Honeycomb Lace
BELOW: Honeycomb Lace

Three Open Mesh Patterns:

Double Faggoting, Delta Faggot, and Netting Stitch

Double Faggoting

DOUBLE Faggoting differs from ordinary faggoting in that the decreases are doubled on every row. Worked in fine yarn, it makes a handsome lace; worked in heavy yarn with small needles, it makes a loose, elastic ribbing. Delta Faggot is a pretty mesh formed of triangular (delta) shapes. Netting Stitch is worked almost exactly like Delta Faggot, changing the position of only one stitch in the first row; but the result is surprisingly different, giving a much more open lace. All three patterns are reversible.

I. Double Faggoting— Multiple of 4 sts plus 1

Row 1—K1, ° yo, p3 tog, yo, k1; rep from °.
Row 2—P2 tog, ° yo, k1, yo, p3 tog; rep from °, end yo, k1, yo, p2 tog.
Repeat Rows 1 and 2.

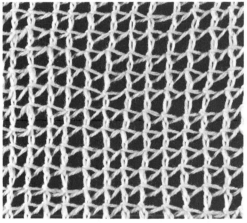

Delta Faggot

II. Delta Faggot— Odd number of sts

Row 1—° Yo, sl 1, k1, pass the yo and the sl-st both together over the knit st; rep from °, end k1. (This row reduces the number of sts to half the original number plus 1)
Row 2—P1, ° yo, p1; rep from °. (This row restores the original number of sts)
Repeat Rows 1 and 2.

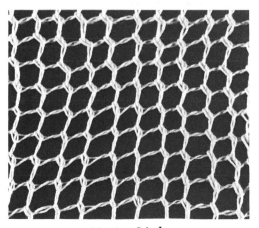

Netting Stitch

III. Netting Stitch—Odd number of sts

Row 1—K1, ° yo, sl 1, k1, pass the yo and the sl-st both together over the knit st; rep from °.
Row 2—P1, ° yo, p1; rep from °.
Repeat Rows 1 and 2.

Open Basketweave Mesh

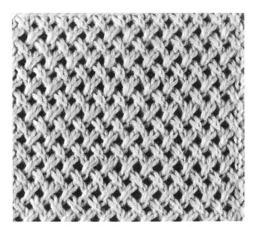

Open Basketweave Mesh

TWIST and yarn-over stitches combine here to make an astonishingly regular and symmetrical diagonal "weave", with open spaces instead of the usual background stitches between the woven ribs. No pattern of the open-weave type has ever achieved this particular illusion with so much success.

Odd Number of sts

Row 1 (Right side)—K1, ° yo, RT; rep from °.
Row 2—P1, ° p2 tog, p1; rep from °.
Row 3—LT, ° yo, LT: rep from °, end k1.
Row 4—P2, ° p2 tog, p1; rep from °, end p1.
Repeat Rows 1–4.

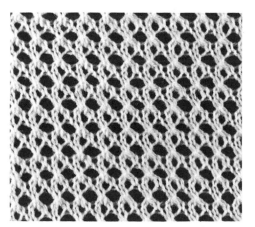

Delayed-Decrease Eyelet Mesh

Delayed-Decrease Eyelet Mesh

VARIATIONS in this pattern can be obtained by substituting other double decreases (i.e., k3 tog, k3 tog-b, sl 1-k2 tog-psso, etc.) for the central double decrease in Row 4. In any case the result is a soft and pretty openwork useful for dresses and sweaters and baby things.

Odd number of sts

Rows 1 and *3* (Wrong side)—Purl.
Row 2—° K2, yo; rep from °, end k1.
Row 4—K1, ° yo, sl 2-k1-p2sso; rep from °.
Repeat Rows 1–4.

Mystery Mesh

UNLESS you are a very clever detective, you will not be able to solve the mystery of this pattern's construction without reading the directions. A reversible fabric with wide open spaces, it looks like either knitting or crochet, or a combination of them. Of course it's all knitting—an unusual stitch that's easy as pie when you know how it's done. Perfect for an openwork vest!

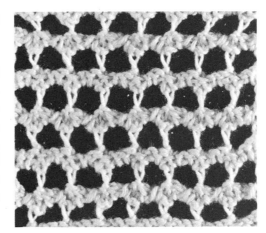

Mystery Mesh

Multiple of 4 sts plus 1

Row 1—K1, ° k2, pass second st on right-hand needle over first st, k1, pass second st on right-hand needle over first st, then keeping yarn in back slip the next st as if to p1-b (inserting right-hand needle from the left into back of st); then once again pass second st on right-hand needle over first st (3 sts bound off); rep from °.

Row 2—K1-b, ° yo, k1-b; rep from °.

Row 3—Knit. (Half the original number of sts now on needle.)

Row 4—K1, ° k1 in the yo space below, k2; rep from °.

Row 5—K2, ° k1 in the same yo space below, k3; rep from °, end last repeat k2. (Original number of sts restored.)

Repeat Rows 1–5.

Tranquility Stitch

THIS pretty mesh looks crocheted; but it is all knitting, and easy knitting at that, in spite of the apparently complicated directions. It works as quickly as the afghan stitch that it somewhat resembles. The wrong side is handsome also, so the pattern can be used for articles that show both sides.

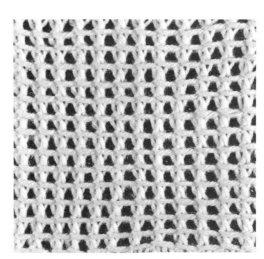

Tranquility Stitch

Even number of sts

Row 1 (Right side)—° Yo, sl 1, k1, then pass the yo and the sl-st both together over the knit st; rep from °. (This row reduces the sts to half the original number.)

Row 2—° Insert right-hand needle from right to left behind the strand lying diagonally across the base of first st on left-hand needle; pick up this strand, place it on left-hand needle and purl it; then purl the first st itself; rep from °. (This row restores the original number of sts.)

Repeat Rows 1 and 2.

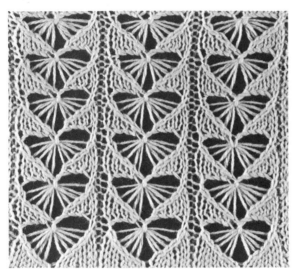

Variation Honeybee

Variation Honeybee

THIS is a way of working the beautiful old Honeybee Pattern that makes a fabric more open and delicate than the original. To cast on the stitches in Row 6, use the cable cast-on; i.e., ° insert right-hand needle between the first 2 sts on left-hand needle, draw through a loop, place this loop on left-hand needle to make a new first st; rep from °. Just before putting the last loop on the left-hand needle, bring yarn through to the front to make a dividing strand between the last two cast-on sts.

Multiple of 12 sts plus 5

Row 1 (Right side)—K2, ° p1, k5, (yo) 4 times, ssk, k4; rep from °, end p1, k2.

Row 2—K3, ° p3, p2 tog-b, (yo) 4 times, drop the yo strands of previous row off needle, p2 tog, p3, k1; rep from °, end k2.

Row 3—K2, ° p1, k2, k2 tog, (yo) 4 times, drop the yo strands of previous row off needle, ssk, k2; rep from °, end p1, k2.

Row 4—K3, ° p1, p2 tog-b, (yo) 4 times, drop the yo strands of previous row off needle, p2 tog, p1, k1; rep from °, end k2.

Row 5—K2, ° p1, k2 tog, (yo) 4 times, drop the yo strands of previous row off needle, ssk; rep from °, end p1, k2.

Row 6—K3, ° p1, drop the yo strands of previous row off needle, turn work; cast on 4 sts to left-hand needle, then insert right-hand needle under the 5 loose strands of the dropped yo's and draw through a loop; place this loop on left-hand needle, cast on 4 more sts, turn work; p1, k1; rep from °, end k2.

Repeat Rows 1–6.

Two Lace-Cable Patterns:

Lace Cross Rib, and Small Lace Cable

I. Lace Cross Rib—panel of 16 sts

CAUTION! In Row 4, after slipping the 4 central sts back to left-hand needle, be careful not to drop the preceding yo. Dropping the first elongated st off the needle will leave this yo loose and exposed. It can easily depart from the needle altogether unless you make sure it is still there before picking up the second elongated st.

CENTER PANEL: Lace Cross Rib
LEFT SIDE PANEL: Small Lace Cable, back cross
RIGHT SIDE PANEL: Small Lace Cable, front cross

Row 1 (Wrong side)—Purl.
Row 2—K2, yo, sl 2-k1-p2sso, yo, k1 wrapping yarn twice, k4, k1 wrapping yarn twice, yo, sl 2-k1-p2sso, yo, k2.
Row 3—P5, sl 1 wyif dropping extra wrap, p4, turn, k4, turn, p4, sl 1 wyif dropping extra wrap, p5.
Row 4—K2, yo, sl 2-k1-p2sso, yo, drop first elongated st off needle to front of work, sl 4 wyib, drop second elongated st off needle to front of work, sl the same 4 sts back to left-hand needle; pick up second dropped st and knit it, k4, then pick up first dropped st and knit it; yo, sl 2-k1-p2sso, yo, k2.
Row 5—Purl.
Row 6—K2, yo, sl 2-k1-p2sso, yo, k6, yo, sl 2-k1-p2sso, yo, k2.
Repeat Rows 1–6.

II. Small Lace Cable—panel of 10 sts

This cable can be twisted to the left or to the right, depending on whether the dpn is held in front or in back.

Row 1 (Wrong side) and all other wrong-side rows—K2, p6, k2.
Row 2—P2, sl next 3 sts to dpn and hold in front (or in back), k3, then k3 from dpn; p2.
Rows 4, 6, 8, 10, and *12*—P2, ssk, yo, k2, yo, k2 tog, p2.
Repeat Rows 1–12.

Tanbark

THIS is one of those interesting little patterns that make half a dozen different fabrics out of minor changes. The basic Tanbark can show either its right side or its wrong side, or it can be worked as a tweedy check by using one color for Rows 1 and 2, another color for Rows 3 and 4. Tanbark Variation can be used either in a plain color or in two colors; and it makes two different color patterns, depending on whether the contrasting color is introduced in Rows 1 and 2 or Rows 3 and 4. Also, the first two rows of the Variation make an imitation tuck, useful when changing from one color stripe to the next, and a pretty turning ridge for a hem.

ABOVE, LEFT: **Tanbark, right side**
ABOVE, RIGHT: **Tanbark, wrong side**
CENTER, LEFT: **Tanbark in 2 colors**
CENTER, RIGHT: **Tanbark Variation**
BELOW, LEFT: **Tanbark Variation with contrasting color in Rows 3 and 4**
BELOW, RIGHT: **Tanbark Variation with contrasting color in Rows 1 and 2**

Odd number of sts

Row 1 (Wrong side)—P1, ° sl 1 wyif, p1; rep from °.
Row 2—P1, ° k1, p1; rep from °.
Row 3—Sl 1 wyif, ° p1, sl 1 wyif; rep from °.
Row 4—K1, ° p1, k1; rep from °.
Repeat Rows 1-4.

Tanbark Variation

Odd number of sts

Row 1 (Right side)—P1, ° sl 1 wyif, p1; rep from °.
Row 2—P1, ° k1, p1; rep from °.
Row 3—Knit.
Row 4—Purl.
Repeat Rows 1–4.

Dutch Knitting

This pattern is a beauty with a single flaw: it tends to pull the fabric slightly bias. The tendency is not strong, however, and can be corrected in blocking. The Variation is very striking. Dutch Knitting can be used both ways—in one color and in three—in the same garment; for example with the three-color portion as a yoke, or as a fancy front to a plain back as in a vest.

ABOVE: Dutch Knitting
BELOW: Three-Color Star Stitch

Multiple of 3 sts plus 2

Row 1 (Wrong side) and all other wrong-side rows—Purl.
Row 2—K1, ° yo, k3, pass the first of the 3 knit sts over the other 2; rep from °, end k1.
Row 4—K3, rep from ° of Row 2; end k2.
Row 6—K2, rep from ° of Row 2 to end of row.
Repeat Rows 1–6.

Variation: Three-color Star Stitch

Work the same as above, using Color A in Rows 1 and 2, Color B in Rows 3 and 4, and Color C in Rows 5 and 6.

Fantastic Stripe Pattern

This pattern gives a rather novel fabric arranged in vertical columns with uneven zigzags of color. The fabric would be interesting as well in a single color. It pulls together quite strongly in the lateral dimension; be sure to cast on enough stitches for required width.

Fantastic Stripe Pattern

Multiple of 6 sts plus 2. Colors A and B.

Cast on with Color A.

Row 1 (Wrong side)—With B, p6, ° sl 1 wyif, p5; rep from °, end sl 1, p1.

Row 2—With B, k1, ° sl 1 wyib, k1, yo, k1, pass sl-st over the 3 subsequent sts (including yo); rep from °.

Rows 3 and *4*—With A, repeat Rows 1 and 2.
     Repeat Rows 1–4.

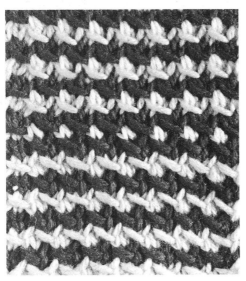

ABOVE: **Indian Stripes**
BELOW: **Variation**

Indian Stripes

THERE are two rather different aspects to this pattern, depending on whether the yarns are changed at the left-hand side or the right-hand side of the piece. The latter method makes the Variation, below, in which the stripes look narrower and sharper. An unusual technique is involved in the knitting of this pattern, which makes an extremely attractive texture, too, when worked in one solid color.

Multiple of 3 sts plus 1. Colors A and B

Row 1 (Right side)—With A, k1, ° sl 1 wyib, k2, psso the 2 knit sts; rep from °.

Row 2—With B, ° p2, insert left-hand needle upward under the sl-st strand that binds the 2 sts just worked, and purl this strand; rep from °, end p1.

Row 3—With B, k2, ° sl 1 wyib, k2, psso the 2 knit sts; rep from °, end k2.

Row 4—With A, p2, rep from ° of Row 2; end p2.
     Repeat Rows 1–4.

Variation

Work the same as above, but use Color A in Rows 1 and 2, Color B in Rows 3 and 4.

Twisted Stripes

Twisted Stripes

Multiple of 6 sts plus 2. Colors A and B

Cast on with Color A and purl one row.

Row 1 (Right side)—With B, k1, ° sl 1 wyib, k2, knit into 3rd st on left-hand needle, then knit into first st and leave on needle, then knit into 2nd st and sl all 3 sts from needle together; rep from °, end k1.

Row 2—With B, p1, ° p5, sl 1 wyif; rep from °, end p1.

Row 3—With A, k1, ° knit into back of 2nd st on left-hand needle, then knit into back of 3rd st, then knit into front of first st and sl all 3 sts from needle together; k2, sl 1 wyib; rep from °, end k1.

Row 4—With A, p1, ° sl 1 wyif, p5; rep from °, end p1.

Repeat Rows 1–4.

Slipped Checks

"Is it possible," a knitter asked me once, "to make a one-and-one check with slip-stitches?" After experimenting, I found it to be quite possible, provided the knitting is done on a circular needle or a pair of double-pointed needles. Not only a one-and-one check can be worked this way, but also a two-and-two check or a three-and-three check; so all three versions are given here. To work these patterns in flat knitting, in rows, use a circular needle or a pair of double-pointed needles and follow the

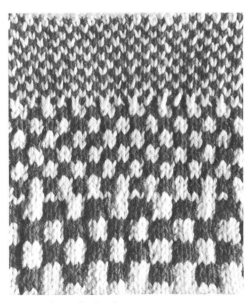

Slipped Checks
ABOVE: **One-and-One Check**
CENTER: **Two-and-Two Check**
BELOW: **Three-and-Three Check**

directions at the end of each row (i.e., either "turn" or "slip stitches to the other end"), always being sure to twist the two strands neatly together at the side edges when changing from one to the other.

All three versions: Colors A and B. Cast on with Color A and purl one row.

I. One-and-One Check—Even number of sts

Row 1 (Right side)—With B, ° k1, sl 1 wyib; rep from °. Sl sts to other end of needle.
Row 2—With A, repeat Row 1. Turn.
Row 3—With B, ° p1, sl 1 wyif; rep from °. Sl sts to other end of needle.
Row 4—With A, repeat Row 3. Turn.
  Repeat Rows 1–4.

II. Two-and-Two Check—Multiple of 4 sts.

Row 1 (Right side)—With B, ° k2, sl 2 wyib; rep from °. Sl sts to other end of needle.
Row 2—With A, ° sl 2 wyib, k2; rep from °. Turn.
Row 3—With B, ° sl 2 wyif, p2; rep from °. Sl sts to other end of needle.
Row 4—With A, ° p2, sl 2 wyif; rep from °. Turn.
Row 5—With B, ° sl 2 wyib, k2; rep from °. Sl sts to other end of needle.
Row 6—With A, ° k2, sl 2 wyib; rep from °. Turn.
Row 7—With B, ° p2, sl 2 wyif; rep from °. Sl sts to other end of needle.
Row 8—With A, ° sl 2 wyif, p2; rep from °. Turn.
  Repeat Rows 1–8.

III. Three-and-Three Check—Multiple of 6 sts

Row 1 (Right side)—With B, ° k3, sl 3 wyib; rep from °. Sl sts to other end of needle.
Row 2—With A, ° sl 3 wyib, k3; rep from °. Turn.
Row 3—With B, ° sl 3 wyif, p3; rep from °. Sl sts to other end of needle.
Row 4—With A, ° p3, sl 3 wyif; rep from °. Turn.
Rows 5 and *6*—Repeat Rows 1 and 2.
Row 7—With B, ° p3, sl 3 wyif; rep from °. Sl sts to other end of needle.
Row 8—With A, ° sl 3 wyif, p3; rep from °. Turn.
Row 9—With B, ° sl 3 wyib, k3; rep from °. Sl sts to other end of needle.
Row 10—With A, ° k3, sl 3 wyib; rep from °. Turn.
Rows 11 and *12*—Repeat Rows 7 and 8.
  Repeat Rows 1–12.

Cottage Check Pattern

SPECIAL NOTE: This pattern must be worked back and forth on a circular needle or a pair of double-pointed needles.

Multiple of 4 sts plus 3. Colors A and B

Row 1 (Wrong side)—With A, purl.

Row 2—With B, k2, ° sl 1 wyib, k1; rep from °, end k1. Sl all sts to other end of needle.

Row 3—With A, k1, ° sl 1 wyib, k1; rep from °.

Row 4—With B, p2, ° sl 1 wyif, p3; rep from °, end p1. Sl all sts to other end of needle.

Row 5—With A, p4, ° sl 1 wyif, p3; rep from °, end sl 1, p2.

Row 6—With B, k1, ° sl 1 wyib, k1; rep from °. Sl all sts to other end of needle.

Row 7—With A, k4, ° sl 1 wyib, k3; rep from °, end sl 1, k2.

Row 8—With B, p4, ° sl 1 wyif, p3; rep from °, end sl 1, p2. Sl all sts to other end of needle.

Row 9—With A, p1, ° sl 1 wyif, p1; rep from °.

Row 10—With B, repeat Row 2. Sl all sts to other end of needle.

Row 11—With A, knit.

Row 12—With B, p1, ° sl 1 wyif, p1, rep from °. Sl all sts to other end of needle.
Repeat Rows 1–12.

Cottage Check Pattern

Diagonal Overlay

THE variation is not very much different from the original pattern here, since the crosswise stripes of Color A are overwhelmed by strong diagonals. Therefore Color B should be a very

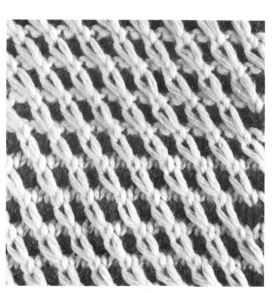

ABOVE: **Diagonal Overlay**
BELOW: **Variation**

obvious contrast. The pattern is handsome in two different textures, such as ribbon combined with yarn or metallic thread combined with wool.

Multiple of 3 sts plus 1. Colors A and B

Row 1 (Wrong side)—With A, k4, ° p1, k2; rep from °.
Row 2—With B, ° k2, sl 1 wyib; rep from °, end k4.
Row 3—With B, p4, ° sl 1 wyif, p2; rep from °.
Row 4—With A, k2, ° drop sl-st off needle to front of work, k2, pick up dropped st and knit it; rep from °, end k2.
Row 5—With A, ° k2, p1; rep from °, end k1.
Row 6—With B, k1, ° sl 1 wyib, k2; rep from °.
Row 7—With B, ° p2, sl 1 wyif; rep from °, end p1.
Row 8—With A, k1, ° drop sl-st, k2, pick up dropped st and knit it; rep from °.
Row 9—With A, k3, ° p1, k2; rep from °, end k1.
Row 10—With B, k3, ° sl 1 wyib, k2; rep from °, end k1.
Row 11—With B, p3, ° sl 1 wyif, p2; rep from °, end p1.
Row 12—With A, k3, ° drop sl-st, k2, pick up dropped st and knit it; rep from °, end k1.
Repeat Rows 1–12.

Variation

Work the same as above, except: Rows 1, 5, and 9—With A, purl.

The Mask

THIS grotesquely grinning fellow is not a "little" pattern, since 44 rows are required to shape him. But he finishes off the Uncharted Miscellany with a juicy set of directions whose variety of stitch counts would make a rather unwieldy chart. Apart from other variations, the pattern begins with 30 sts, but one stitch is removed on Row 10 and never restored, so the final count is 29 sts.

If you want to make a real ski- or Halloween mask out of this pattern, it isn't hard to do. Use a fairly heavy yarn and large needles so that 20 stitches will reach across the face. A contrasting color will do nicely to accent the eyebrows or to add a fringe of hair. If you cast on 7 new stitches in Row 20 instead of making 7 stitches from one, the bottom of the nose will be open for the wearer's breathing convenience, and the mask can be worked in one piece with an entire hood. It will also look clever on the back of a (lined) mitten or a pillow.

Panel of 30 sts

Rows 1 and *3* (Wrong side)—Knit.

Row 2—Purl.

Row 4—P11, k8, p11.

Row 5—K11, p8, k11.

Row 6—P10, RT, k6, LT, p10.

Row 7—K10, p10, k10.

Row 8—P9, RT, k8, LT, p9.

Row 9—K9, p12, k9.

Row 10—P8, RT, k3, k2 tog, yo, ssk, k3, LT, p8.

Row 11—K8, p4, p2 tog-b, yo, p1, yo, p2 tog, p4, k8.

Row 12—P7, RT, k2, k2 tog, yo, k3, yo, ssk, k2, LT, p7.

Row 13—K7, p3, p2 tog-b, yo, p5, yo, p2 tog, p3, k7.

Row 14—P6, RT, k1, k2 tog, yo, k7, yo, ssk, k1, LT, p6.

Row 15—K6, p17, k6.

Row 16—P5, RT, k1, k2 tog, yo, k9, yo, ssk, k1, LT, p5.

Row 17—K5, p19, k5.

Row 18—P5, k9, sl 1 as if to p1-b, k9, p5.

Row 19—K5, p9, sl 1 wyif, p9, k5.

Row 20—P5, k9, (k1, p1, k1, p1, k1, p1, k1) in next st, making 7 sts from 1; k9, p5.

Row 21—K5, p25, k5.

Row 22—P5, k16, (turn, p7, turn, k7) 3 times, k9, p5.

Rows 23 and *25*—K5, p9, sl 7 wyif loosely, p9, k5.

Rows 24 and *26*—P5, k9, sl 7 wyib loosely, k9, p5.

Row 27—Repeat Row 21.

Row 28—P5, k11, sl 2-k1-p2sso, k11, p5.

Row 29—K5, p23, k5.

Row 30—P5, ° k3, k2 tog, (yo) 3 times, ssk, k3, ° sl 2-k1-p2sso, rep from ° to °, p5.

Row 31—K5, p2, ° p2 tog-b, (p1, k1) 3 times into the long yo loop, p2 tog, ° p5, rep from ° to °, p2, k5.

Row 32—P5, k1, k2 tog, k6, ssk, k3, k2 tog, k6, ssk, k1, p5.

Row 33—K5, ° p2 tog-b, (p1, yo) 5 times, p1, p2 tog, ° p1, rep from ° to °, k5.

Row 34—P5, ssk, k9, k2 tog, k1, ssk, k9, k2 tog, p5.

Row 35—K5, p2 tog, p7, p2 tog-b, p1, p2 tog, p7, p2 tog-b, k5.

Row 36—P5, k1, p7, k3, p7, k1, p5.

Row 37—K5, p1, k7, p3, k7, p1, k5.

Rows 38, 40, and *42*—P5, k19, p5.

Rows 39 and *41*—K5, p19, k5.

Rows 43 and *44*—Repeat Rows 1 and 2.

The Mask

Index